GAIL GRECO'S

NEW *Secrets of Entertaining*

TIPS FROM AMERICA'S BEST INNKEEPERS

"Once again Gail has captured the essence of that astounding knack of innkeepers for capturing a sense of their place by creating a unique experience with specific practical methods. Innkeepers have become the gurus of hospitality in this century. Gail has found a way to reveal their secrets in this readable, easy-to-use handbook."
—PAT HARDY, CO-EXECUTIVE DIRECTOR,
PROFESSIONAL ASSOCIATION OF INNKEEPERS INTERNATIONAL, SANTA BARBARA, CA

"Entertain like a real pro."
—USA TODAY

"Full of great ideas from an expert segment of entertainers . . . open to nearly any page, this book will offer a useful hint or idea for do-it-yourselfers."
—TRIBUNE, OAKLAND, CA

"A homey package filled with wisdom and guidance. A most unusual and useful book."
—COUNTRY ACCENTS MAGAZINE

"Innkeepers have shared their best tried-and-true ideas along with special touches and bits of wisdom for hosting, decorating, and renovating. Helpful for starting a B&B or entertaining friends in your home."
—INN BUSINESS REVIEW

"With her Country Inn Cooking *television series on PBS and her many books, Gail Greco is truly an expert when it comes to country inn ideas you can use to better your life every day."*
—NORMA STRASMA, PUBLISHER, *INN MARKETING*

OTHER BOOKS BY GAIL GRECO

Gail Greco's Little Bed and Breakfast Cookbook Series:
Vive La French Toast
Autumn at the Farmer's Market
Recipes for Romance
Chocolates on the Pillow

❧

Country Inn Cooking with Gail Greco:
Companion to the Public Television Series

❧

Great Cooking with Country Inn Chefs

❧

The Romance of Country Inns: A Decorating Book for Your Home

❧

Tea-Time at the Inn

❧

Breakfasts and Brunches (formerly *A Country Inn Breakfast*)

❧

Bridal Shower Handbook

❧

World Class Cuisine of Italy and France:
Cooking with Recipes from the Provinces

❧

World Class Cuisine: Great Adventures in
European Regional Cooking

❧

World Class Cuisine: Tales, Tastes, and Techniques from
Europe's Most Celebrated Chefs

GAIL GRECO'S
NEW *Secrets of Entertaining*

TIPS FROM AMERICA'S BEST INNKEEPERS

Second Edition

by
Gail Greco

The Globe Pequot Press

Old Saybrook, Connecticut

Cover and text design by Saralyn D'Amato-Twomey

Library of Congress Cataloging-in-Publication Data

Gail, Greco.
Secrets of Entertaining: tips from America's best innkeepers / by Gail Greco :
— 2nd ed. p. cm.
Includes index.
ISBN 1-56440-991-0
1. Entertaining. I. Greco, Gail. Secrets of entertaining.
II. Title.
TX731.G687 1996
642'.4—dc20 96-12839
CIP

Manufactured in the United States of America
Second Edition/First Printing

❧ DEDICATION ❧

For you, Dad

I miss hearing the excitement in your voice for new adventures—mine as well as yours. You had your hands in my work because you wanted to help but also because you wanted us to be together. What a compassionate cheerleader you have been for me, as well as for the family and so many who knew you. As one of your colleagues put it, "your loyalty, friendliness, and 'can do' attitude are impossible to replace." You were an unheralded genius and a formidable example of how someone can beat adversity for a life worth living. Knowing you so well taught me so much.

I want to dedicate this book to your memory because it is complementary of the way you and Mom graced your home for the company of others—something I am continually reminded of year after year by my friends and yours. And also because you were such a romantic at everything you did and thought about—passionate and playful.

I wrote this to you years ago, and now in your passing, I need to say it again: "I wonder if you know how many times your faith in me made the difference between giving up and trying again . . . when your love helped me find a strength I didn't know I had. I could never begin to thank you enough."

You have only one thing left to do now. Be with Mom and make her eternally happy.

Giving Thanks

In 1995 I lost both my parents. They were young and vibrant, passing away before their time. They had devoted their lives to their family, so we were very close friends.

Mom and Dad passed away within four months of each other, shortly after I signed a contract for this book. I didn't know how I could start the manuscript, let alone complete it. Ironically, the work turned out to be a blessing. Joyful communication with innkeepers who responded to my requests warmed my heart and helped me get through. Writing about how they work at making others happy filled my heart with great joy and eclipsed some of my sorrow. I thank the innkeepers across America for their help with this book and for their unconditional devotion in providing all of us with sanctuaries for that which ails as well as that which prevails.

Since the first edition of this book, I have written several more inn books. It is time to extend my thanks to those who have been so generous and encouraging with each and every new book. The booksellers in America have embraced my books. I am ever grateful. I also want to thank those merchants who have supported me personally in my home state of Maryland.

Jack and Debi Parkin and their delightful Homeplace Everlastings in Hagerstown, Maryland. What an honor it has been to sit among the unusual and outstanding dried arrangements created by Debi. Your shop is indeed a home place where everyone who enters wants to stay. Your country talents are material for a book in itself. I want to thank you both for your unfailing support over the years and for your caring and genuine interest in my life and my successes. It is a simple pleasure just to browse and be among the unique charms of your shop. I advise my readers to stop there and do the same for a soothing moment.

Carol Bills, you have been incredibly uplifting over the years, and I consider myself so fortunate to be among the chosen few in your exquisite shop, Julia's Room in Gaithersburg, Maryland. Carol, you are a role model, having persevered through your own personal hardships. You have the respect of the community for your outstanding antiques and select gifts.

Marty Shaw for finding a home for me—year after year—in your comforting Pine and Patches store in Laytonsville. It has been worth putting out a new book each time, just as an excuse to see you and your place, with all its inviting country accents.

Pat Sugg, you were the first, locally, to stop and say, "I want your book in my shop," without blinking an eye. You and Jim and the girls have been so encouraging. I have always felt a special place was there for me in your Potpourri of Old Town in Gaithersburg.

I also want to thank all of those in the inn industry's national associations, who have been so helpful and supportive to me from the time I wrote the original edition of this book right up to the gathering of information for this new edition and beyond. In particular, my sincere gratitude goes to Executive Directors Pat Hardy and Jo Ann Bell and the Professional Association of Innkeepers International (PAII) in Santa Barbara, California. Thank you for hatching the idea of how PAII could help me gather information. I'll always remember our dinner together at San Ysidro Ranch. I would also like to thank Executive Director Norm Kinney and the Independent Innkeepers Association (IIA) in Marshall, Michigan for helping out so quickly and readily.

Appreciation also goes to my great friend Lester Anderson and his family (his wife Joanne and wonderfully precocious children Brian and Karen) for the cheerleading as well as the multifunctional office equipment support from Ricoh Corporation to keep me and my business going strong year after year.

Finally, I thank assistant editor Cindi D. Pietrzyk for her professionalism, open mind, and great insight and understanding; and Bruce Markot, the editor whose vision for this book was right on target.

❧ CONTENTS ❧

CHAPTER 8

THE JOY OF DECORATING: Creating Adventurous
and Peaceable Places / 167

CHAPTER 9

BRINGING HOME THE SEASON: A Gathering of Quiet Pleasures,
Thoughtful Feasts, and Days of Grace / 185

❧ INTRODUCTION ❧

Come Stay with Us . . . The Language of Hospitality

*L*ittle acts of kindness which we render to each other in everyday life are like flowers by the wayside to the traveler: they serve to gladden the heart and relieve the tedium of life's journey.

As soon as I know I am paying a call to a bed and breakfast or a country inn, my mood brightens. The very essence of the Shaker quote above sent to me by The Montford Inn in Norman, Oklahoma, begins to delineate why. Some of my many former visits to inns—cottage mornings, country weekends, and enchanted evenings that are forever pressed in my memory—reel forward, and I am in anticipation of another memorable adventure and an assortment of soothing moments that ease my life's journey, for sure.

I begin to skylark lightheartedly among the rigors of the day, and the abundant paperwork on the top of my desk suddenly seems to shrink with insignificance. I am enkindled by the vision of a peaceful, romantic visit that holds with it the promise of a new way of looking at things. That is the very nature of innkeeping itself—fulfilled by visionaries who bring to us something new and exciting to share. One of the most wonderful examples I have encountered in my travels is a place called A Teton Tree House in Jackson Hole, Wyoming. It was the fancy of innkeeper Denny Becker to create a B&B at the top of a hill, seemingly at eye's level with the famous, 13,000-foot-high Teton mountain range across the valley. This enterprising artist of sorts did just that, and the result is a wonderfully imaginative winding, twiggy sort of house, with all the comforts of home and views outside every romantic window and deck. You are living among the trees when you stay here. What a joyful place!

Other poetic images come to mind, like this one from Gaye Curran of Riversbend B&B in Mancos, Colorado: "Juice is available for guests who want to start their morning before breakfast in the hot tub, watching the stars make way for the sun." Do you begin to see why I get to musing so over inns?

Even the names of some of the inns make me begin to drift off—Whispering Waters B&B, Morning Star, Meadowlark Manor, Willow Brook Inn, Window on the Winds, Roses and the River, Run of the River, Inn at Willowbend—I'm ready to pack my bags. Hearing the names of the businesses brings on a rush of hope, comfort, and beckoning.

Innkeepers, like those who host us in their own homes, are happy to give. This is why I turn to these disciples of hospitality time after time for inspiration and ideas for hosting at home.

Room names are also evocative and sometimes have become legendary, with people asking for them specifically. "One of our guest suites, the Foothill Lupine Suite, has become a real favorite for our guests and always gets glowing write-ups in the guest book for the stars at night," says Doris Beckert of Foothill House in Calistoga, California. Can you imagine . . . rooms getting star billing and being written up! What do they do for an encore?

Inns are spas for the heart and soul where guests are treated as though they are the only important thing on the face of the earth. "Let us share our dreams with you," is how they put it at The Manor House on Cape Cod, Massachusetts, and they set out to do everything possible to make your and my fantasies come true—and I mean everything.

Now I want to again give you the opportunity to savor with me, in this book, the gentle, rewarding art of entertaining just as romantically in your own home. I think there is great merit in taking home tips from innkeepers, as is evidenced by this quotation from eighteenth-century writer William Shenstone and shared by the Mt. Juneau Inn in Alaska: "Who'er has travel'd life's dull round, whate'er his various tour has been, may sigh to think how oft he found his warmest welcome at an inn."

During my fourteen years of writing about inns, one thing has really struck me most prominently. While gathering information for this latest book, it hit me how there are a lot of people out there who are devoted to making a lot of other people feel good—the innkeepers. No detail is left out in the process. Innkeepers think through everything they do with their guest's comfort and happiness in mind; it's the language of hospitality at work, and it speaks of everything they approach. When decorating one of the bedchambers at The Arcadian Inn in Edmond, Oklahoma, foremost in Martha Hall's mind was, "I like to add depth to a room—high beds, thick comforters, big pillows, rich colors . . . decorate all the way to the ceiling, canopies, borders."

There is no larger a group of folks so dedicated to the mission of bringing happiness to those who step beyond their front door. What a blessing for all of us. For me it is a celestial touch just to hear from them, let alone visit them. Dean and Holly Ramseyer, of The Old Church House Inn in Mossville, Illinois, have often said, "Our ministry is to do for others what they don't take the time to do for themselves." This is a good thing to keep in mind when preparing to host people in your home. Thinking about what might interest your guests, but what you know they won't take time for, will result in satisfied visitors and certainly a strengthening of your friendship. Diane Carroll of The Federal House in Ithaca, New York, sums it up succinctly, "The most important thing you can give to your guests is yourself."

Among some of the innkeeper's letters I received while putting this book together, was Maureen Magee's from Rabbit Hill Inn in Lower Waterford, Vermont. She wrote rather apologetically, "Gail, I can't imagine you reading through everybody's stuff." Yes, Maureen alone sent me more than seven typed, single-spaced pages of her ideas. Hundreds of other innkeepers joined her and, like Maureen, are humble thinkers. They never brag about or think about the impact they have on others. They just do what, for them, comes naturally.

Reading through the epistolary of fervent verse and thoughtful philosophy underscored the importance of entertaining as a joyful art. Each letter offered the blush of the unexpected, a sense of leisure, and put smile after smile on my face, as I expect will happen to you as you read through the pages of this book.

Who has time to entertain at home? may be the question, but the answer is, Who can afford the time not to? or else miss out on rejoicing in the pleasures the innkeepers say they receive from being hosts. There is nothing like "extending yourself—loving and caring and thoughtfully providing for another's comfort," which is how Bob and Mauranna Sherman approach their work at their Mansion Inn B&B in Lynchburg, Virginia. Or, from Mary Timmins at the Butterfield B&B in Julian, California: "Our inn is in its eighth year, and every day I am surprised how many fun things happen; how many romantic things happen; and how we enjoy helping to make this happen. Seeing people at their best has made our entire outlook on life different . . . they continue to give us the best gift of all."

Statements such as these make you ask yourself what you are missing when you fail to invite a friend, a relative, or even a virtual stranger to your house. Giving to others at home may not take as much time as you think. You will find that innkeepers know short-cuts that are still elegant and easy and make a grand impression.

This new book not only contains updated information on hosting, cooking, serving, and decorating for special occasions as well as for everyday visits, but it also has taken a few steps further in extracting all sorts of life-style tips, many that are heartfelt, from innkeepers. The chapter Rhapsodies of Romance offers countless ideas that have been done at inns or by the innkeeper/partners themselves in the privacy of their own home. They are ideas that you can provide for yourself and your guests. Life's Little Treasures is a chapter about how to take time out for simple pleasures and make every moment feel good. These are new chapter additions, but the other chapters are also filled with lots of new thoughts and easy but elegant shortcuts that make entertaining in your own home not only fun but desirable.

Perhaps we can learn something here from the way in which innkeeper Bill Putman relieves the stresses of entertaining his guests at his Simmons Homestead Inn in Hyannis Port, Massachusetts: "I treat my guests as, say, a brother-in-law or someone who is a best friend of someone I knew awhile back. They are family of sort. I have to entertain them up to a point, leaving absolutely nothing to chance, but then they are on their own. If they want another glass of wine, they can just head to the icebox and get it. In the mornings they get their own coffee and teas from a sideboard, head to the kitchen for juice, and then I do the rest. Most take their plates to the kitchen when they are done. They feel at home here. They like it, and that's all I want."

Each inn has its own way of implementing its philosophy of entertaining, and you can develop your own as well. The key is not to feel burdened by having people over but to look forward to the event. That's the innkeeping way, and as I've always preached, the innkeepers know best, as they do this every day. They are the role models to look up to when entertaining anyone at home. Frances McClanahan of Sassafras B&B in Hernando, Mississippi, defines a good hostess as someone who senses the needs of others and acts on them as quickly as possible. "This way they will feel you care about them and want them to be at ease and enjoy themselves," Frances says.

I think that what I have seen with my family and friends these days is a fear of committing to having people over. One day you feel you are free to entertain; another day you are sorry you made the commitment. Innkeepers, like you and me, are not insensitive to the fact that entertaining is hard work. Bonnie Statz of The White Lace Inn in Sturgeon Bay, Wisconsin, offers a solution: "In our own personal home, we'd go way too long without company if we always set our entertaining goals as high as we used to." Bonnie and her innkeeper/husband, Dennis, have two children, and they run two businesses. "Now, sometimes we have to settle for a clean and mostly picked-up house before company arrives. But we can still do many other things to make them feel special." I think one must adopt an attitude that you can entertain without so much effort that the result is a pressure and a feeling that you just don't want to have anyone over.

Bonnie gets the kids involved. She may have them pick herbs from the garden to add to a vase, and when dinner guests arrive, the children may help with the coats and ask everyone what they might like to drink. She adds that a guest room should be free of family clutter, and she introduces cedar for a fresh room scent. The Statzes feel that hosting can be kept simple without compromising guest pampering.

Another way to look at it is as Joseph Saunders III does at his John Brady Inn in Muncy, Pennsylvania. Joseph reminds us that you cannot be all things to all people. "Do the best you can. Be prepared to think on your feet and roll with the punches. If you feel that you have provided the best you can for your guests, then you shouldn't have a worry."

I think what constantly attracts me to innkeepers as experts in home life-styles is their sense of truth. They are real and unpretentious, and they are innkeepers because they love it and it affords them a living. Although they go all out for their guests and you see lush pictures of inns and guest rooms, they also know what is most important: It is not the appearance of something but what is at the heart of the matter. Gretchen Fairweather at The Half Penney Inn in West Hartford, Vermont, exemplifies what I mean. "Have good mattresses and box springs. All the fluffy pillows and flowery comforters will not make the impression a good night's sleep will." I think this is an essential and symbolic philosophy to be mindful of when hosting at home.

Another aspect innkeepers teach us is that we must be cognizant of our own personal needs. "If you truly want to enjoy your guests," explains Karen Owens of King's Cottage in Lancaster, Pennsylvania, "you must take care of yourself and be well rested." Taking that cue, I remember visiting the Davy Jackson Inn in Jackson Hole, Wyoming, and walking into my room for the night. There was a tapestry-tufted fainting couch at the foot of the bed in front of the fireplace. It made me laugh inside at all the times I have entertained and after a long, hard time of it, felt like lying back and falling into a faint sleep. The inn's couch reminded me to take time out. I guess if I do take time out and yet still continue to offer those little acts of kindness that the Shakers alluded to and that the innkeepers do, I am sure I will never regret having said to someone, "Why don't you come stay with us. . . ."

Innkeeping with Their Spirit,

Gail Greco

Chapter 1

HAPPY TO GIVE

A HOME IN ANTICIPATION OF COMPANY

Whenever you invite someone for dinner or an extended visit, you like to roll out the red carpet. In other words you want to make your guests' visits memorable.

Incidentally, this hospitable expression has firm roots. Red carpets really were unfurled for kings and other nobility during public and private appearances. The practice is still carried out today among the world's remaining royal families. And figuratively speaking, a different type of red carpet is turned out today in American homes—a carpet of hospitality. Someone is hosting someone else every minute of every day from the most humble to the grandest of households.

Colloquially, the old catchphrase means we want the best for our visitors, who deserve nothing less. But you need not do palatial curtsies to make someone's stay a regal one. Stylish slumber is often created by the littlest touches that make a guest's stay special.

The innkeepers know this well, and they supply their home and guest rooms with the most thoughtful touches. At the Ravenwood Castle in New Plymouth, Ohio, for example, you'll find a flashlight on bedstands for guests' use when padding to the bathroom in the middle of the night. Not all houses have private baths in guest rooms, so a flashlight seems an appropriate aid for those who are not familiar with your home.

Flashlights are also in use at The Fairhaven Inn in Bath, Maine. The inn makes sure there is one outside the front door so that guests staying out late can find their way back to their room. What a good idea. I wish we had thought of that at our house when we were teenagers. A front-door light was left on, but inside, we groped around in the dark, not turning on lights for fear of waking someone who would notice curfew had passed!

Another thoughtful but less pragmatic nicety at inns has become a tradition—mints on the pillow at turn-down time, or fruit, as they do at O'Duach'ain Country Inn in Bigfork, Montana. "Fresh fruit in season," says innkeeper Tom Doohan, "makes a neat pillow surprise." Guests often find baskets of toiletries in their room. At The Governor's Inn in Ludlow, Vermont, the Butler's Basket contains such trial-sized goodies as toothpaste, shampoo, deodorant, cough drops, razor, soap, mending kit, chewing gum, and lip balm.

There is great reward in making the traveler feel comfortable and right at home. Staging rooms for guests is the innkeepers' specialty. You hear them offer this sentiment repeatedly, "We want guests to feel as though no one has ever stayed in this room before."

Innkeepers know how to serve and entertain guests and how the host can be a part of

> *Your guests, whether friends or family, thrive on individualized attention.*
>
> —Whispering Waters Bed and Breakfast

the fun. Some inns even go to the length of greeting guests in costume. At Randall's Ordinary in North Stonington, Connecticut the innkeepers sometimes greet guests in Colonial period garb. Visitors may be met by a knicker-clad gentleman or a mob-capped lady. That's when they cross the bridge through time and enjoy eighteenth-century hospitality.

You may not go to these great lengths to entertain your guests, but such ideas instill a sense of escapism, which is possibly the best gift you can offer your own houseguests. Your reward is the pure joy of entertaining. You are happy to give, and your rewards are contented people who go away with some of the most pleasant memories they will have in life. Just reading how some inns suggest we entertain at home is enough to make you give pause and feel a sense of relaxation and good spirit.

Once you get into the habit of preparing for your guests in the spirit of the innkeepers, you will wonder why you didn't think of these niceties before—and not only for guests, but for your family and for yourself. It's really not hard to do. As Adella and Bob

Schulz of Sweet Adeline's in Salida, Colorado, put it, "There aren't too many secrets to innkeeping or hosting your own guests at home. Just open your heart, and the rest will take care of itself."

THE PAMPERING SPIRIT

❧ As host, make time for yourself. Get a good night's sleep and luxuriate in a whirlpool once each day. Then you are refreshed. Having guests is only work if you'd rather be doing something else.

Hospitality at home, like innkeeping, is an expression of the intangible through the tangible. Thus, while the accumulation of thoughtful, specific, sensual details that meet the guests' needs is essential, don't get so lost in stuff—the perfect bedding, flower arrangements, etc.—that you forget a relaxed, welcoming, happy go-with-it attitude, which truly embraces those who honor you by visiting or eating in your home. –*Dairy Hollow House*

❧ Create a relaxing environment for your houseguests. In order to do that, you must be relaxed yourself. Peace and relaxation at home can always be achieved by not taking life too seriously. All problems miraculously work themselves out. —*Black Dog Inn*

❧ Relax and do what you do well. Don't try to offer your guests an experience that doesn't really reflect you and your style. Remember, there are other places they can go to experience other things, but you are unique.—*Sooke Harbor House*

❧ Consider your guests' interests, not your own, when entertaining. Nothing is more boring to them or inconsiderate than forcing your guests to do things they'd rather not be doing.

Participate in your guests' activities if possible. In the event that you just can't stand to go through the county's Civil War museum for the twenty-third time, help your guests get there and perhaps ask the museum to give them some special attention in exchange for some volunteer work you can do for them later. In other words, if you do leave your guests on their own, just make sure they are well taken care of as though you were right there with them. —*Langdon House*

❧ Remember, the world isn't interested in the storms you have encountered, but rather, did you bring in the ship. Don't share the storms in the kitchen with your guests.

Keep your lip up, your sails trimmed, and bring in your guests with smooth sailing. —*The Groveland Hotel*

❧ Most important is your attitude! Whatever you do, do not lose your sense of humor. If you have some guest frustrations, vent them with laughter and love. —*The John Brady Inn*

❧ Never tell tales about other guests. Be there for them but don't be intrusive. —*Barry's Gull Cottage*

❧ Treat yourself as a guest in your own home. It works. Drag out your best things and use them often. If they break, they break. At least you had the pleasure of using them. —*Governor's Inn (Vermont)*

❧ Ministering to our guests is a sure cure for our blues or blahs. Need a pick-me-up? Have a guest to your home. —*Roaring Lion*

❧ Hosting guests is hard work. But remember that when they arrive at your door, they are on a holiday, and that spirit is contagious. Sometimes the arrival of guests can turn around a day that had previously gone awry. —*Quill and Quilt*

❧ At the time of their arrival, your guests should be your most important concern. Put yourself in their position and try to anticipate their needs. Be sensitive that your guests may have immediate concerns that you know nothing about. If they have been traveling for hours, they may have more pressing things on their mind than talk. Don't hesitate to ask what their needs might be. Provide them with the opportunity to briefly freshen up before going into extensive dialogue.

Put yourself in a position to be at ease when your guests arrive so that you can give them your attention. Get to a stopping point with whatever task you are involved in.

Don't have your dog or other pets run out to greet your guests. Put them aside until your guests settle in. Don't make your pets the center of attraction. —*Langdon House*

❧ When getting a room ready for a guest, approach it as though your mother-in-law were coming for a visit (even if you don't have a mother-in-law). —*Davy Jackson Inn*

❧ Allowing yourself extra time in the morning for hair and makeup, nice jewelry and something attractive to wear gives you a lift, even if all heck is breaking loose behind the scenes. And when things are running smoothly, it gives you that extra confidence to greet guests. —*Bramble Inn*

It often happens that you have just finished polishing your nails when a guest rings the doorbell. If you are in a hurry to go somewhere and can't wait any longer for your wet nails to dry, run them under cold water. They dry instantly. Then go answer the door or go paint the town. —*Palmer Inn*

Pace yourself in preparing for guests. Entertaining can easily turn into much more than you had imagined. Intersperse your periods of preparation with periods of something fun. Any guest would vastly prefer a relaxed host over the perfect table setting or flawless soufflé. —*Kedron Valley Inn*

You put out a lot of time and energy to entertain guests, but it is personally rewarding when you know you can effect a change in someone's life. Always go out of your way to pay attention to your guest's needs. For example, we had a guest who was on a family-roots mission. His grandfather had lived in our area in 1904, having worked in a mine that closed in the early 1920s. I called the local historian, and, together, the three of us trampled through the woods on a rainy day to a long-abandoned mine shaft. Our guest was just thrilled to be on the spot where his grandfather had descended to work each day so long ago. We were able to give our guest an experience he would not have been able to get elsewhere. These are the kinds of things that help create memories for you and your guest. —*Trezona House*

Don't peer from behind the curtain. Rush out there and greet your guests before they reach the porch. You know you have been preparing for hours, so why act so surprised when your guests arrive? Why make them ring the bell and then count to ten before opening the door and ushering them in? —*Tyler Hill B&B*

Gail's Touch: Leave room for enjoying yourself while you prepare for visitors. Light scented candles in the kitchen to add some romance and sensuality to your day in the kitchen. Choose sweet food flavors such as strawberry, vanilla, and cinnamon.

Few things make a guest feel more at home than being greeted by name. —*Shire Inn*

It is nice to have a welcoming sign in your foyer announcing guests' arrival. Our

12-inch-high house mouse is dressed according to the season, with a writing board that lists the name of our arriving guests.
—*Seymour House*

❧Just before your guests arrive, spray a natural scent around the house. We use a mixture of vanilla and water and just spray. The vanilla is so refreshing and pure. Add water to a sprayer bottle and add vanilla or vanilla extract according to desired strength. Add slowly—a few drops of extract will go a long way. —*Abriendo Inn*

❧These days, overnight guests often have to work very hard just to get away from home. They spend several hours cooped up traveling. Put out a split of champagne, as it encourages them to relax before doing anything else, including unpacking. We do this often at the inn. —*Kedron Valley Inn*

❧The "lights, camera, action" of preparing turndown for guests is "lights on, heat turned up, sheets folded back, shades drawn." —*The Maine Stay*

❧For those guests who are truly special in your life, hide a short note or card on the pillow under the bedspread. Write about how

happy you are that they are visiting and share with them how much they mean to you. It is just a little gesture, but these little unexpected things are often the mementos we save for years after. —*Oceancrest House*

Gail's Touch: Buy yourself a copy of Alexandra Stoddard's *A Gift of a Letter*. This little book is a flower garden of ways to send special messages and why it is so important to give such a gift.

❧When confirming your guests' plans to visit, send a handwritten note letting them know you are anxious about their arrival. We do this at the inn all the time and have declined sending off a form letter, writing it by hand instead. —*Two Sisters Inn*

❧It's good to have an icebreaker as guests arrive to get things going. Our answer to that is that we placed a life-sized soft-sculpture doll in a rocker by the fireplace. We introduce her when guests come inside. She manages to elicit a smile as soon as she is introduced. —*Prince of Wales B&B*

❧A sweet touch is to send off a short note to an invited guest, sharing your joy as you await their visit. This serves to heighten your

guests' anticipation as well.

It's fun to find just the right small, personal gift for arriving guests. This can be set at their place at the table or in their bedroom (if staying overnight). Make it a thoughtful little present. For example, remembering that they just did a room in their house in new colors, one could give a packet of stationery, cocktail napkins, a small collectible bottle, or such—one of these items to match the colors in the room.

As with everything, presentation of the gift—a ribbon, a sprig of foliage tucked inside, perhaps—is important. Don't we each cherish small signs of acknowledgment that indicate friendship and love?
—*Rabbit Hill Inn*

Gail's Touch: If you bake apples on a tray in a slow oven all day, by the time your guests arrive, the whole house will bear the natural scent of a comforting welcome.

When your guests arrive, give them a tour of the house as soon as possible so that they feel comfortable and know where everything is. —*Jakobstettel Guest House*

When expecting your guests at home, leave some low-level lighting on in their guest room. Also turn the radio on to a classical or jazz station to set a warm ambience upon arrival. —*Doanleigh Wallagh B&B Inn*

Make a welcome banner for the guestroom door. See their eyes light up. —*The Grey Whale Inn*

We try to treat every guest who walks through our doors as if he were the first we ever had. The most difficult part of innkeeping (or entertaining any guest) is staying fresh continuously. Be sure to greet your guests cheerfully, even if you're having a bad day. —*Inn on Golden Pond*

We provide the guests with a goings-on list—everything from local concerts and performances to someone giving a talk at the local library, to festivals and parades, even including such things as the annual Humane Society Doggie Shop Thrift Show. This way, guests may know their options, follow their inclinations, and maybe even have some fun doing something totally out of character.

Sometimes the simplest of small-town goings-on has great appeal to someone on vacation from a metropolitan area—and vice versa. Be proud of what and where you are, and remember that what's commonplace to

---

✺ PORTRAITS OF INN-SPIRATION ✺

The Gift That Keeps on Giving:

In November 1995, we hosted three couples from Michigan who lodged and dined with us as they fulfilled their plans to attend a Penn State–Michigan football game. As they waited for their table in the dining room, they chatted with four Penn State fans, also waiting to dine. After dinner the Michigan crew nestled into the coziness of our living room before retiring. My husband, John, came in to inform us that the Penn State fans had just departed and that before doing so, they gave him $50 for a friendship bottle of champagne for the Michigan-gang-of-six. It seems that several years ago, the donor had been embarrassed in State College when local residents treated some Michigan visitors rudely. He wanted to make amends in the only way he could—a random act of kindness that inspires and becomes contagious.

Nancy Showers, The Inn at Olde New Berlin

---

you may be special and unique to your houseguest.—*Dairy Hollow House*

✺We decorate with pineapples around the inn because they are the symbol of hospitality. We purposely named our inn after the famous fruit because we wanted to send the message that we are all about hospitality.

Some people place fresh pineapples outside the front door. This tradition harkens back to the days of the traveling, early American sea captains. When they stopped at home before going on another journey, they first wanted time alone with their family. When that time had elapsed, fresh pineapples were placed in front of the house, signalling to neighbors that it was all right to visit. When you have guests coming, place a couple of pineapples outside your door or around the house and entertain them by relating the story of the tradition.—*Pineapple Hill*

Overnight guests, especially those who have been traveling a long time, may not want to carry in their luggage right away. Encourage them to come on into the house first and settle down, freshen up, and then perhaps take a beverage in the parlor.

Finally, a memorable visit for your guests would be one in which you are giving them something different from what they can get at home—a surprise around every corner. That's good to keep in mind when planning for company. —*Edge of Thyme*

We have an extensive inventory of brochures, articles, pamphlets, and maps to assist our guests. Chance are you, too, have a lot of travel information at home. We can't stress how efficient it is to keep this information in order. When you're ready to become guests somewhere else, you'll know where to begin looking to set up a travel agenda—especially should the opportunity to take a trip materialize unexpectedly. Indeed, file folders are one good way of keeping your information at hand.—*Bechtel Mansion*

You can have everything in life you want, if you just help enough other people get what they want.

—The Maples Inn

If you have a lot of guests visiting you throughout the year, it helps to have some activity supplies available, even if you personally don't use them. We keep binoculars on hand; a bike rack; backpacks, fannypacks, and umbrellas.—*Shire Inn*

Complimentary port in a decanter is always in our Winston Churchill Library for a small after-dinner refreshment.—*Over Look Inn*

If you're entertaining guests at home, and they are celebrating an anniversary, birthday, or other special occasion, you may want to do what we do. Place wine and glasses in their room before arrival.—*Mason Cottage*

For a guest celebrating an anniversary or birthday, we place antique postcards in their room, with a handwritten congratulations note. Your guests will want to take it home with them and keep this greeting in a scrapbook, as our guests have done. —*Kingsley House*

A large basket of fresh apples sits in the lobby—fun, healthy, unexpected. —*Carter House*

For honeymooners, we pin little brass bells—engraved with their wedding date—on the mattress.—*Robins Nest*

In case a guest takes a fall and needs minor first aid involving ice, fill a balloon with water and then freeze it. This makes a neat and clean, hand-held ball to rub on an affected area. We're near a ski resort, and occasionally a guest returns to the inn needing such assistance.—*Center Street Inn*

We clean every day. Otherwise it gets out of hand. Dust and vacuum in the morning, and the rest of the day will be free. If someone calls unexpectedly, you don't have to worry about rushing around picking up things.—*Countryside B&B*

An antique child's chalkboard is used to post the day's weather forecast for our guests when they come to breakfast. It's a nice touch for house guests who are likely to ask about the weather when they sit down to breakfast.—*Captain Lord Mansion*

Bird feeders just outside the breakfast window provide natural enjoyment for our guests. But we enhance the fun by leaving a bird-identifying book on each table. What a conversation starter!—*Trillium House*

A HAVEN FOR THEIR PRIVATE PASSIONS

SETTING UP THE GUEST ROOM

When setting up a guest room, imagine that you are the guest and try to provide everything that you can for your comfort or pleasure. This will give you hints of what might be needed. For example, good reading lights and two extra pillows on the bed are what we discovered was needed.—*Four Chimneys*

The overall feeling of the guest room is important. You want to be sure that there is no reminder that someone else has inhabited the room recently. This is especially important for an at-home guest room. Remove any items from the room that are personal family effects. It will make your guests feel that the room is really for them. Make sure the room is not in any way cluttered.—*Alexander's Inn (New Mexico)*

❧Tasteful signs in the room, with instructions such as "Remove quilts and shams before retiring," help guests feel more comfortable about what is expected and also put you at ease, knowing that your things are well taken care of. Our signs are quality, artistic directives on wood plaques. —*Churchtown Inn*

❧Before your guests arrive, check their room. Especially at home, when you may have guests less frequently than at an inn, you need to be sure the room is clean—free of spider webs and the like. Don't assume that the room is as you left it weeks or months ago. Turn a few lights on to give guests a warm welcome. —*WinterGreen Country Inn*

❧An attractive clothes tree in a guest bedroom provides added space for clothing, especially if you have limited or no closet space.—*Silas Griffith Inn*

❧We always have a small, nonglaring light

Shakespeare wrote, "Our happiness is greatest when we contribute most to the happiness of others."
—The Montford Inn

on in the hallways, drawing room, parlor, and each bedroom and bathroom. A dark inn or home has no sense of welcome. Yes, we have high electric bills. But when you are welcoming guests, lights spell warmth to those who are visiting. The same goes in your own home if you have guests coming over.
—*Chestnut Hill on the Delaware*

❧We have a welcoming letter in the room. Perhaps in your home there can be a scaled-down version, handwritten to explain some unusual things. If you have a hard time finding the bathroom light switch because the switch is in an unusual place, your guests might, too. Make them aware of this nuance. You might personalize the note with the guests' names and put it on the dresser. Other things you can explain are what bathroom they may use, where to put their used towels, and what other niceties you have for them in their room and throughout the house.—*Hill Farm Inn*

❧Spend one night in your guest room to determine if the furniture is placed in the best arrangement. This offers clues to any missing amenities.

Familiarize your guests with their accommodations, and define the space available for their use. This also gives you some much-needed privacy during their stay. —*Shellmont B&B*

Never move guests belongings when you clean their bedroom. If you must pick up something to dust or vacuum, place it back in the same spot. It is their room while they are staying with you. Let them decide where their things should be.—*Willow Brook Inn*

BEDTIME STORIES

Use quality mattress pads instead of the type that has only a flat top and four skinny elastic straps. The better pads stay securely on the bed and make doing up the bed easier.— *The Manor House*

To keep bedrooms looking fresh, use down comforters with duvet covers. We use white with Battenburg lace at the inn. Since the duvet covers are changed with each guest, the rooms always look clean and fresh. —*La Maison*

We enjoy playing with quilt folds to add interest to a bed. A quilt folded into a triangle

or square can be placed on the bed. The unexpected angle adds drama.—*Rabbit Hill Inn*

A queen bed is much more romantic than outfitting your guest room with two twin beds. If you must, keep a queen in the room but add a daybed that can be set up as a sofa. This way, you have the best of both worlds in case you have guests who need two beds.—*The Maine Stay*

Keep beds quiet—no squeaks allowed. It may help to glue or attach carpet scraps to the backs of the headboards so that they don't scuff the walls.—*The King's Cottage*

Mounting the headboards to the wall will prevent any rattling.—*The Seal Beach Inn*

Here is the anatomy of a perfect bed. Start with a top-of-line Posture-Pedic-style mattress and box spring with the extra quilting for cushioning. Add an egg-crate foam mattress cover and then place a sheep's-wool mattress cover on top of that because it comforts and soothes, reflecting heat, but it breathes so that you do not sweat. Use 200-count-thread quality sheets, not for beauty so much as comfort and wear. Our guests tell us that they sleep better at our inn than at home and want to know the anatomy of our bed making to the final detail. We know it's a magic combination.—*Casa de las Chimeneas*

If you don't do anything special with your bedding at home, at least try using a quality egg-crate foam mattress pad. This special pad reduces stress on body pressure points, resulting in comfort and a soft, floating feeling. For very hard mattresses, you may want to use two of the egg-crate pads. The reward will be an incredible night's sleep in blissful comfort. —*Alaska Ocean View B&B*

Always have clean bedding. At home, especially, you may not have guests constantly turning over in your guest room. Clean the sheets anyway if they have been sitting there for a long time.—*Conover's Bay Head Inn*

Our linen closet is organized by tieing like bedding together with a ribbon. This makes it easy to make up a room, especially at home when each room, like our inn, is individually decorated.—*The Montford Inn*

For those who hate to make the bed because it hurts your back, buy an old-fash-ioned bed that is high off the floor with a high mattress and you'll be amazed at how much less stress there is on your back when you go to make it up.—*Victorian Oaks B&B*

Two mattresses on top of the box spring will give you height and that antique-bed feeling.—*The Seal Beach Inn*

In addition to pillows at the head of the bed, we often place pillows at the foot of the bed, propped up against the foot-board. It just adds more of an invitation and suggestion for luxury and comfort.—*WinterGreen Country Inn*

Let the other person feel important, if they have to.
—La Maison

We make our beds using three sheets—one fitted and two flat sheets. In between the flat sheets, we use a lightweight goose-down comforter, folding the bottom flat sheet about 6 inches over the comforter and the top flat sheet to protect the comforter. —*Shire Inn*

To have distinctive sheets and pillow-cases and save time and money, buy solid-colored linens and have your initials embroi-dered on them in contrasting color. This may be done at a local embroidery shop where they sew on names of teams on shirts and jackets.—*Abriendo Inn*

❧Close the end of a pillowcase with a decorative napkin ring. Stand it up behind the pillow sham to create a dramatic setting. It's like a finial for a pillow. You could choose a napkin ring that fits the theme of the room. Do it with two rings if you have two pillows or more. —*Truffles B&B*

❧Our theme is Bavarian, so we set out feather pillows as though they were the Matterhorn. Two pillows sit at the head of the bed, with foil-wrapped chocolate disks sitting in the pillow. Turn the pillow upside down in the pillowcase, pushing the feathers into one corner. Grab the opposite corner and push it into the other corner so that you are forming a cone. Turn the pillow upside down. Fold up the bottom, tucking excess pillow into the cone. Stand the pillow up onto the bed. Push the pointed tip down, by pressing your hands on either side of the point. Place a chocolate in the rim.— *Schumacher's New Prague Hotel*

Our job is to make innkeeping look easy so that when we're too tired to do it any longer, you are lined up waiting to buy the inn.
—The Inn at Merridun

❧For a bed with headboard, footboards, and side rails, use a fitted sheet instead of a dust ruffle to avoid the hassle of tucking in the dust ruffle with the sheet every time you make the bed. Use a fitted sheet on the box spring of a bed made up with a bedspread. This will give a polished, decorator look. —*The Inn at 410*

❧If buying a feather pillow for the bed, the nonstitched ones fluff up more elegantly.—*Truffles B&B*

❧Drape canopied beds in netting. Secure the fabric loosely at the corner posts to easily untie and cocoon.—*Under Mountain Inn*

❧Make sure your guest room contains feather and foam pillows. Many folks are allergic to feathers. —*Doanleigh Wallagh B&B*

❧We make up all of our beds in the twenty-eight rooms with designer ruffled sheets. As a result, we have to launder them ourselves. Commercial launderers won't touch them. But we aren't dissuaded. The extra effort and time is worth it to us, and it will be for your own house guests, too. We want our guests to experience an elegant home and our hospitality, right down to the sheets. —*Kedron Valley Inn*

❧Good mattresses are a must. Although all of our beds are antiques, we make sure the mattresses are firm. And we use only English cotton-flannel sheets for warmth and cozy comfort.—*Hilltop Inn*

❧For marvelous bedding, ironed sheets are a must. Sorry, there's just no comparison, no matter how wrinkle-free the sheets are that come out of the dryer.—*Captain Dexter House*

❧If you require extra beds but don't have the space, any bed with legs and a clearance of 14 inches can house a pop-up trundle bed with a good innerspring mattress, versus the foam mattress on a rollaway. —*Grant Corner Inn*

LITTLE AFFECTIONS

❧A friend kept a male and female spray cologne on a dresser for her guests' use at her house. So now, Safari and Polo colognes are on each one of our guest-room dressers.

Since we are in ski country, we have boot-warmer stands in each guest room. Guests really appreciate this touch to warm their shoes or boots before going out into the cold.—*The Painted Porch*

❧Put a Funsaver camera in the room with a note to use during their visit. You can then have the pictures developed and mail them to your guests for a holiday or other gift.—*The Maine Stay*

Gail's Touch: I use pretty ceramic toast holders for keeping a bookmark or two, scrap paper, pens, and postcards on a nightstand in a guest room. It keeps things organized and gives guests plenty of needy supplies at hand. Mail dividers can also be used.

❧Scented drawer liners leave your dressers with a scent of their own rather than that of the previous guest. —*Captain Nickerson Inn*

❧Offer your guests a newspaper, wrapped in white paper and tied with a ribbon, as we do every morning here at the ranch. —*San Ysidro Ranch*

❧Most home guest rooms don't have a telephone. Have a portable phone in the guest rooms so that guests can make calls at any time.—*The Inn at Depot Hill*

Old cut-glass or pressed-glass oil and vinegar cruets make nice sherry decanters; they hold just about the right amount for one or two people.—*Rose Manor*

Since robes are always too bulky to pack, provide them in your closet. Be sure they are clean. Hang them and tie them with the sash, cinching the waist. They look very romantic that way.—*Crystal Rose Inn*

Forget those complicated digital radio/alarm clocks for guest rooms. Your guests will get frustrated trying to figure out how to make one of them work. Set out a battery-operated or wind-up alarm clock with a glow-in-the-dark dial. If you are stuck with the radio/alarm, offer to set it for them before they go off to bed.
—*WinterGreen Country Inn*

Place a copy of *Life's Little Instruction Book* by the bedside table.
—*Adams Edgeworth Inn*

Another reason for using battery-operated clocks is that if the power goes out during the night, your guests may not be too happy if they miss their flight or some other commitment.—*Kingsley House*

Guest-room closets seem to be a catchall place for the family's clothing. Be sure to check out the closet before your guests come and weed it out so that they have a place for their clothes. Make an obvious spot for them to hang things up.
—*Crystal Rose Inn*

Keep a hamper in the guest room closet and explain to your guests that this is where they can put their wet towels. It answers a dilemma for them, and it almost ensures that a wet towel won't be hung over your antique headboard or dresser to dry.
—*Thompson Park House*

A pincushion with pins, safety pins, and one or two needles plus thread in your guest room allows guests to make emergency repairs to clothing while they are away from home.—*Inn on Cove Hill, Rockport*

Gail's Touch: My friend Lester Anderson suggested I put a card by the radio/alarm clock designating the call letters and numbers and music choice of local stations.

Keep a supply of easy-to-read books and magazines in a guest room, keeping the male species in mind by getting current magazines men might like, such as *Smithsonian* and *Time.*—*Folkestone B&B*

🦋Lots of decorative pillows are a great asset to a guest room. Consider putting an empty trunk at the foot of the bed for storage of those pillows at night.—*The Maine Stay*

🦋A stuffed toy and some books placed on a child's bed prior to arrival can go a long way to making a strange place seem much more secure and inviting. —*Hilltop Inn*

🦋Antiques make great luggage racks. We use a wringer washing machine for one. A suitcase can be placed on either side, where the tub used to go. And an old, wooden potty seat serves just fine for suitcases when the lid is down.—*Wildwood Inn*

🦋We place books in guest rooms. If we know a guest's particular interest, we try to find a book about that subject. This may be easier for homeowners who know most of their overnight guests.

We also have small book lights available,

"To invite a person into your house is to take charge of his happiness for as long as he is under your roof." (Brillat-Savarin)
—North Garden Inn

so guests can read comfortably in bed without disturbing their partners.—*Roaring Lion*

🦋We use steamer trunks for luggage racks. They also are excellent for storing extra blankets and other linens.

In each guest room is an antique meat platter, which is used as a tray for organizing two wine glasses, napkins, small carafe for water, corkscrew, and chocolates. —*Captain Lord Mansion*

🦋Guests on vacation may not want to read a book that will take them a long time to get through. We leave a copy of *Tales for Travellers* in each bedroom. The book contains short stories by famous authors printed in a format like a folded road map. —*Balcony Downs*

Gail's Touch: Padded hangers are great for protecting clothing, especially a garment's shape. Coordinate them with colors in the room. Sew a label containing your name on each hanger to remind guests that the hangers are your property, or tie a ribbon around the neck base, as they do at Holden House.

If by accident one is taken home, it's a nice souvenir, reminding them to visit you again.

You can buy old books cheaply at flea markets and garage sales. They're nice to keep around. If guests become interested in one, you can tell them (as we do) that they can take it home.—*Summerland Inn*

We have a hot-water bottle hanging in each guest room to help bones and muscles relax.—*Blueberry Hill*

We place flannel nightshirts in the rooms for our guests to use while they are with us. Even if they don't wear them, people are touched by the gesture. Chances are they don't wear nightshirts at home, so if they do try one on, it's usually good for some laughs and a snugly night's sleep to boot. —*Tyler Hill B&B*

When we prepare a room for a guest, the crisp linens are turned down to create a welcoming sight to the eye.—*Sweetwater Farm*

The world is run by the people who show up. (Pat Lile, Leadership of Arkansas)
—Dairy Hollow House

Put a glass and a carafe of ice water by your guest's bed to quench a midnight thirst. Place them on a tray with a cloth napkin. —*Winters Creek Inn*

To make our guests feel welcome, we have sparkling water and chocolates in the room. We also put extra blankets and pillows in the closets.—*Ash Mill Farm*

We provide guest rooms with small portable ironing boards. This prevents anyone from ironing on the bed or dresser. An ironing board and iron in the closet of your own guest room at home will prevent your having to lug out the household ironing board for a guest and taking time to set it up while you're in the middle of fixing a lavish dinner.—*Heartstone Inn*

To make guests feel more at home, I go up to their room at night with a small basket containing home-baked goodies.—*Locust Hill*

Handmade stuffed lambs, with woven hats and scarves, sit on each guest bed to welcome guests. Some say the lambs help them not miss their pets so much.
—*Six Water Street B&B*

FOR MORE INFORMATION ON INNS LISTED IN THIS BOOK, SEE THE DIRECTORY BEGINNING ON PAGE 203.

BATHED IN DELIGHTS

To put it simply: The bathrooms must sparkle.—*Victorian B&B*

A pillow for the tub adds to a luxurious bath for you or your guests.—*Hannah Marie Country Inn*

Tiny paper cups in the bathroom are sanitary and practical.—*Thompson Park House*

Fancy bathroom soaps are fine for the ladies, but make sure you also have a man's soap in the bathroom.—*Folkestone B&B*

Shelf space seems to be a universal bathroom problem. We solved the problem at our inn by cutting out the wallboard between the studs for the space we needed. We then installed shelves into the new-found space. They take nothing away from the look of the bathroom and add a world of usefulness. —*Black Dog Inn*

Decorate extra toilet paper with ribbon tied around the center.—*Doanleigh Wallagh B&B*

Peg rails, similar to those the Shakers used, are in our bathrooms and guest rooms.

The racks are handy catchalls for your house guests and for your own family. You can buy them or have a local craftsman or carpenter design one to fit the length of one wall or to wrap around the entire room.—*Two Brooks*

Gail's Touch: We have towel racks on the back of the guest room door. One rack holds clean towels, and a double hook, close to the top of the door, gives guests a place to dry the towels. We always leave clean towels in the room so that when company is coming, it's one less matter we have to take care of to prepare for their visit.

Small baskets lined with material that matches the guest room colors contain extra soap and shampoo.—*Inn on Golden Pond*

When you have guests, it's nice to leave small sizes of toiletries in a basket in case they have forgotten something. We leave such things as shampoo, hairspray, and even bubble bath.—*Freedom House B&B*

Custom-crafted, stained-glass nightlights are in each bath for our guests' convenience.—*Captain Lord Mansion*

Big towels of the bath sheet kind are

very important for guests. There's nothing worse than offering guests towels that do not wrap all the way around them.—*Cobbs Cove*

Gail's Touch: Fresh towels every day pamper guests. But if you prefer to change them only every other day, make sure each guest sharing a room has a different colored set of towels.

If your guests will be sharing the bathroom down the hall with family members, use a quilt rack in a corner of the guest bedroom for hanging towels to dry.—*The Inn at 410*

Provide at least one large bath towel, one hand towel, and one washcloth per person.—*Connover's Bay Head Inn*

Turning down your guests' bed at night provides the chance to also remove damp towels and replace them with clean, dry, fresh ones.—*The Half Penney Inn*

Extra towels are made accessible to guests. They are in an armoire in the hallway. Tell your guests where your extra towels are, just in case they need one.—*Main Street B&B*

Consider using a brass front-hall coat

tree instead of towel racks.—*Victorian Rose Garden B&B*

Towels are placed in decorative baskets in each room. The guest may then use the basket to carry toiletries to the bathroom. —*Benner House*

SCENT-SATIONAL FLOURISHINGS

Each of our female guests receives a small bag of homemade sachet. You can do this for your own house guests. Here's what you need:

3 ounces lavender flowers
1 ounce powdered orrisroot
4 drops lavender oil

Mix the ingredients together in a bowl and place them in a sealed container for at least two weeks. Fill small bags (you can make your own fabric bags) and tie with a bow.

Added bonus: After the lavender has dried, the stems are used to make incense sticks. Here's how: Soak stems in a mixture of one tablespoon of saltpeter and one cup of water for thirty minutes. Dry completely. Light a couple of the stems in rooms that need refreshing. They will smolder long enough to perfume a room. You can wave them around the room or stand them in a glass and watch them smolder. Don't leave them unattended.—*Horatio Johnson House*

A bowl of honeysuckle in a bedroom with the door shut will emit a wonderful fragrance when guests enter the room. —*Balcony Downs*

Sew up a small, thin, cloth bag. Fill it with rosemary, mint, or lavender and add one teaspoon of crushed cinnamon stick. Attach it to a hanger and place in a closet. It makes a spicy moth bag.

Pierce the skin of a lemon or an orange with a meat skewer, making several holes close together. Push whole cloves into the fruit to make a pomander. Then place it in a closet or a drawer.

Make an herb cushion by cutting muslin to desired size and sewing up three sides. Fill with crushed herbs such as peppermint, sage, lavender, and lemon balm. Sew up the fourth side to close.

Eucalyptus makes a pleasant scent in the house. At our inn, we have bunches of it in the hallways.—*Fairhaven Inn*

Attitudes are contagious. Be sure yours is worth catching! —Blue Harbor House

In early times beds were often musty smelling, so early settlers sweetened their nocturnal comforter with scented sleep bags. Today we put the practice to use for the sheer enjoyment of guests. Here's how to make a sleep bag:

3 cups dried rose petals
1 cup spearmint leaves
1 tablespoon powdered cloves

Mix the ingredients; you will have enough for many bags. Place a few handfuls of the mixture into a tiny muslin bag. If you sew up your own bag, stencil over it for design. Place on a bedroom pillow. —*Victorian House*

Gail's Touch: To dry flowers for potpourri, place petals or blossoms in a shallow box in a car trunk, where the heat will dry them and the darkness will help keep their color. In about a week remove them and place them in a plastic bag. Mix the petals with spices and essential oils.

A handful of dried fresh lavender under the mattress pad sweetens the guest's bed. —*Robins Nest*

For more information on inns listed in this book, see the directory beginning on page 203.

❧ PORTRAITS OF INN-SPIRATION ❧

Because our inn is located within two blocks of the Atlantic Ocean and a beautiful lake, our guests who come from the hustle and bustle of the city welcome the peace and tranquility of our surroundings.

During our first summer season, a young family of seven from New York City visited the inn. Mom, dad, and five children—four boys and one girl, ranging in age from six to twelve! They were a delightful family who were thrilled to be spending a few days at the shore.

There were a few pillows that I wanted to replace. One was a very firm pillow, which was in the boys' room. The next morning when the boys and their sister came down for breakfast, one of the boys was raving to the others about how much he liked his "rock pillow."

And so, they passed the next few days just being kids and having fun with mom and dad.

On the last morning of their stay, my husband was driving to work along the ocean at about 6:00 A.M. He said he saw a family up on the boardwalk with their arms encircled around one another. That family was our guest, who later told me that they had arisen early to watch the sun rise (the sun rising . . . just an everyday spectacular occurrence that most of us take for granted).

We truly enjoy all our guests, yet the memory of this family's delight in simple pleasures will endure through the years as one of our fondest.

Rosemary Volker, The Inn at the Shore

In the winter we put cinnamon sticks in a teakettle filled with warm water. It smells just wonderful throughout the house. —*Mill Farm Inn*

Apples, cinnamon, and cloves boiled in a medium-sized saucepan of water will fill the house with an inviting aroma. Later, the apples can be made into applesauce by removing the cloves and mashing the apples with a potato masher.—*Britt House*

To provide a wonderful scent in the inn during the winter, we offer hot spiced cider in the evening. We take a bottle of apple juice, two pureed apples, cinnamon, and nutmeg, and simmer for a few minutes. The aroma spreads everywhere. —*Palmer House*

A good way to have a nice scent in a room is to place a light-bulb ring around one of the bulbs in each room and put several drops of scented oil on the ring. As the bulb heats the oil, it fills the air with aroma. Light-bulb rings are available in home improvement stores.—*Captain Dexter House*

Potpourri in your rooms lends a pleasant, welcoming odor to your home. We've used antique porcelain cups to hold potpourri.—*Arcady Down East*

REMAINS OF THE DAY

Think about sending your house guests off with something from your kitchen. A nice bag of homemade cookies is frequently our choice. We often place a note in their hand about an upcoming event so that we indirectly suggest they return.—*Inn at Manchester*

As we are a seaside inn, we send our guests home with a seashell. It's fun to collect them and place in a large, clear bowl. Think about what is particular about your area and do the same.—*Bay Moon B&B*

Don't wait for your guests to send you a thank-you note after they leave. Get out your pen and send them a letter letting them know how much you enjoyed their stay and how much you look forward to seeing them again.—*Willow Brook Inn*

We had note cards made from the line drawing of our inn. They make very inexpensive souvenirs for visitors.—*Heartstone Inn*

Gail's Touch: I'll never forget being sent off

from The Whitehall Inn in New Hope, Pennsylvania, with a delicate fabric sack full of dried, sweet-smelling roses. This dainty reminder of my visit there lingered in the car all the way home, and so did my smile.

✒Inn guests sign out in our guest book and often leave comments about their visit along with their address. We use it for business purposes and as our own ledger. But it is a particularly good idea to have one in your own home. Have dinner and overnight guests sign your book. This gives you an automatic Christmas-card list. Also refer to the book when you're trying to remember when a guest last visited. A guest book can also thwart an embarrassing situation. if a friend brought a guest for dinner, you may have forgotten his or her name. Refer to the book and you will find the name that eluded you.—*Corner Cupboard Inn*

✒After guests have gone, we send them a friendship card and enclose a sealed tea bag along with tea-making instructions. It's a reminder to them to relax with a cup of tea and remember the good times shared together. This is a nice thing to do for your own guests.—*Hannah Marie Country Inn*

Gail's Touch: Artists often offer to sketch private homes. Although you would probably like to have it done, the practical voice in you asks what in the world you will do with it. Well, have the sketches made into postcards. When your guests come to visit, offer them the postcards to send to their relatives and friends back home. They will love them.

Chapter 2

RHAPSODIES OF ROMANCE

WHIMSIES, ADVENTURES, AND ELEGANT GESTURES

I'm not sure that anyone can define romance. The dictionary talks about chivalry and fairytales and fantasies and love affairs, but I walk away from the great book unsatisfied. I guess that's because you can't really put your finger on a definition for romance. What is romantic? Who is romantic? And yet, romance, with all its inexplicable "idyllisms," is all around us. One does not have to be married, living with someone, or even be in love with someone to partake in the triumphs of the heart.

Because romance is not something you can see—you only feel it with your essence—it is understandable why it is so hard to define. But all you have to do is look out a window that fronts on nature and you can better grasp its presence. You can see romance—the harmony of trees with the sky, the animals, or the shapes and textures of whatever the scene may be in front of you—from a lone golden meadow singing in the wind to a looming and variegated forest inviting mystery and discovery. It doesn't matter where you are, even in a city slum, you will find something romantic if you look for it. Somewhere in the midst of everything we see, feel, and do is romance, in the form of art or poetry.

Once you allow romance into your heart, it will fulfill you plenty. Sharing those feelings with someone you care about only enhances the aspect of romance, and that's what I think being in love is all about—but who am I to say?

If anyone has a clearer sense of what

romance is, it is the innkeepers, who not only see it every day but are its biggest proponents, creating it at every turn.

"They have fallen in love in our hot tub, honeymooned in our lover's suite, celebrated their first anniversary with us, and have conceived their first child with us," an exuberant Vivian and Bob Barry boast of their Barry's Gull Cottage bed and breakfast in Dewey Beach, Delaware. They speak for the majority of small inns who set out to inspire romance in everything they do. In fact, country inns and bed-and-breakfast inns are synonymous with the subject and may even be at the very heart of the matter. Inns certainly can be some of the most important places to set the stage for romance of any kind.

In the preceding chapter, you read about how innkeepers play Cupid, preparing their venue with all the mood-enhancing attributes from garden to dining room and bedroom. In this chapter they tell you what to do to put yourself into the scene and ensure a romantic time.

At Kedron Valley Inn in South Woodstock, Vermont, they have a multitude of fireplaces that have been wooing people for more than a century, for the inn was formerly a stagecoach stop. As Merrily Comins of the inn observes, "Nothing inspires romance like a fireplace—a wood-burning fireplace." Maintaining the fireplaces—cutting the logs, storing the wood, cleaning, and all of the other chores of keeping up a wood-burning fireplace—is an enormous job, but the innkeepers feel that there is nothing akin to the sound of snapping logs and the glow from the hearth to illuminate relaxation and warm exchanges, and whatever follows that is up to their guests.

FUN AND FLIRTY

Put Kenny G's "Breathless" on the CD player. You know what to do next.
—*The King's Cottage*

Gail's Touch: Instead of filling your room with flowers for your guy or gal, buy buckets full of edible flowers. Let your imagination do the rest—and the flowers are even better dipped in chocolate!

Go to your airport and pick any departure gate. Kiss good-bye. Everyone else is doing it, then don't go.

Soak in a hot tub. There is much to say for being warm and wet anywhere. When you're sharing a five-foot circle—you have no choice but to look eye to eye.— *Queen Anne Inn*

A Vermont company makes a product called, Chocolate Body Paint. Need we say more?—*The Inn at Merridun*

For those who have forgotten what stars look like, take a flashlight and a moon-lit walk. —*Rowell's Inn*

Play a romantic game such as Enchanted Evening (World Wide Games). This romantic quiz provides a series of questions for you and your partner to answer, opening the door to loving communications. Set the mood by lighting scented candles and playing soft music. Prepare a small feast of your favorite wine, cheese, and chocolate-dipped strawberries. Men love this game as much as women do!—*The Inn at 410*

Draw hearts with your finger in the steam on the bathroom mirror before your spouse comes out of the shower. —*Lynchburg Mansion*

All our rooms with whirlpool come

with a copy of *An Affair to Remember* propped up against the pillow. Many a couple have snuggled watching that classical romance.—*Clements Inn*

"I might understand all mysteries, have all knowledge and all faith, so that I could remove mountains, and might bestow all my goods to feed the poor, but if I don't have love, I am nothing." (Corinthians 13:2–3)

—Mansion Inn

Plan a weekly date and each time, act as though it was your first: Carefully pick out what you're going to wear, hold hands, sit close, and walk arm-in-arm.—*The Arcadian Inn*

Playing strip poker, chess, or darts in front of the fire during winter can be fun!—*The King's Cottage*

This may sound like a cliché but there is nothing like holding hands. Truly. Energy, warmth, and reassurance are transmitted electrically palm-to-palm.—*Kedron Valley Inn*

Travel separately. This gives you the opportunity to really miss each other and to really appreciate the "grounding" that you provide to each other as a couple. You can also explore your disparate interests without offense.—*Kedron Valley Inn*

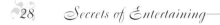

INTIMATE SURPRISES

❧Place gold-foiled Hershey Kisses on a small candy dish next to the bed with a card that says, "A Good Night Kiss."—*Victorian Rose Garden B&B*

❧Catch the sunrise at any park. Take a wool blanket, firewood, and matches. Build a cozy fire in a barbecue pit.— *Queen Anne Inn*

❧Tuck "sweet nothing" notes in unexpected places: the egg carton, medicine cabinet, underwear drawer, and toes of shoes. —*The Inn at Merridun*

❧Smile!—*Adams Edgeworth Inn*

❧Shovel your spouse's car out of the snow—or at least make a happy face in the snow on the windshield.—*Lynchburg Mansion*

❧Sprinkle fresh rose petals in the empty bathtub—fill your rooms with fresh flowers. —*Alaska Ocean View B&B*

❧Send a Valentine on any other day but February 14th.

Buy her a rose once in a while, for no reason at all.—*Shire Inn*

❧Tell him (her) that he (she) smells good.—*Adams Edgeworth Inn*

❧Buy him a plant for the office; buy her a dozen roses for no particular reason. —*Queen Anne Inn*

Gail's Touch: Place sexy notes among his or her clothing in the suitcase to luxuriate in when traveling. Or, do as they do at Lynchburg Mansion. Get a ten-second message recorder. When the one you love must go away, leave a caring message and stick it in his or her suitcase as a surprise.

❧Rose petals made into the bed is a sweet surprise when your guests pull back the sheets.—*Langdon House*

❧Pack the kids off for a night without telling your spouse—leaving you both an unexpected evening together.—*Shire Inn*

❧Surprise your significant other with a bottle of champagne. Chill it in a bucket and serve the bubbly in your best flutes with a strawberry in each glass.—*La Maison*

For more information on inns listed in this book, see the directory beginning on page 203.

PASSION ON THE MOVE

Get away. Even if just to a museum picnic or canoe trip. —*The Half Penney Inn*

Make plans to go somewhere for just one night. Keep the destination a secret and only tell your significant other what dates to set aside and what to pack. This special get-away adds extra excitement to the relationship and the location. —*Crystal Rose Inn*

Shop for antique jewelry. Buying is not as important as looking. Sometimes it's less threatening to look at previously owned rings in an antique store than diamond wedding rings in a modern jewelry store.

Learn line dancing together, or whatever the current craze—at the country-western dance hall.

Visit a greenhouse in winter. Seeing things growing instead of groaning has a cheering effect.

Sample the wine at your nearest winery, a unique before-dinner treat.

Step back in time for an afternoon. Visit the oldest house in town and thank your lucky stars that you two are together now instead of then.

Split a beer sampler late in the afternoon at the brew pub.

Watch quietly as the geese and mallards in the lake partake in the spring courting.

Pack a picnic lunch and head for peace and quiet in the park, on a high hill, or beside a lake.

Take a walking tour of your town, hand-in-hand of course, to see a part of its future as well as its past.

Go to a pet shop. There is something about cozy, cuddly puppies and kittens that is contagious.

Visit a zoo during the winter— see how happy you make the animals and they make you.

Spend a quiet afternoon reading romantic novels while sitting side by side on the floor of your favorite bookstore.— *Queen Anne Inn*

Walk a beach from end-to-end, collecting driftwood to commemorate your time together.

Visit a bird sanctuary and observe these beautiful creatures in the quiet of nature.

Browse at the one-of-a-kind treasures in your town's unique shops and galleries.

There is only one happiness in life . . . to love and be loved. —The Mockingbird Inn

Stop by a travel agency and browse through brochures. Plan your dream vacation, even if only a dream!

Learn a new sport together. Take scuba diving, wind surfing, or jet skiing lessons.

Walk the canals of Naples.—*Seal Beach Inn*

There's nothing more romantic than a moonlight snowshoe hike. Take a hand-made walking stick and a lantern, and head to your nearest lake. You'll see stars like you've never seen them before.—*WinterGreen Country Inn*

Take long walks—not for the purpose of exercise. These are "walk-talks"—slow-paced long rambles to explore and enjoy each other and some portion of the world. A walk-talk helps you both unwind; getting out of one environment and into another—a kind of psychological and spiritual deep breath—time out.—*Shire Inn*

Get yourself a tandem (built-for-two) bicycle and see how much romance you can create!—*Barry's Gull Cottage*

Enjoy a horse-drawn carriage ride down town at night.

Take off at dawn on a soaring balloon ride. So quiet, so serene, you'll whisper your feelings for fear of being heard on the ground below.

Hire a limousine—they're in the Yellow Pages. Take it to dinner, to the theatre, wherever. And, most importantly, have it wait for you.

Take a train ride to anywhere and perhaps make it an overnight in a bed-and-breakfast inn.—*Queen Anne Inn*

Gail's Touch: Take your favorite someone on a date to the nearest observatory for real star-gazing.

Make snapshots of your present surroundings at home and work. Send them to a dear friend whom you haven't seen in a long time.

Visit an antiquarian book store together and just thumb through books you both read as kids, such as Hardy Boys and Nancy Drew.

Do something unexpected. Take breakfast to a nearby park.

Book a ferry boat ride.

FOR MORE INFORMATION ON INNS LISTED IN THIS BOOK, SEE THE DIRECTORY BEGINNING ON PAGE 203.

AGLOW AT HOME

❧Take a nap together in the afternoon. It may be more romantic than going out that evening.

Attempt the Sunday newspaper cross word puzzle in front of the fire, on the living room couch, or on the garden chez. It really doesn't matter how you do, rather that you tried.

Surprise your lover with a champagne breakfast.

Engage a private harpist for yourself and friends in your own living room. It doesn't cost much more than a fine bottle of wine.

Just talk one evening. Sit in front of the fire instead of the television.—*Queen Anne Inn*

❧Spend the night in one of your guest rooms. It will feel as if you are somewhere else.—*Shire Inn*

❧Have a massage therapist come to your home with a portable table and world-class relaxation. Nothing smooths out the raw edges like a massage.—*Black Dog Inn*

❧Make sure to hang your bird feeders outside the kitchen window. Fill the feeders just before breakfast. Watching the birds while you're eating is a wonderful conversation topic, and very romantic.—*WinterGreen Country Inn*

❧Read a bedtime story to each other. —*The Inn at Merridun*

❧Arrange a night of romance in black and white. Use no electric lights, just candles, even in the powder room. Play harp or classical guitar music before dinner, jazz during dinner, and soft piano music to slow dance after dinner.—*Inn at Playa Del Rey*

❧Put a bottle of wine on ice, order in some fried chicken, place the chicken in a basket, and have a picnic in the bedroom. —*Adams Edgeworth Inn*

Gail's Touch: Love is a magnet; it attracts the best of everything. It attracts the most positive of relationships, because nothing less will do. When you are a loving person, you don't have to look for meaningful relationships. People are drawn to you. They can be themselves with you, so they want to be in your loving space. (Susan L. Taylor, *In the Spirit*)

❧Reading to your spouse is one of the

most intimate, romantic activities there is.
—*The Lovelander*

❧Dimmer switches beckon romance. Install them in the bathroom and the bedroom for instant ambience.—*Holden House*

❧Arrange small branches in an unused fireplace—attach tiny glass Christmas bulbs. —*Under Mountain Inn*

❧Everything looks better by candlelight! —*Willow Brook Inn*

KEEPING IT HOT

❧To keep a hearty fire, always keep the pieces of large dried wood in a pyramid shape—this creates the necessary draft around the logs (for example, if using six pieces, place three on bottom, two next, one on top). The top piece will always burn the fastest and should be moved down when you put on a new piece.—*Boydville The Inn at Martinsburg*

Gail's Touch: When acquiring wood for the fireplace or wood-burning stove, the aroma of the burning logs is nicest from woods of fruit and nut trees, such as apple, cherry,

beech, hickory, and pecan. You do pay a price for this nostalgic effect. Fruit wood is more expensive and harder to find.

❧Firestarters can be useful and decorative. Gather pinecones small enough to fit into muffin tins. Dip the pinecones in a kettle of hot paraffin. Let them cool. Fill each muffin cup with two teaspoons of sawdust and hot paraffin. You can add different colors of food coloring. Place a pinecone in each muffin cup. When cool, remove the pinecones and place them in a wicker basket, set next to the fireplace.—*Heritage Inn*

❧If you don't have kindling wood, use newspaper knots to start the fire. Roll two to three full sheets of newspaper lengthwise and then into a single knot. This is an old Scandinavian trick that really works. —*Out-the-Inn-Door*

❧The tendency is to clean out the fireplace every time you use it. It is, however, better not to clear out the ashes, as a bed of coals helps produce more heat for the next fire you build. Leaving the coals will warm the room more.—*Corner Cupboard Inn*

FOR MORE INFORMATION ON INNS LISTED IN THIS BOOK, SEE THE DIRECTORY BEGINNING ON PAGE 203.

PASSAGES TO ROMANTIC SPACES

❧Take a big tub, add a bubble bath and a mirror, and you have a romantic room.—*Olallieberry Inn*

❧Make a rule: No business discussions in the bedroom!—*The King's Cottage*

❧Creating a romantic atmosphere means setting a stage: fireplaces, candles, and soft music. Always include an unexpected surprise among the props.—*The Notchland Inn*

❧There is always light in our fireplaces at the inn, and that includes summertime. We burn tea-light candles in little round glasses and place them on the floor of the hearth, about six in each fireplace. The little lights burn for hours—it is almost like a real fire. —*Victorian Oaks B&B*

❧Display sentimental books at the bedside. Include poetry and romantic suggestions.—*Willow Brook Inn*

❧Fill the room with flowers. I'm not talking a bunch or two—I mean fill the room.

Negotiate a bulk-rate with your local florist for unarranged, right-off-the-truck flowers. Or, collect pickings from your neighbors' gardens. (Ask first, of course.)—*Langdon House*

Gail's Touch: You can create all the romantic moods you want and have great intentions, but without both of you first reading John Gray's, *Men Are from Mars, Women Are from Venus,* there shall be no deeper meeting of the hearts or the minds.

❧Drape canopied beds in netting. Secure the fabric loosely at the corner posts to easily untie and cocoon.—*Under Mountain Inn*

❧Last Christmas, we hung miniature white lights along the upper edge of our eight-foot redwood fence in a swag design. The fence runs across the back and side of our property and ends behind our Victorian gazebo.

During the holidays, we use a lighting pattern regulator which allows the bulbs to blink or change patterns. For the remainder of the year we use the lights in a non-blinking mode as a backdrop for evening parties or for guests who enjoy sitting in the gazebo after dark. Because of the structure of the landscaping, the light strings are almost invisible by day. But in the evening, the lights add romance to even the bleakest winter nights.—*Durham House*

❧Romance would be enhanced if only we went to our bedroom before we were exhausted, had a place to sit, read, chat, and just catch up on the day's events.

Our rooms encourage romance. We should all design our bedrooms the way bed and breakfasts do. But alas, we don't. Why? Must be those dirty socks on the floor, or the thought of having to make our beds every morning. The bedroom should have the things that make a couple comfortable with each other, and not just be a place for sleep: a recliner, a fainting couch, a cozy place to read or talk.—*Davy Jackson Inn*

Gail's Touch: Find old cards you've collected from a significant other, and frame them as a surprise. Hang them on the wall.

❧Place a small terracotta angel somewhere in each guest room to serve as guardian to all who stay within those walls. The angel's mission is to watch over your guests while they are with you. When they leave, guests take the spirit of the angel to forever watch over them.—*Riversbend B&B*

RECIPES FOR ROMANCE

❧Create a cozy bedroom picnic for two. Spread a red and white checkered cloth on the bedroom floor and turn on a continual play CD of romantic instrumental music.

Place scented candles on the cloth and around the room for soft lighting. Lay out silk robes, beautiful napkins, special luncheon-size plates, crystal goblets, and tiny silver forks, spoons, and spreaders. A small bouquet of flowers in the center and your table is complete.

The menu can be gourmet or fast fun! But always in small portions—making it easier to share and feed each other. Start with grapes and cherries, strawberries with sour cream and brown sugar, or cheese and apples. Then, smoked oysters, pickled herring, hot wings, and always a loaf of fresh French bread—unsliced and no knife. There's something so sensual about breaking bread together. A good herb butter and fresh cheese assortment are delicious accompaniments. Dessert can include rich chocolate tidbits, soufflé, crème brûlée, or bonbons. Of course the meal is not complete without a sensuous bottle of wine!

These are just a few suggestions. Choose your favorite foods, but don't eat too much.

You don't want to feel stuffed for the final course. . . . —*Kirschke Hour B&B*

⚜Prepare an aphrodisiac:

CHOCOLATE COVERED STRAWBERRIES:

1 tablespoon shortening
1 cup semisweet chocolate chips
1 pint strawberries, washed, dried, stems
    intact

Cover a cookie sheet or baking tray with waxed paper. Measure the shortening and chips into a medium-sized microwavable bowl. Heat the chips in the microwave on medium-high heat, 20 seconds at a time until completely melted. Stir every 20 seconds. Dip the strawberries into the melted chocolate. Set the chocolate-covered strawberries on the waxed paper tray. Allow the chocolate to cool and harden before serving.—*The Inn at 410*

⚜Have a sidewalk cafe lunch. Remember how to be alone together in a crowd.

Partake of "high tea" wherever it is served, even your own home. There's something genteel about tea and scrumptious tidbits. The proper time is usually 2:00 or 3:00 P.M. so don't plan an early dinner.

Laborare est orare. (To work is to pray.) (From the ancient orders of the Benedictine monks)
—Dairy Hollow House

Cook a dinner together at home. That means both of you participate, perhaps each preparing a different course.
—*Queen Anne Inn*

EMBRACING THE MOOD

⚜Give the gift of time to the one you love. Romance is rarely spontaneous in this age of busy schedules. Set aside time to just be together—a regularly scheduled event blocked off on the calendar. Make a rule prohibiting business discussions, this is an important date after all. You'll find yourself looking forward to this special time. . . . a true sign that romance is blooming again.
—*Oceancrest House*

⚜This from an inn that was voted one of the best places in which to kiss in southern California:

If someone cares enough to plan a special outing with you, this is a very special gift. So take the time to make the time. Don't ask questions. Go and enjoy the moment. Time spent with someone—especially someone you love—is precious and should not be

---

❧ PORTRAITS OF INN-SPIRATION ❧

One guest wanted to make his marriage proposal memorable. He spoke with us several times before his arrival to request special champagne, flowers, and other surprises for the occasion. He ordered a gourmet dinner in the Victorian courtyard garden, served by waiters in black tie. The engagement ring was resting on a dollop of whipped cream on the dessert. When the time was right, the man knelt at the woman's feet and, accompanied by his guitar, sang the proposal song he had written. She accepted. They were married in the courtyard six months later, and they return each year for their anniversary.

Lanaux House

---

weighed against the place or event to which you have been invited. Even a phone call to say hello is a significant gift and can make anyone's day.—*Butterfield B&B*

❧Every now and then, think back and remind yourself of the qualities in your partner that attracted you in the first place. No biggie, no fanfare—just a simple activity that goes a long way toward keeping the glow alive.—*The Hutchinson Mansion*

❧When you make the effort to do something special make sure it is just for that person. It can be something as simple as rubbing his/her back or feet. Whatever it is, do it with focus—love and tenderness. —*Grace Hall B&B Inn*

❧Imagination is the key to romance. —*The Lovelander Inn*

❧My husband, Tom, and I have been married thirty-two years and have three married children. We also have four (soon to be five) beautiful grandchildren!

We have known each other since we were teenagers, and through the years, we have grown more deeply in love. Our married life has had many pleasures as well as challenges. One of the biggest challenges is keeping romance in our lives.

We schedule a special "date night" for ourselves. On that night we'll go out to dinner and a movie, or see a play. We take turns picking out the restaurant and show. Or, we simply stay home, prepare a favorite dinner, listen to music, or rent a good movie.

This date night allows us to concentrate on each other—to appreciate all those qualities that attracted us in the first place.

But the best romantic tip, which my mom gave to us (and really works) is: "Never go to bed mad at each other."—*The Inn at the Shore*

❧Stay healthy and attractive. While it sounds basic, it's important to look good—not just for guests—but for yourself. You need to take care of yourself on a daily basis.

Decorate your champagne bucket by festooning it with netting, and add pretty ribbons to the stems of the champagne glasses.—*Pratt Guest House*

❧Inspire romance by the mere mention of a special experience. Ask a couple about their quiet times together. What was their most romantic twilight, dawn, or rain walk?

Then share your own experiences with them.—*The Notchland Inn*

❧Visit the tip-top of the highest building in your town. The view is well worth the effort.

Sit on the highest hill you can find. Marvel at the past and discuss the future. —*Queen Anne Inn*

❧Take care of your spouse's needs. Even anticipate them.—*Lynchburg Mansion*

❧Keep saying and doing romantic things for the one you love.—*Queen Anne Inn*

MELODIOUS INTERLUDES

❧Use music as a mood setter, but personalize your choice according to the age of your guests. For some, Vivaldi's *The Four Seasons* is just the ticket; for others, the Beatles or Pearl Jam lend the proper aura. Lighting also adds to the romantic ambience. Use soft, indirect lights mixed with scented candles. (If using scented candles, make sure the aroma doesn't clash with your potpourri—or worse, your own perfume!)—*Lanaux House*

For more information on inns listed in this book, see the directory beginning on page 203.

ROMANTIC MUSIC SELECTIONS

❧ *Jewel Lake* (Bill Douglas)
—*Pratt Guest House*

❧ *Reflections of Passion* (Yanni)
Mist and Stone (Maggie Sansone)
Music for Oboe and Harp (Claude Achille Debussy)
Shepherd Moons (Enya)
—*Twin Gates B&B*

❧ *Somewhere in Time* (John Barry/Roger William)
Best of Roberta Flack
—*The Doctor's Inn*

❧ *A Man and a Woman*
Sax at the Movies
—*The Inn at Ormsby Hill*

❧ *My Favorite Works, The Romantic Guitar* (Andrés Segovia)
Return to the Heart (David Lanz)
Jazz Round Midnight (Bill Evans)
Dinner for Two (CBS Masterworks Dinner Classics)
—*Shire Inn*

❧ *Celtic Harp* (Patrick Ball)
—*The Grey Whale Inn*

❧ *Brava* (Sally Harmon)
—*Antique Rose Inn*

❧ *Springtime Reflections* (Gary Prim, pianist)
—*Truffles B&B*

🍂Piano music at breakfast is a joy for all—even those who are not romantically disposed.—*The Winter House*

LASTING IMPRESSIONS

🍂Save the corks from bottles of wine you share. Write the date and place on the cork and keep them in a basket. Great memories!—*Clauser's B&B*

🍂Even during the winter months we seek the romance of childhood memories. We set up rocking chairs and blankets around our century-old fireplace and roast marshmallows and serve hot spiced cider.—*Governors' Inn*

🍂When I am through in this life, I want to be able to have more "glad I dids" than "wish I hads."—*Crystal Rose Inn*

🍂"The real secret of happiness is not what you give or what you receive; it's what you share." (author unknown)—*Holden House*

🍂The perfect gift for a honeymoon, anniversary, or any memory-making moment is a sweetheart gift basket filled with a massage kit, cherub magnets, a picture frame, scented floating candles and other items for the bath, a miniature book on "love," and of course—chocolate candies.—*The Mockingbird Inn*

🍂Find a different restaurant one day each week. Trying something new creates memories that last.

Have a picture taken in a photo booth. It's a simple memory of a happy time that could come to mean as much as your wedding picture.

Plant a tree together. Make plans to come back in ten years to mark how the tree and your love has grown.

After dinner, go out for a banana split or multi-scoop yogurt cone, and remember the fountains of your youth.

Lean back, relax, and hold hands in the movie theatre. Remember when you were teenagers.—*Queen Anne Inn*

LOVE INN-SPIRED

🍂The three most important words are not "I am sorry" or "I love you," but "You are right!"—*Madame Dyer's B&B*

🍂Spend a night or two at a country inn. Leave the kids with grandparents or friends. Relax and be pampered—ask for a room with a canopy bed and a wood-burning fire-

place. **Hint:** Select a small inn during their off-season and receive extra-special treatment. For instance, if you're our only guests, we serve you dinner in front of the fireplace in the parlor.—*Shire Inn*

Take care of your guest's kids for a night so they can check into a local B&B for a romantic evening alone.—*Langdon House*

Chapter 3

LIFE'S LITTLE TREASURES

SOOTHING MOMENTS AND SIMPLE PLEASURES

hy do we do it? Why do we race around trying to accomplish this and that? What will we have to show afterall? Will we ask ourselves if we regret not having spent more time working? I don't think so. Life is not a beginning or an end. Life is a process, and to work so hard and ignore all of the finer things along the way is really missing the whole point.

Now, this is not saying we should not work hard. Work can be fun and rewarding and challenging in and of itself. Most of us are conscientious, but we do need a moment of peace. However, more often than not, we all tend to unbalance the scales. I am merely pointing out that during the process of working hard, we need to pay attention to every single thing we are doing. If we just work toward an end and not enjoy the middle, we are not fully experiencing the rewards that everyday life has to offer.

Elizabeth Barrett Browning once wrote that the earth is crammed with heaven. "Crammed," she said. To me that means heaven is everywhere—in every nook and cranny if only we look for it. Heaven may be experienced more often then we could ever imagine—that is, of course, if we ever allow ourselves the time to do any imagining!

If we do not pay attention to the peace and joy and pleasures along the way, we really miss out. Here is a prime example of what I mean. It tells of what might have been lost if two people didn't stop a moment. Liz Latshaw of The Manor House in Cape Cod, Massachusetts told me that at her inn, relaxation is something that is encouraged, not only among the guests but also between she and her husband, and they practice what they preach.

"As the sun goes down, or in the early morning, my husband and I have always tried to get in a walk down by the water where we seem to do our best talking and thinking," she said. "We use the time to talk about ideas—our hopes and dreams," Liz revealed. "It really gives us the chance to get back in touch with why we are together."

Wouldn't you know that is was during one of these dedicated rituals that Liz and Rick came up with the idea of starting their very own bed-and-breakfast!

Taking a walk along a beach is a simple pleasure that can suddenly open up a whole new world. You bet Liz and Rick feel a touch of heaven every time they walk along the shore. The result of taking time out and paying attention to what is really going on inside of you is essential.

Soothing moments and simple pleasures

A real conversation stopper occurred once when a new bride came downstairs to the dining room one morning wearing only her nightgown. We tried to carry on normally with breakfast, but . . .
—Captain Ezra Nye House

offer all of us the chance to get back in touch with our inner self. When we do that, we become more focused and centered and actually enrich what we are doing. The time we spend creating something fresh and artistic should not be rushed. As you go through what you are doing, walk, don't run.

It is good to keep a journal to record your day's activities. See how much time you are spending thinking about everything but your inner soul and spirit. In your journal, as you make changes and record activities and observances, you will find yourself getting in touch and centered. Inns have guest books. These journals record a visitor's impressions and beckon us to write about what we learned by staying at the inn. You would be surprised how informative, revealing, and inspirational they can be.

One of the most impressive guest books I have ever seen is at October Country Inn in Bridgewater Corners, Vermont. Here Richard Sims and Patrick Runkel have volumes of large, bound and unlined books where guests have not only documented their impressions and insights in verse, but also in art. The innkeepers leave out thin magic markers of all colors to inspire such creativity. The books are exciting and energizing to read. I remember spending a cold, blizzardy afternoon by the fire, poring through the books, looking for a new revelation. All of the expressions from strangers—people I never met but have sat where I was sitting—were teaching me a whole lot about simplicity and the joys of paying attention to my inner self. Next time you sign a guest book at an inn, realize that you are taking a step toward finding your soul and offering others something to think about, too. It is a simple pleasure to sit at an inn and read a guest book all day.

Soothing moments are everywhere for the taking, especially at inns. One day during one of my visits to Clifton Country Inn in Charlottesville, Virginia, I was working on a new project—this time in the garden. Suddenly, I spotted a few very large blueberry-colored morning glories climbing up a brick wall to one of the inn's enchanting cottages. Of course, I was under a tight schedule and filled with the stress of getting the job at hand completed. In glancing over at the flowers, I thought of the oft-repeated cliché, "Take time to smell the flowers." And so I took it literally. I thought, "C'mon, why don't you do it for a change?" So, I told the folks I was working with that I needed a minute—too bad about schedules. I walked over to one of the flowers and put my face right into its wide trumpet-shaped mouth. I breathed deeply. The beauty of the moment—sensing the velvet of the petals on my cheeks; looking at the flower's life-bearing potential where the seeds are produced and the pollen is generated; and the touch—cupping such a gentle living thing in my hand—it was all a bit overwhelming. I was brimming with good feelings. The flower didn't have a sweet smell—in fact, it didn't have a scent at all! But I got the message of the old maxim anyway, and so the rest of the day went along stress-free and on time.

One of the simple pleasures suggested in this chapter comes from the Willow Brook Inn in Canton, Michigan, suggesting that we plant a butterfly garden. I wouldn't have known what the inn meant if I had not seen one recently at Glen-Ella Springs Inn in Clarkesville, Georgia. We were filming a sequence for my TV show, *Country Inn Cooking with Gail Greco*. My director turned to one of our cameramen and instructed, "Get Gail goo-gooing with the butterflies."

❧ PORTRAITS OF INN-SPIRATION ❧

Our cottage was rented by a lovely lady for her fifteenth wedding anniversary. She spared no expense: The creative woman rented a limousine and picked her husband up at work—she wore nothing but a mink coat and a jeweled tiara! She asked me if I would go along to record the surprise on video. Of course, I accepted. When the limousine arrived at her husband's office, the woman waited until people began leaving the building. She then opened the sun roof and jumped out with a bottle of champagne and yelled, "Happy Anniversary, darling!" Talk about some envious men. She was definitely a charmer, and everyone was excited for them both.

Sassafras Inn

So, I got behind this patch of flowers where dozens of small butterflies were dancing around, unmindful of our crew and me. I was fascinated by the flight of fancy they took around and around. I had never seen anything like it. Usually when I go chase a butterfly, the winged creature is off in a flash. Well, our cameraman, Tony, shot video for a good five minutes. The job was done and he was off. I lingered as long as I could. But later that evening, I felt a bit saddened that Tony hadn't put his camera down and Richard his directorial urge aside, and taken a moment to just sit there with me and watch the waltz of the butterflies.

I think this is a good example of why this chapter is so important. Even though life's little treasures are all around us, we have to be reminded of what they are and to go ahead and indulge in them. Butterflies *are* free and truly, so are you! And besides, remember that the butterfly does not count by months, only moments—and he has enough time. So do you.

SOOTHING MOMENTS

Don't think about tomorrow, next week, or next year—live for today. Too often we loose sight of the simple joys by planning and living in the future.—*Abriendo Inn*

Hang a moon calendar (showing the phases of the moon) near your back door. Glance at it as you come and go, noting the date of the next full moon. Plan an outdoor activity such as an evening stroll, a cross-country ski, go camping, or just spread a blanket out on the lawn in the moonlight.
—*The Inn at 410*

Have someone else make the coffee and deliver it to you in bed.

Have someone else take care of the kids' needs first thing in the morning.
—*Langdon House*

Rock away the "worries of the world" in a padded hammock.—*The Inn at Merridun*

Brush a horse.—*Cedarcroft Farm*

Take a tray of afternoon tea into the garden. Find a beautiful spot and just relax.
—*Blue Lake Ranch*

Gail's Touch: Frame a recipe written in your mother's or grandmother's hand and hang it in your kitchen.

❧

Buy book plates and enjoy browsing through your book collection, putting your own I.D. on the inside cover.

❧

Look through a drawer or scrapbook of past accomplishments and good times had to remember how pleasant and rewarding your life has been.

❧

Line your closets and drawers with scented pretty paper for great satisfaction every time you have to decide what to wear.

❧

I keep little books of sayings and thoughts in my car console. I read a saying or two at a stoplight. Even looking down at them now and then gives me happy thoughts as I toodle along the roadways.

❧

When you're feeling low, go out and buy greeting cards. There's always someone who is either having a birthday or a celebration, or just a friend you need to keep in touch with. Browsing through the cards will give you a lift.

❧

Pick up a tin of new watercolor paints and dabble a little bit on paper, doing any design you wish whether you can paint or not. The feeling of brushing color onto a surface is restful and yet exciting and who knows, you might even find a hidden talent.

❧

Change your routine by traveling to a typical destination, but taking a different route, even if it is a little longer.

❧

String big bells with ribbon and hang on your front door so that each time you open the door, a joyful sound fills your ears.

❧ Lace is a simple pleasure to look at. Collect a few small lace doilies, handkerchiefs, and napkins from craft shows or antique shops. Arrange these delicate adornments inconspicuously around the house. Hang one over the edge of a shelf, arrange one on your dining room buffet. Just a few pieces of elegant lace here and there subtly soften any room.—*The Inn at 410*

Live each moment to the fullest, relish every task no matter how mundane, and take time to treasure the simple pleasures of life.

—Alexander's Inn

❧ Make a simple lap quilt with scraps of curtain fabric: Make a fabric sandwich in the size you desire. The top slice is the curtain fabric, the sandwich center is a sheet of bating (available at any fabric store), and the bottom slice is a complimentary fabric—such as the good section of a worn sheet.

Carefully fold in the edges of the two outside fabric layers on all four sides and pin to secure. Then hand-stitch all four edges and remove the pins.

Purchase crewel thread with complementary color at a fabric or needlepoint shop. Use this to "hand tie" your quilt at measured intervals. (You'll need a crewel needle to bring your thread through all three layers of fabric and back up to the top.)

Finally, cut the thread leaving enough to allow the formation of a knot on the top surface. These knots not only secure the three layers of fabric and stabilize your quilt, but they make a truly unique design.
—*Rabbit Hill Inn*

❧Forego the modern hot tub, and learn the art of taking an old-fashioned bath. Soak until your toes wrinkle.—*Ashling Cottage*

❧Sit in your town's central plaza and enjoy an ice-cream cone.
—*Alexander's Inn (New Mexico)*

❧Spend an afternoon in a bookshop that serves herbal tea. Browse through books, listen to music, and sip relaxing tea.
—*The Grey Whale Inn*

❧Float along a lazy river.—*Queen Anne Inn*

❧Take a nap. When travelling allow yourself time to rest. You'll be refreshed and ready to explore.

Feel comfortable. Run around in your socks or bare feet!—*The King's Cottage*

❧Take a walk with your dog, if you don't have a dog, get to know your neighbor's dog and take a walk with it. Dogs share companionship in a different way: they seem to appreciate your simple presence and shared time, regardless of the activity.

Start a journal. Each day, write down what you love most about someone: The first day, your mother; the second day, your dad; and so on until a daily entry becomes second nature. Keep it a happy, loving journal. You are and will become what you emphasize in your life.—*Adams Edgeworth Inn*

❧Listen to wind chimes and sip lemonade while sitting under an apple tree.—*Willow Brook Inn*

❧Sleep in late.—*The Inn at Merridun*

❧Take a trip down memory lane to the old swimming hole in town. No designer bathing suits here—just kids and adults floating on rafts, sharing picnics, and enjoying the river as it winds by.—*The Inn at Maplewood Farm*

❧Look for small pleasures that happen every day. And not for fortune or fame—infinite treasures that lie along the way, like a candle waiting for a flame.—*From Ben Franklin in Paris, The Inn at Olde New Berlin*

❧Enjoy your coffee with the fresh morning air, out in the garden or on the front porch.—*Madame Dyer's B&B*

❧Catch an old television show.
—*The Arcadian Inn*

Read a good book on the porch in a rocking chair when it's pouring rain out on a summer day.—*The Manor House*

Take a trip to scout out lighthouses. —*The Shelburne Inn*

SHARING HANDS AND HEARTS

The simple pleasure of keeping friends provides many opportunities:

Offer to help a friend before they need to ask; give him or her a present for no reason; remember birthdays, anniversaries, hobbies, places they like to go, music they like to listen to; pitch in with chores when dropping in for an unexpected visit; send funny or seasonal cards—it's always nice to open your mailbox and find a bright colored envelope.—*Butterfield B&B*

Fill your house with nature's bounty. Place a bowl of fresh, crisp apples in the guest room and sitting room of your home. —*The Maine Stay*

Read something soothing to someone.—*Langdon House*

Do anything you enjoy doing—together or alone. My husband enjoys fishing. While he's fishing, I'm quilting. When we're together, we both enjoy exploring flea markets and sitting on the gazebo porch listening to the frogs serenade. Couldn't be simpler. —*Candelite Inn*

Collect golden aspen leaves and send them to a loved one far from home.—*Black Dog Inn*

Gail's Touch: Call someone on the telephone. I know this sounds like a telephone-company line, but the cost of a phone call is really cheap. And on the same subject, please get rid of call-waiting if you have it in your home or business. This is one of life's little destruction devices.

Make the biggest decision of a guest's day, choosing a freshly baked oatmeal or chocolate-chip cookie before bed.—*Willow Brook Inn*

Remember, everyone wears an invisible badge with the letters MMFI—Make Me Feel Important. If more people did this for others, the world would be a much better place.—*Truffles B&B*

When we see the smiles on our guests' faces, we know we are doing something right. That brings us great joy.—*Sassafras Inn*

We keep a sheet of paper in an old 1940s typewriter and invite our guests to type a line or paragraph. As guests continue adding to this ongoing story, I hope to someday have an interesting collection of ideas that our guests have personally created. —*Duggan Place*

Have an "I'm-Feeling-Blue Party" in January. Invite guests to dress as beatniks. Render meaningful philosophies with the Blues Brothers playing in the background. —*The Meadowlark Manor*

It's not the decision you make, but that you make the decision. —*Dairy Hollow House*

"Let the Nothing Begin." This phrase coined by one of our long-term guests, has definitely become our slogan. It reflects the atmosphere we try to create for our guests: elegant, relaxed surroundings that allow our guests to forget their everyday concerns, to feel pampered and indulge themselves in the freedom to do anything or nothing. —*Manor House, Connecticut*

Gail's Touch: There are many kite-flying clubs out there. Find one in your area and check out one of their exhibitions. Or, just on your own, take a friend out for a silly afternoon of kite-flying at a nearby park.

Hold a tea and storytelling afternoon. Invite friends to bring their short tales or yarns and read them to the group while sipping tea.

Invite friends over for an old-fashioned Sunday afternoon dinner.

One summer I invited my sister out for a surprise afternoon. It included a trip to a local park where a mere 50 cents to ride an old-fashioned carousel was the best money I had ever spent on her!

Go berry-picking with the family, then go home and make a pudding or pie.

Whenever you send out a special letter to someone, add a teabag inside.

FOR MORE INFORMATION ON INNS LISTED IN THIS BOOK, SEE THE DIRECTORY BEGINNING ON PAGE 203.

The art of conversation is practiced here, where art, music, and the world come together over steamy hot muffins and coffee. From the living room and dining room, sailboats can be seen slipping silently across the bay. Lewis Carroll, Tolstoy, and Buckminster Fuller are equally comfortable here. Satisfying the mind with stimulating conversation, the body with delicious food, and the senses with unhurried views make this a totally comforting experience.
—*North Garden Inn*

Gail's Touch: In the dead of winter, enjoy the fruits of nature. Grab a friend and two baskets and scavenge a nearby wild forest for berries and other plant life. Exchange ideas on how to decorate with these new findings.

Accentuate the sense of smell with inexpensive indulgences: Open windows for a breath of fresh air, place seasonal potpourri or a bouquet of flowers from the garden in guests rooms, provide fragrant bubble bath.—*Isaiah Hall B&B Inn*

Put all your photos in a pretty basket. When friends and family come by, invite them to rummage through and keep the pictures they like.—*Adams Edgeworth Inn*

Serve a long, leisurely breakfast. Use your finest china and play soft music in the background.—*The Manor House*

People love to feel pampered. Ask your guests to relax in the parlor. Serve them coffee or tea in a china teapot with matching cups and saucers, doilies, and a small plate of cookies. The look on your guests' faces will show you how special they feel. It doesn't take much to bring unexpected joy to someone and the reward is a wonderful sigh of contentment.—*Windermere Manor*

We constantly work with taste, touch, sight, sound, and smell to subtly impact the senses all around the inn. Flowers, lace, art, fragrances, bubbling sounds of water, peaceful nooks—ah, simple pleasures.
—*The Seal Beach Inn*

FAVORITE THINGS . . .

Decorating with a childhood theme brings back many pleasant memories for our guests and creates an atmosphere of peace and tranquility.—*Willow Brook Inn*

Display your favorite whimsical collectibles in and on top of a multishelved glass cabinet. Include stuffed, quilted, and chenille animals; art and children's books; hand-stitched pillows; a folded quilt; antique toys; framed quotes.—*Pratt Guest House*

❧Always have on hand Play-Doh, squirt guns, and bottles of bubbles for blowing in the yard, in addition to the usual board games.—*Trezona House*

❧Play in the snow, build a snowman, ride a sled down a hill, make snow ice-cream.

Put a picture puzzle together. Keep one started to encourage guests.—*Shire Inn*

❧Turn your bathroom into a secret garden: Paint the ceiling blue and extend down the walls about five inches. Apply white paint with plastic grocery bags to create puffy clouds. Add a painted trellis with stenciled ivy. Hang silk ivy plants from the ceiling and wrap more ivy around the medicine cabinet.—*Willow Brook Inn*

❧Play hide and seek with your child. —*Alexander's Inn (New Mexico)*

❧Sit on the beach and dig into a container of Ben Jerry's Toffee Crunch Ice Cream.—*La Maison*

Gail's Touch: A favorite anonymous saying: "Happiness is like a butterfly. The more you chase it, the more it eludes you. But if you turn your attention to other things, it comes and softly sits on your shoulder."

❧Host a tea party for children. Make teacup invitations and invite children to come dressed up like grown-ups. They can wear hats, old wedding dresses, and carry handbags. Read "The Legacy of the Teacup" from Emilie Barnes's book *If Teacups Could Talk.*—*The Meadowlark Manor*

❧Encourage guests to watch, catch, and release fireflies. This summer, we had a guest from Las Vegas who had never seen these curiosities of nature. She was fascinated for an hour just watching them. —*Pheasant Field B&B*

❧Jump in a pile of leaves in autumn.

Chase lightning bugs on a summer evening.

Catch a winter snowflake on your tongue.—*The Half Penney Inn*

❧From the moment guests walk in, they are reminded of school days past: Large prints of pages from the *Fun with Dick and*

Jane reader series, the school bell, little slate writing boards, original blackboards, and antique school desks. Guests are greeted with their names written on big hearts taped to the blackboard and are offered a traditional after-school snack of homemade chocolate-chip cookies and milk.—*School House B&B (Missouri)*

Roast marshmallows in your fireplace. To prevent marshmallows from falling off skewers, serve them slightly stale by leaving them out to dry for a few hours. Pack them in festive little cans and leave by the fire for a chilly night.—*The River House*

Have a good, old-fashioned scavenger hunt with friends from out of town. This enables your visitors to see some spots in your area that they would ordinarily not get to see. The object is for the participants to get to some out-of-the-way places, enjoy a nature drive, and stop at a cafe and some fun spots.

First, you need to plan a route for them to take. Make a list of some of your favorite spots (scenic or otherwise), local parks, restaurants, shops, and other assorted points of interest. Spend the afternoon riding around and checking these places out. Design the route so that all you tell them is

---

🎭 PORTRAITS OF INN-SPIRATION 🎭

On Valentine's Day, a guest asked us to snap a picture of him and his lady friend after removal of their salad course. Right on cue, the scene was indelibly captured as the unabashed young man got on his knees—in a full, albeit dimly lit, dining room—to formally propose. Their vegetarian alternative of fondue-for-two that evening may have absorbed a tad more salt than expected. Tears of joy and memory making were flowing all around—beautiful and inspiring to all observers.

The Inn at Olde New Berlin

left and right turns, street names, and landmarks.

In addition to picking the spots, you need to make up questions that the participants have to answer so that they get a closer look at stops they need to make along the way. The questions add fun, competition, and enrichment. For example, some of our queries have included the following: How many steps to the top of the lookout tower at Peninsula State Park? What date was the downtown Sturgeon Bay Bridge built? There is a piece of antique equipment in the lobby of the White Gull Inn—what is it used for? On the wall of the Bayside Tap, there's a picture of a man holding a book—who is he?

The questions get our guests in conversations with local people, which also can be educational. Once you develop the hunt—its routes and questions—you can use it for all your friends. You can even do this for friends who live in your area but not your neighborhood. They will discover places they never knew existed only a stone's throw away from where they live. Be sure you provide directions with each route and send along a good map, just in case they get lost.
—*White Lace Inn*

FOR MORE INFORMATION ON INNS LISTED IN THIS BOOK, SEE THE DIRECTORY BEGINNING ON PAGE 203.

Listen for the sounds of blades skating across the ice.

Swim in a river gorge pool so cool that you huddle together on the rocks in the sun to warm up.—*The Notchland Inn*

Put a deck of cards in each room. Play a child's game. What could be more simple? —*WinterGreen Country Inn*

Go outside with a piece of chalk and play hopscotch on your sidewalk. —*Lynchburg Mansion Inn*

ALONG THE GARDEN PATH

Take a bike ride through a historic neighborhood.—*Madame Dyer's B&B*

Smell the air when the earth breathes a sigh at dusk.—*Kedron Valley Inn*

Wade in a cool mountain brook on a hot summer's day.—*Black Dog Inn*

On your next hike, take along a snack, a small camp stove, and preparations for coffee or tea. Find an out-of-the-way place to spread out, brew up a fresh cup, and breathe in nature. Take along a good book or just take a nap. You'll return to your day truly refreshed.—*The Inn at 410*

⚘Mother nature is the most enjoyable and pleasurable of anything available, simple or complex. Inhale a sunset, or a tree turning color in the fall. Watch a kitten sleeping, a mother duck with her ducklings, a blade of grass or a single leaf. It's all free for the walking.—*The Mockingbird Inn*

⚘I invite my friends for a cup of tea and conversation, and we just sit on the front porch and absorb the warmth of the sun . . . not fancy, but I give them my undivided attention and listen with ears that open into my heart. —*The Meadowlark Manor*

⚘Find a visually impressive spot and invite friends to join you for a simple picnic supper. Watch the sun go down, watch the birds fly by, or just listen for sounds of the season.—*Sweet Onion Inn*

⚘Always keep extra fishing gear (and a welcome invitation) on hand. The day's catch

makes for a fun barbecue. Don't forget the homemade ice cream. What barbecue is complete without it?—*Mt. Juneau Inn*

⚘Plant a butterfly garden and furnish it with a bench, where you can sit and enjoy the colorful show.

Coordinate colors in your flower gardens with colors in your rooms in the house for an overall visual delight inside and out.

Sip a glass of wine while watching the sunset from the porch.

Enjoy a good book or magazine in a rocking chair beside the wood stove on a cold winter day.

Keep a pair of binoculars and a bird book on hand to watch birds at bird feeders and bird baths.—*Willow Brook Inn*

⚘Savoring the wilderness surrounding our inn:

Guests enjoy the challenging hike to the Raptor's Ridge where hawks nest and eagles soar. The stony hedgerow isn't far—where chipmunks hide in berry brambles and wild flowers. The "Spinney of Woods" north of the farm shelters the red fox, but for sheer heaven, watch the fireflies perform their

> *Search for happiness and you may never find it, but help others to find it and you shall be truly happy.*
> —Old World Inn

meadow ballet every July night.

Bring a hammock, quilt, or Indian blanket to make a grassy slope even more comfortable and quietly observe the moon in all its phases.—*The Chatelaine B&B*

Measure the height of your grandchildren on the same door or porch post every time they visit. Mark their name and the date. As the years go by, this will become a greater and greater pleasure for all.—*Adams Edgeworth Inn*

If you have gardens of edibles, send your guests out to harvest the greens for your dinner. They will enjoy the soothing moments of snipping something for the tables. Edible flowers, vegetables or fruits may also be gathered. They will be entertained while you take a breather and a soothing moment for yourself.—*Kedron Valley Inn*

Get to know a few edible wild plants and gather them in season. Persimmons, for example, are an unexpected gift from nature. Growing in hedgerows and weedy patches from Connecticut to Florida, persimmons bear small, round, purple-cast orange fruit. Just before autumn's first frost, the fruit is perfect for snacking: soft, ripe, and very

sweet. Pick a handful off a tree or from the ground—and just start eating! You'll enjoy, in addition to the taste of the fruit, a sense of a happy conspiracy with nature.—*Dairy Hollow House*

Walk around the village, roller blade beside Cape Cod Canal, stop and chat with the fishermen, sit in a chaise lounge and read a book, walk on the beach and collect sea shells.—*Captain Ezra Nye House*

Lay on a dock at midnight and gaze at the stars. Put on a raincoat and walk in the warm rain.—*WinterGreen Country Inn*

Popcorn cooked in the fireplace or wood stove always tastes better!—*Pheasant Field B&B*

Listen to the rain fall on a tin roof. —*Adams Edgeworth Inn*

Take an evening walk in the cold, crisp air of winter. The silence of the forest and the brightness of the snow in the dark is so overwhelming—it just melts your cares away. —*Mt. Juneau Inn*

New crayons. Warm cookies. Feeding

birds. Old bathrobes. Farmers' markets. Wild flowers. Breezes. Old books. Church bells. Seed catalogs. Waving at folks.—*Clauser's B&B*

A cat curled in your lap. Walking along a wooded creekside. A child's hug. A smile on Grandmother's lips. A "thank you." —*The Inn at Honey Run*

Our breakfast room overlooks rolling fields and a meadow, with the South Mountain as a backdrop. Most mornings, guests are entertained by cheeky chipmunks scampering up the trunks of century-old maple trees that surround the inn. Pheasants can be seen wandering through the giant pumpkin patch, while an assortment of hawks, woodpeckers, and blue jays savor their breakfasts in the woods.—*Fairfield Farm Inn*

Relax in an Adirondack chair on the bank of a river. Watch the birds, read a book, or just take a nap.—*Shire Inn*

Dig in the earth by gardening or planting trees.—*Kedron Valley Inn*

Transport yourself to another world— walk in the woods. The quiet and serenity is so rejuvenating and there is nothing like the thrill of a seeing a newborn deer.—*L'Auberge Provençale*

"Take your time and do it right the first time." (The Ten Commandments of Human Relations) —*Chicago Pike Inn*

THE LUXURY OF COMFORTABLE THINGS

Gail's Touch: Get rid of anything you really don't like and replace it with something you do like. If you don't give it the heave-ho, you will suffer with it forever. Be positive and move on.

Don't use manila folders when there are so many pretty colored ones for your office or household files.

Sit under shady summer trees, dreaming to the tunes of nature.

Smell the scent of a wood fire that fills the mind with distant memories.

Use a printer's box not only for small collectibles but also to place inside a dresser drawer to hold jewelry. Knock out a few sections, if necessary, for storing larger jewels.

❧There's no better place to munch on a bowl of warm, buttery popcorn, than by a crackling fire.—*Old Church House Inn*

❧On a chilly night, sit by the fireplace with warm apple pie a la mode and a good listener. Share what's important or what's troubling you.—*Campbell Ranch Inn*

❧Return home to warm cookies and hot chocolate after snowshoeing on a full moon night.—*Black Dog Inn*

❧We leave seasonal messages on our answering machine such as this one: "Colorful leaves and pumpkins—it's fall at Willow Brook Inn. Cranberry bread and baked apples for breakfast, then hot cider and doughnuts before you climb into cozy flannel sheets for a good night's rest. We look forward to having you as our guests."
—*Willow Brook Inn*

❧Sit in front of the fire with a pot of tea and a good gossiping girl friend.—*Adams Edgeworth Inn*

❧Watch a very pink sunset.—*Kedron Valley Inn*

❧Spend a lazy afternoon in a hammock. Enjoy the quiet, interrupted only by a bird's song or a squirrel's chatter.—*Orchard Hill Country Inn*

REVERIE WITH OLD THINGS

❧Our inn's signature—part of its Gothic Romanticism—is the unexpected use of antique objects. Audacious effects surprise guests at every turn. One of those surprises is towels offered on antique, wooden, store-mannequin arms.—*Red Castle Inn*

❧A preacher's pulpit is in our guest registration area. You can use one in your home as a dictionary stand or a place for a guest book.—*Inn at Mitchell House*

❧A former church pew makes a nice bench in any room. Decorate it with an old hymnal, a pair of cotton gloves, and a basket of flowers.

An antique doll carriage is a decorative accent for a room and can hold magazines and books.—*Benner House*

We use wooden drier racks for drying herbs and flowers or to hold current newspapers and magazines.—*Riverwind*

We made a coffee table from a hatch cover on an old freighter.—*Silas Griffith House*

Gail's Touch: If there's a vintage book you want, but it is mildewed, don't shy away from buying it. You can remove a good part of the mustiness. Set the book in the sun. Fan the pages frequently. Then brush off the dried mold.

A popular spot is our coffee corner, where a 1915 gas stove is the butler for coffee any time of day. Coffee is made in an automatic, drip coffee maker on top of the stove. Stove drawers hold spoons. Cups can be found in the warming oven. —*Schoolhouse Inn*

Shopping at salvage sales is a great way to bring some unusual old items into your home. We've purchased several different porch railings, for example. If you like the item, buy it. You'll find a use for it eventually. —*Zachariah Foss Guest House*

Revive an old lampshade frame with a doily.—*Hutchinson House*

Stylish old clothes can be used as decoration. An old lace nightgown on a padded hanger is draped across the foot of one of our beds.

Those delicate hankies of old can be put to good use by placing them over an old Bible or a book of verse on a bureau or small table.—*Thompson Park House*

> *We too often love things and use people, when we should be using things and loving people.*
> —Sassafras Inn

Using clothing from the Victorian era reinforces the time period we're creating. A period bridal gown and a dried bouquet hang in one of our guest rooms. Lovely, funny, old hats, including flapper clothes, are on stands and bedposts in guest rooms. They give our guests plenty of giggles when they try them on.—*Heartstone Inn*

We have a few old Victorian swimsuits hanging by the hot tub. Some guests want to know if they have to wear them in order to use the hot tub. Other guests just try them on for fun.—*Audrie's Cranbury Corner*

FOR MORE INFORMATION ON INNS LISTED IN THIS BOOK, SEE THE DIRECTORY BEGINNING ON PAGE 203.

An antique dress hangs on an old dress-maker's form in one of the bedrooms. We've wondered if guests have ever tried it on during the course of their stay.—*Ilverthorpe Cottage*

Gail's Touch: Old doll clothing mounted in a picture frame makes an attractive accent in an appropriate room.

Chapter 4

OH, TO BE IN THE GARDEN

A WONDERFUL MISSIVE DIGS UP NEW WAYS TO SEE THINGS

The other day an innkeeper sent me a card. Whenever I receive a communication from an inn, I know there is something pleasant inside, a few well-chosen words or phrases, an invitation, or an announcement. (You may know what I mean if you are on any guests-of-inns mailing lists.) You can count on the note being poetic in verse, pretty to look at, personalized to you, and inviting. While writing this book, one such missive was delivered to me and it left quite an impression. It will become a lifetime keepsake. I may even mount and frame it for what it represents.

The communique was from The Southern Hotel, a charming eight-bedroom country inn in the quaint French-historic Missouri village called Ste. Genevieve. It was a notecard. Inside, innkeepers Barbara and Mike Hankins were letting me know that they were sending along a "... cuddle and a hug, we're thinking of you. . . ." (Innkeepers are like that . . . concerned about their guests long after they are gone.) But I thought of them and their special inn filled with the romance of the past portrayed through a combination of whimsy and sophistication. The outside of the card has the same effect.

The card is a soft watercolor of the inn's garden, done in shades of greens, browns, and terracotta. The moment I set eyes on the painting, I put myself inside of it. There I was smelling the rows of colorful blossoms and herbs Barbara has so lovingly tended for many years. I shuffled along the brick pathway, passing flowers seemingly planted with no particular logic but plenty of insight. The capricious and lyrical layout of the garden even brought a song to mind, a tune by The Moody Blues about leaves "swaying to a breeze that's playing on a thousand violins and bees that are humming to a frog that's strumming . . . and a mouse playing a daffodil, while all the band was really jumping. . . ."

At the far left hand corner of the painting, my journey through the eyes was coming to a close. But first I stopped at the old summer kitchen that Barbara now uses as her artistic room for painting and potting. The old brick shed is a delight for the senses and is filled with great garden trinkets to buy. An old leafy tree bends toward the little brick out-building and a farm bell on a wooden pole tilts its head in acknowledgment of the tree's gesturing glance. Everything has a mind of its own in this garden.

I walk out of the painting, but I'm still in the garden. Past the shed I know there's a bench under a shade tree and lots of garden flowers and curiosities Barbara has set out. It's only a painting, but it has proven an enchant-

I'll tell you something partner. If you don't like what you do for a living, you won't like anything else." (Ben Brooks, our local commercial fisherman)
—Langdon House

ment and certainly an inspiration. The garden at The Southern Hotel is one of my favorites and, like many inn gardens, reminds all of us why it is so important to have our own things to nurture and care for—a big message that having a garden teaches.

On one of my visits to Ste. Genevieve, I can remember Barbara telling me how she is impassioned by the sound of the spade hitting the earth and the warmth of the sun on her shoulders and how opinions and issues of the day matter not as she turns the earth with her shovel. Despite heavy duties as an innkeeper who also makes the breakfasts, dinners, answers phones, and makes reservations, she still makes time to be in her garden.

We cannot all have gardens, but we can visit someone else's, and we can bring the fruits of another's horticultural labors into our homes. Cut flowers and potted plants are gifts from the garden that your guests at home will find add romance and warmth to their visit. Meanwhile, it is at best rewarding to romp through the following secrets of the innkeeper's gardens.

Gail's Touch: A favorite quote of mine: Flowers are here to remind us of our inner garden. They are purveyors of color, beauty, and life. We can't postpone our appreciation of flowers for some future time; a daylily lives only one day. Flowers urge us to look at them, and by the brevity of their lives, they force us to examine what it means to be on this human journey. (Alexandra Stoddard, *Tea Celebrations*)

THE PROMISES OF A GARDEN

❧If you don't have land for a garden, and besides, you aren't the type who likes to mow the grass and till the soil, a rooftop garden is the answer. We built a redwood deck on one of our roofs with a covering and a totally enclosed solarium. The solarium has a fireplace, so we can sit and have breakfast out here even in cold weather. We have hanging plants all over the outdoor section and plants in large standing pots.—*Healdsburg Inn on the Plaza*

❧Don't let the lack of planting areas stop you from planting a garden. Use clay pots and large barrels filled with a mixture of potting soil and topsoil, and watch your garden grow above ground!—*Inn at Starlight Lake*

❧Purchase colorful plants in bloom. Petunias and snapdragons in 4-inch pots work well. Mass them together in a shallow container or basket. Disguise the top of the plastic pots with sphagnum moss. A tight circle of 4-inch pots works well around the base of deciduous trees. After the blooms are spent, the plants can be set out permanently in the garden.—*Red Castle Inn*

❧Because our time is precious, gardening must be fairly maintenance-free. One of our techniques: Bark mulch in beds looks nice, keeps down weeds, and holds moisture. —*Bramble Inn*

Gail's Touch: Fill an old wooden wheelbarrow with colorful flowers in the summer. Display the cart on your front lawn. In the winter the wheelbarrow can hold potted plants indoors.

❧Anyone can have a small pond in a garden. Dig a deep hole the depth and size you want. Buy a heavy-duty plastic liner at any hardware store. This forms your pool for holding the water. The dirt from the hole can be used as an embankment around the pond.

It doubles as a dam. Clean out the pond once a week. Keep it stocked with goldfish (to alleviate mosquitoes), snails, and aquatic plants.—*La Maida House*

Gail's Touch: Anyone can have a garden. A garden is one of life's simplest pleasures. Try it once and you'll be hooked.

❧Enhance garden space with a hot tub. Use an ozonator as well as chlorine. You guarantee sanitation and avoid odor and red eyes.—*O'Duach'ain Inn*

❧The key to raising bulbs successfully is good drainage. Prepare the soil well so that water does not sit around the bulbs, causing them to rot. Planting bulbs in raised beds is a good idea if you don't have good drainage. —*Cedarym B&B*

❧Don't skimp when buying good bulbs. Buy high-quality bulbs from a reputable supplier. Remember that you're making a long-term investment.

Plan your garden well. The tallest growing bulbs should be in the back, bordered by shorter ones in the front. Early-blooming bulbs are fun to plant where they will be easily seen from your windows or be adjacent to frequently traveled walkways, so you can enjoy a sensation of spring when little else is blooming.

Remember that bulbs have different growing and flowering periods. Plant accordingly so that your garden will bloom throughout the full growing season.

Bulbs can be used to bring early color to a perennial garden when planted in clumps of five or six throughout the garden.

Early or mid-season daffodils add a nice touch to a field or around the edge of a pond, if planted in clumps 5 to 10 feet apart or at random, to look as though they grew on their own.—*Kedron Valley Inn*

❧To attract butterflies, plant flowers such as zinnias and marigolds. There are also numerous varieties of butterfly bushes and flowers, which were grown during the Victorian era, that are planted specifically to attract butterflies.—*The Bechtel Mansion Inn*

❧Plan your garden to include an evening-fragrance garden, especially if you live in an area conducive to strolling or you have a patio. Use mostly white flowers. They are luminescent during the nighttime. Nicotiana is a favorite. It's white and fragrant, and its blooms open at night.—*Bungay Jar*

If you have two loaves of bread, sell one and buy a flower. —*The Seal Beach Inn*

Gail's Touch: To make gardening easier, take a tool caddy along with you. Create clever caddies according to your needs. One idea is to take an old golf bag and fill it with rakes, hoes, and shovels. Use the smaller pouches for tinier tools.

The hotter and drier the soil, the more pungent the herbs. Although they will not look as nice as herbs growing in moist soil, they will be perfectly pungent.—*Park House*

The best time to pick herbs is in the early morning, when they are fresh and have not withered from exposure to the sun. —*Carter House*

When you first plant your herbs, don't cut them back too much in the first year. You are providing growth for the rest of their life.—*Churchtown Inn*

Our large herb garden grows prolifically, so when we are short on greenery, we cut herbs to fill out a pot of flowers. The aroma refreshes any room, including the bedrooms.—*The Montford Inn*

EVERBLOOMING EXPRESSIONS

Nothing shows more than flowers that you are happy your guest is with you. Even when they are unseasonable, we put pots of flowers outdoors so that they can be seen out the sliding doors of every guest room. —*Canyon Villa*

To give cut flowers longer life, cut the ends on an angle. Make sure no leaves are below the water level. Change water daily. —*Isaiah Hall B&B*

Bleach will help fresh flowers and the water in the vase look fresher. Add about one-half teaspoon per quart of water. —*Ash Mill Farm*

Flower vases dulled by brown film can sparkle again. Chop a small potato into very small pieces and place them in the dulled vase. Add one-half cup vinegar. Shake well. Wash in soapy water and rinse.—*Britt House*

Wildflowers make wonderful bouquets in the summertime. Pick them late in the day when it's cool. As soon as you pick them, soak them right up to their necks in a bucket of water. Let them stand overnight before arranging. This way, they will keep for up to a week.—*Inn at Gristmill Square*

▸Use a meat/poultry baster to add water to vases and potted flower arrangements to prevent water damage to antique tables and other furniture.—*Red Castle Inn*

▸When buying flowers, ask the florist when they came in or how long they have been at the shop. If the flowers are faded, it could be a sign that they are old. Ask if that is so, as some flowers only have the appearance of being faded.

When dried flowers look old, dust them lightly and spray them with hairspray. The spray helps hold them together and slows down crumbling or falling apart.

To make flower arranging easier, make a small ball of tangled chicken wire that fits into the bottom of the container. Insert the stems of your flowers, and they will be held in place. You can also crisscross the top of your container with transparent adhesive tape, making small areas in which to insert the flowers. Make sure the tape doesn't show.—*Blossom Tyme*

For more information on inns listed in this book, see the directory beginning on page 203.

▸The stems of roses will hold the weight of the rose, without bending over, if you place one tablespoon of epsom salts around the base of each rosebush and water it in. I don't know why it works, but it really does. A guest gave us this tip, and it has worked for all eighty of our rosebushes.—*Lamplight Inn*

IN BLOOM WITH THE PAST

▸An antique tricycle in our front flower bed serves as a trellis for our climbing flowers.—*Ellis River House*

▸Antique scales make great plant hangers. We have one over a bathtub.—*Arcady Down East*

▸We hang plants in little buckets from each spoke of an old yarn winder. —*Birchwood Inn*

▸Small, glass mason jars are vases on our breakfast table.—*Silver Maple Lodge*

▸Antique bottles can be used as flower vases.—*Pudding Creek Inn*

▸We disassembled an old chimney when we first arrived and have used the bricks for

PORTRAITS OF INN-SPIRATION

A guest reserved the nicest room available at the inn for himself and his significant other on December 5. He had a special gift or surprise for her every day until Christmas. The man could hardly contain himself with what he had done and what was ahead and shared a few of the impending surprises with me:

The answer to the riddle, "It looks like a snowflake, but lasts forever" was a diamond ring. He followed me to the kitchen to divulge more of his planned surprises. I was taken aback by the elaborate lengths this man traveled to impress this woman. Curiosity forced me to ask what was going to top everything on December 25. He replied that he had ordered 1,001 roses—all but one would be red. The single rose would be coral, her favorite color. Santa Claus would be delivering the flowers on a horse-drawn sleigh.

As time passed, I often thought about the couple who stayed with us that Christmas and wondered what the outcome of the events had been. About a year later I saw the man and asked if he and the woman got married. He simply replied, "No." Was I surprised? Not really. No matter how much we like to control our lives and try to make things happen, some things are just not meant to be.

Abriendo Inn

different projects. They make excellent borders around flower beds.
—*Inn on Golden Pond*

✂An ornate bird cage of yesteryear is great for housing a plant. Hang the cage from the ceiling, or put it on a stand or table.—*Benner House*

✂Antique apothecary jars are great for

filling with potpourri.—*Boydville The Inn at Martinsburg*

✒ Desks from old schoolhouses can double as plant stands; those with lids can be used as display cases for collectibles.

Just because a wicker chair seat might be worn with age doesn't mean the piece no longer can function. Use it as a plant holder.—*Glenborough Inn*

✒ Maple-sugar buckets, which have been put to rest when they can no longer be used for sugaring, are indispensable in the garden. We use them to sit on, carry tools, cover tender plants from frost, make supports to hold up shading frames or berry netting, to stand on to reach tall trees, and to gather ashes from the fireplace to spread on the garden.—*Windfields Farm*

✒ Horse-drawn sleighs are filled with seasonal flowers and plants outside the inn.—*Middlebury Inn*

✒ An old stone pediment from a building

"Don't walk in front of me—I may not follow. Don't walk behind me—I may not lead. Walk beside me and just be my friend." (author unknown)

—Shire Inn

column has made a great plant stand for a Christmas cactus.—*Boydville The Inn at Martinsburg*

✒ We use old children's chairs to hold plants.—*Victorian B&B*

✒ Any antique that you admire but can't find any use for can be converted into a vase or container of some kind. Place a glass jar inside the container, such as in high-top button shoes, and you have a unique flower holder.—*Red Castle Inn*

✒ If you're looking for lovely antique vases, don't overlook glassware originally intended for other purposes. We've found that topless apothecary jars make wonderful flower holders. With their stoppers intact, these jars can be quite expensive, but if purchased topless, they're a bargain. One of our most admired vases is an 1895 light-blue apothecary jar that cost us only $3.00. With the top it would have been about $20.00 to $25.00.—*Quill and Quilt*

✒ Antique strawberry boxes make great

vases for dried arrangements. We have some complete with original advertising: "Seagraves Strawberries–Elsah: The Place to Get Quality."—*Green Tree Inn*

❧Painted milk cans hold dried flowers. Antique gravy boats hold potpourri.
—*Greenbriar B&B*

❧I do the things I want to do and I make excuses for everything else.
—*The Groveland Hotel*

❧Old shoe-drying racks are the best we have found for holding large tools in the garden. The pegs support the handles of rakes, hoes, shovels and garden hats. The racks were always on wheels, so you can find them in antiques stores.—*Settlers Inn*

❧Antique family teacups serve as tiny vases for flowers. You also can use them on a vanity to hold cosmetic puffs or cotton balls.—*Inn on Golden Pond*

Chapter 5

WHERE ALL HEARTS GATHER

ENHANCEMENTS FROM THE KITCHEN TO THE TABLE

I remember the first time I sat down at the table of a country inn. It was an autumn night when the air in the mountains in upstate New York had caught a cold. Candlelight illuminated lace and linens and crystal stemware, but more than that, my imagination and my sense of well-being were enlightened. The room was an oasis for those who wanted quiet chatter, eclipsed only by the ting of a silver fork hitting a bone-china plate. Other small tables and a gentle fire were coaxing a mood. I still feel the peacefulness of that table after more than fifteen years and so many, many gracious tables afterwards.

Sitting at a table to eat and join in a communion of taste, texture, and sound is truly one of my greatest joys in life, whether at an inn or at home. To me, dining is poetry—the chance to look into another's eyes for intimate or any other type of conversation and to focus, seeing much more than myself, seeing the beauty of another. "Dining is and always was a great artistic opportunity," wrote architect Frank Lloyd Wright. I think sitting at a table with one or more people enables us to be like an artist, thereby being in touch with our own nature, and as an artist, being able to free our spirit. It seems as if any subject is elevated to sacred status by being placed on the dinner table. Food and the ceremony of eating keep the conversation in balance.

Depending on the occasion the conversation can be anything from subdued to uproarious or have no uniformity at all. I like tables for two, but just as passionately, I also find that sitting down family-style is a very centered, settling experience. Inns offer us the rare opportunity to come away from a meal not only having nourished our bodies, but our hearts and souls. Many inns serve breakfast family-style.

The breakfast table is home base; freshly brewed coffee in the morning makes the inn come alive and triggers anticipation. Some inns even seat guests at a long table for dinner. Joining with hearts who have gathered but do not know each other expands the mind and is always uplifting. At The Mainstay Inn in Cape May, innkeeper Sue Carroll (who with husband, Tom, opened one of the first bed and breakfasts in America in 1971) encourages comradeship among breakfast-goers with place cards that tell two sides of the story: The first name of each guest is printed on the back side of the card, as well as on the front, thus enabling other guests to know who's who. Makes perfectly good sense, and I wonder why I hadn't

"You are welcome, very welcome to the shelter of our roof, and to show you're well contented, may we ask this little proof? Put away all thoughts of strangeness and in quiet slumber rest, till tomorrow brings renewal of glad welcome to our guest."
(author unknown)
—Kingsley House

thought of doing that at my house. It is becoming a cliché in the bed-and-breakfast industry, but this much is true: Sometimes you walk away from the breakfast table with new friends for life. Indeed, you always walk away having spent time with shared comforts that go a long way in bonding even a casual acquaintance.

Meanwhile, in the kitchen, is a relaxed innkeeper who has everything under control, making an arduous task look simple. Actually, innkeepers are perfect scientific models of hosting. What they tell us is that it is just as rewarding to be behind the counter in partaking of the great ritual of dining as it is to be out in front of it. The exuberance they feel about preparing a feast for their guests is admirable. I love this description by Sallie Clark of how she prepares for dining at her inn. The emphasis is on the details; everything is considered. Listen to the strength of hospitality in her reverent portrayal of breakfast at Holden House.

Breakfast is a special treat. In the morning we start with fresh fruit cup, using the best seasonal produce available. Colorful fruits are used in combination to give eye appeal and freshness. We cut our fruit into bite-sized pieces and place the fruit in fluted dishes. We top our fruit cups with honey and a vanilla yogurt made locally here in Colorado. Garnish may consist of kiwis, strawberries, raspberries, whatever looks best at the market. Color mixtures are very important in making the meal look inviting.

The table is set attractively and includes lace or linen placemats, linen napkins, napkin rings, fine silverware (fork, knife, teaspoon, butter knife, demitasse spoon), china, crystal knife rests, cut-glass plates (to set the fruit cups on and allow for muffin space), juice stem glass, fresh ice water, coffee cup and saucer, butter slices set on a crystal dish, cream and sugar, and a variety of teas. A beautifully set table makes the initial presentation of breakfast more appealing to guests. We brew freshly ground almond-Amaretto-flavored coffee each morning—the aroma luring the guests out of their comfortable beds to the breakfast table.

First, the juice and ice water are poured, the fruit cup served, and a basket of muffins is presented at the table. Our guests begin their meal. When some time has passed, we bring out the piping-hot entree as a second course. This gives our guests the opportunity to relax and enjoy their dishes at a leisurely pace while listening to classical music and conversing with other guests.

The kitchen is the hub of activity behind the scenes at almost every inn. Some kitchens are busier than others, with several more food preparations than breakfast on their plates. Afternoon tea, pre-dinner get-togethers, picnics, and dinner itself keeps a kitchen staff on full time. Organization is essential in making the job look easy, and some of the ideas in this chapter will help you get underway in your own food-preparation space.

My kitchen is a place of peace. To me, the preparation is part of the art of eating, and I've got to be in aesthetic surroundings to do my work. This is true of whatever room I'm in, but particularly in my office and the kitchen, where I spend most of my time.

Things can get really muddled and out of hand. I need to be visually stimulated and satisfied in my work space. I surround myself with things that make me feel good: fruit, grains, beans, pasta in glass jars, plants, colorful plates, teapots, framed art work, books here and there, and always African violets. All utensils (except my knife block) are invisible. I'd rather take the extra time and hassle to pull appliances out from under than to have to look at them every day. And there are always flowers in the kitchen, fresh when possible.

At the end of each television episode of *Country Inn Cooking with Gail Greco*, I offer a quick tip from the inn we have just featured. One memorable suggestion was one that came from Rowell's Inn in Simonsville, Vermont. Innkeeper and chef Beth Davis told me the only advice she has for others is that you surround yourself with love in the kitchen. For Beth that meant a framed portrait a la stick figures from her granddaughter, a decorative bracket that was formerly in her mother's home, her collection of cookbooks, framed photographs of her family, and her Bible. All these loving trinkets were contained in a very small country inn kitchen. I walked viewers through this kitchen of love; it made me feel good, and I'm sure the viewers felt the same. Doing the same in my kitchen makes me feel loved with every stir at the stove.

Getting ready for feeding family and friends and gathering at the table can be a pleasurable experience every day from beginning to end—one that holds promise of a great day ahead or a wonderful evening's repast. I like ending my thoughts on this subject with this refrain taken from Doris Beckert of Foothill House in California:

Our wine-appreciation hour is a special time for guests to gather before dinner. It gives them an opportunity to meet the other guests and to get to know their hosts a little better. This time is for relaxing, conversing, and sharing. We do appetizers and pair the wine with the food we are serving. Once again, a great deal of thought and care is given to ensure that the guests have the best. On beautiful summer evenings the time may be spent on the patio, with the waterfall as background music and lovely views of the gardens. On chillier evenings the sunroom becomes a cozy space. The fireplace is lit, soft music is in the background, and the laughter and pleasure of our guests create a time to remember. Guests will then leave to go out for dinner, and we will continue the pampering at the Foothill House with our evening turndown service.

ARDENT LESSONS

❧A warm, simple, good meal, lovingly prepared and served by a relaxed hostess, is much better than an elegant repast if doing said repast stresses the hostess out. Having nice, hot, made-from-scratch-soup waiting along with good bread, a salad, maybe cheese, fruit, or a simple dessert is a simple feast that instills comfort and reassurance. —*Dairy Hollow House*

❧Most houseguests don't want to feel as though you are waiting on them; they don't want to "be a bother." Include them in the meal preparation. They would probably love to help but don't know what to do.—*The Inn at Depot Hill*

❧Remember that your guests have feelings and opinions, too. They should be made to feel comfortable and the center of your consideration.—*L'Auberge Provençale*

❧Include your guests in your regular, everyday activities. If you walk or if you belong to an organization, ask guests to accompany you. The guest is then privileged to share your life, to meet your friends and business associates.—*The Grey Whale Inn*

❧Relax. If you are relaxed, your guests will be. The more things they can help themselves to, the easier it is for you.—*The Half Penney B&B*

Gail's Touch: I believe in name tags when it comes to a large party at home. You may know everyone who's been invited, but your guests don't know one another, and you need an icebreaker. I not only spell out the person's name but I usually add a tagline about their interests or occupation. A tag might say, "John Smolak . . . I make dough rise." In fact I once used this very phrase. John is a chief financial officer at Lechter's Kitchen Stores, and he enjoys baking his own bread. You might say, "I'm Kathy, ask me about tomatoes," for that friend who has an incredible vegetable garden.

❧It's nice for each guest to have his or

her own salt and pepper shaker in front of his or her place setting. This way, guests don't have to interrupt conversation at the table. —*Madame Dyers B&B*

Inns are like cats. Get a hundred of them together and you've got a hundred very distinct personalities and styles of entertaining. Every inn becomes what the folks that run them want them to be. That's my advice for entertaining at home. Be yourself. —*The Simmons Homestead Inn*

Flexibility is key in entertaining with charm and good spirit. If someone is late for breakfast, so what. Guests should be accommodated.—*La Maison*

Being a host is like being in love—you have to think of the other person. We didn't make this up, but we live it and think it's a good idea to do at home.—*The Inn at Ormsby Hill*

Guests at Ash Mill Farm have plenty of lighthearted conversation between courses.

PORTRAITS OF INN-SPIRATION

A young man asked that two glasses of champagne be brought to his table after he and his companion had placed their dinner orders. He had pre-arranged for us to slip an engagement ring in the woman's glass—a treasure at the bottom of the bubbles. Because we didn't want his future wife to inadvertently choke as she sipped, we took the liberty of presenting the ring in a shallow sherbet glass filled with champagne. Easily seen, carefully retrieved, readily accepted!

Another man brought his ring to the inn early in the day. We had plenty of time to honor his request: He wanted the menus presented as scrolls. As the woman unrolled the menu, the ring was revealed inside the scroll.

The Inn at Olde New Berlin

Everyone gets chatting once the innkeepers begin asking where everyone went for dinner the night before.

If you have a dinner party with people who don't know one another, a good way to break the ice is to start talking about some good places where you have dined.
—*Ash Mill Farm*

Don't let your guests know how hard you've worked to set the beautiful table or cook the wonderful meal. All of this will be obvious. There is nothing worse than a hostess who complains about the toil.

When introducing your guests at a dinner party, we suggest you don't bother with last names. Take your time with the introduction so that the guests clearly hear each name. They may remember names better that way. Also, if you know the person's interests or occupation, mention that, too. Then there won't be any problem with getting a conversation going. When planning whom to invite to your party, especially a small dinner get-together, carefully select guests who are compatible.

And consider that when it's time to pour the coffee, whether for breakfast, lunch, or dessert, it's a nice touch to have the man of the house do the honors.—*Edge of Thyme*

THE KITCHEN EMPORIUM

When following a recipe, it is most efficient to set out all your ingredients first. This is called the *mise en place* (pronounced meez on plaz). Use small muffin tins or cupcake-sized pans, instead of individual ramekins or ingredient bowls, to measure out spices and herbs and other ingredients. This way you have one more manageable source for all your little goodies, and it also makes cleaning up afterwards a lot easier.—*Old Drover's Inn*

Gail's Touch: To intensify the flavor of many rolled-cookie recipes, dust the work surface with powdered sugar instead of flour.

By the way, don't let a lack of cookie cutters stop you from making interesting cookies. Trace shapes you like from a picture book onto cardboard. Place the cardboard on the dough and cut around the shape with a sharp knife.

Cook pasta in a lot of water and you won't need to add oil. The water, if there is enough of it, dilutes the starch that causes the stickiness, as it is dissolved during cooking.

If you want to perk up the flavor of your

fresh red-pasta-sauce recipe, add some feta cheese to the pan as you finish sautéing the tomatoes, olive oil, basil, and garlic.—*The Checkerberry Inn*

Forget potato chips. Vegetable chips are the new snack to accompany or garnish your plates. Use anything from sweet potatoes, beets, or carrots to zucchini and turnips or other root vegetables. Use your imagination. Peel the vegetables and use a mandoline to shave the vegetables paper thin. Using a sieve, sprinkle cornstarch over the chips. This prevents them from curling when cooking. Place the chips into very hot oil (about 250°) and fry until lightly crisp. Remove the chips to a paper towel to drain. Season with salt and serve in a nice fabric-lined basket.—*Stonehedge Inn*

Use a potato peeler to peel broccoli stalks.—*Glen-Ella Springs Inn*

To keep your blueberry pancakes from turning blue, add the small Maine frozen blueberries to the pancakes just after you pour them onto the griddle. This requires a few extra seconds of cooking so that the dough around the blueberries cooks.

For a new twist on carrots, blanch them in water in a skillet with a tablespoon of maple syrup and a dash of mace. Cook them over medium heat until much of the water is gone. Test with a fork for doneness.—*Shire Inn*

Gail's Touch: Nonstick cookware is a must in the kitchen nowadays for reasons of health as well as expediency. Nonstick kitchen helpers come in all forms and styles from cookware and bakeware to stove-top appliances. Choose only quality nonstick pans, such as DuPont SilverStone, with trusted names and labels for long wear. It really does make a difference. Some companies now even have lifetime warranties. I use nonstick for all my kitchen needs, not only for sautéing and deglazing but also for simpler cooking needs, such as cooking pasta.

Our guests appreciate our concern for their health. We don't go overboard, but here are some substitutions for a healthier pantry:

🍂 Sauté turkey sausage in orange juice

> *Twelve words keep a family together: I was wrong. I am sorry. Please forgive me. I love you.*
> —Campbell Ranch Inn

instead of oil. It adds flavor and keeps the dry meat moistened.

❧ Apple juice may be substituted for oil in a recipe. Use twice the amount called for in oil. The juice doesn't seem to change a recipe as it does quite a bit of evaporating.

❧ Two egg whites will take the place of one whole egg.

❧ Whirl 1 1/8 cups oatmeal in a blender to a fine grind to use as a substitute for 1 cup white flour.

❧ Substitute evaporated skim milk for cream in coffee as well as in recipes.

❧ Use lowfat yogurt in place of cream sauces. Season with spices.

❧ Chocolate equals 4 tablespoons carob powder, plus 1 tablespoon margarine.

❧ One cup sugar equals 2/3 cup honey. Reduce one of the liquids in the recipe by 1/4 cup.—*Twin Gates B&B*

Gail's Touch: Skim milk can have the added consistency of whole milk without the added calories by mixing it with nonfat powdered milk. Stir in small amounts of powder until you get the consistency you want. By the way, dry milk added to yogurt will cut the acidity of the yogurt.

❧ A little touch of a cinnamon/sugar mixture, kept in a spice shaker, when sprinkled over muffins prior to baking, adds crunchiness to the tops and fills the kitchen with a wonderful smell.—*Holden House*

❧ An easy breakfast or dessert idea is to layer different types of fruit in a stem wineglass. Be sure to have a variety of colors in there. Top with sliced bananas and a slice of kiwi. Serve with vanilla yogurt in a sherry goblet. Top the yogurt with a cherry. Makes the table look festive and elegant.
—*Clements Inn*

❧ Sifting powdered sugar over fruit cups or around the edges of serving plates can make any fruit course special.
—*Duggan Place B&B*

❧ When you don't have lemon juice available, here's another way to protect fruit from browning in the open air. Use about 1/4 teaspoon salt to 2 cups water. Add sliced fruit to the mixture; drain and pat dry.

So that carrots won't have that dried-out look when prepared ahead of time, peel them and cut to desired length. Place the cut carrots in a plastic container with a teaspoon of sugar and fill with water. Change the water every other day and use as needed. Before serving, cut as desired, then cover with a damp paper towel.—*The Jabberwock*

To refresh limp parsley, place the vegetable in a bowl of water with only *a drop* of liquid dish detergent. The dark green color will be restored, and the parsley will be like new again. Rinse, dry, and serve.—*Trail's End Country Inn*

To help keep the edges of your knives sharp, store them in a wooden knife block, blade-side up. This way, every time you pull out a knife, you won't be dulling it.

To crush garlic in a press, leave the skin on. It is then easier to clean the press.—*The Jabberwock*

Before some meals, sometimes during a meal, and always at the end of a meal, we pass around washcloths that have been dipped in rose- or lemon-scented water (warm in winter and cool in summer) and wrung damp. Having lived in Japan for a while, we brought this custom to the inn.

Also, we use our collection of chopstick holders for knife rests.—*The Inn at Merridun*

Gail's Touch: Some of my fondest pictures of my parents and family are those taken in the kitchen. I keep my camera in a drawer. So much fun goes on in the kitchen, where precious and fun-filled moments—from failed recipes to magical creations and funny incidents—occur.

❧ PORTRAITS OF INN-SPIRATION ❧

A gentleman reserved our most romantic room for himself and his wife of thirteen years. He arrived early with a gift of sexy lingerie. About 7:00 p.m., a boudoir photographer, hired by the couple, arrived and stayed several hours. By breakfast the next morning, the couple had the glow of newlyweds. But we still haven't received a photo of them for our family parlor!

The Inn at Merridun

Organization is important in any size kitchen. No matter what its size, a kitchen is only a good one to work in if there is no mess. My country kitchen and dining room face each other, so I must keep my kitchen neat. Here are some suggestions for better preparation in your kitchen:

Keep the cutting area in close proximity to sink and stove.

Use separate drawers for cooking utensils, measuring spoons, cups, spatulas, and knives.

Ceramic jars are always good for holding wooden spoons and other cooking implements. If there's no counter space, hang a deep basket on the wall near the stove for the utensils.

To make your food preparation seem effortless, clean up after each dish you make. Never pile dishes in the sink.

When following a recipe, put away your ingredients as you use them.

Keep staples, such as baking supplies, together to cut down on unnecessary steps in the kitchen.—*Ujjala's B&B*

Use a person's first name often. It makes people feel acknowledged, and it is the one big thing in the world that is truly theirs.
—Willow Brook Inn

Gail's Touch: It is easier to measure out honey by spraying the measuring cup first with a nonstick vegetable oil.

A pinch of freshly grated nutmeg takes the raw-tasting edge off of flour in cream sauces.—*Arcady Down East B&B*

When measuring shortening, it is by far easiest to do it in cold water. For example, if you need 1/3 cup of shortening, put 2/3 cup of cold water in a one-cup measure. Then submerge shortening in the water until the water level reaches exactly 1 cup. Pour off the water, and you have the right amount of shortening, and it comes out of the cup easily.—*Hill Farm Inn*

We have no housekeeper, but we serve breakfast far away from the kitchen. Thus, when guests sit down with china, candlelight, soft music, and delicious food, they can't see the dirty pans, spilled flour, and opened juice containers that went into it all or hear us washing dishes and putting everything back in order.—*Six Water Street B&B*

FOR MORE INFORMATION ON INNS LISTED IN THIS BOOK, SEE THE DIRECTORY BEGINNING ON PAGE 203.

If you have more than one cook using your kitchen, and that individual(s) is considerably taller or shorter than you are, you may develop back pain from the height of your baking counter. Make an adjustable baking center. Our baking counter was designed for me (Annie), and I am 5 feet tall. Our summer chef is 6 feet tall and nearly broke his back leaning over to knead dough on the low counter. We placed supports at two different heights on the ends of two cabinets (leaving about 4 feet between the two cabinets) and slid a smooth-surfaced shelf. When I bake, I slide the shelf onto the lower supports. The shelf is easily removed to raise or clean.—*Glacier Bay Country Inn*

I do the things I want to do and I make excuses for everything else.
—The Groveland Hotel

It's more efficient to store liners inside and at the bottom of the kitchen trash can. Remove the filled bag and you just slip up a liner.—*Clayton Country Inn*

If you're going to prepare something in the kitchen whereby your hands will become gooey, and there's no one in the house to answer the phone if it rings, place a medium-sized plastic bag beside the phone to slip over your hand before reaching for the receiver. —*The Decoy*

THE ART OF GETTING READY

When deciding on your menu, be sure to ask guests if they are allergic to any foods. Keep index cards on guests, noting these matters and also what you served them. The next time you have them, you will be assured you are not serving the same things.

Plan your menu one week in advance. Select items that can be made ahead. There are many gourmet dishes that can be pre-cooked and still give the illusion that you've cooked all day.—*Edge of Thyme*

If you have gardens of edibles, send your guests out to harvest the greens for your dinner. They will enjoy the soothing moments of snipping something for the tables. Edible flowers, vegetables, or fruits may also be gathered. Your guests will be entertained while you take a breather and a soothing moment for yourself.—*Kedron Valley Inn*

⅋Do a few things perfectly. Too often people think that when they entertain they must have many things to serve. I am sure everyone has been to parties where the table is covered with many items, all in various containers. These usually represent the host's repertoire of favorite recipes and perhaps a few experimentations. What generally happens then is that nothing much stands out or is memorable, but, even more sadly, the host is rather worn out trying to shop and prepare for so many items.

At our inn we focus on making each item served a memorable one in terms of both the food itself and the presentation. Menus are coordinated to provide variety and balance, but we don't' serve everything we know how to make at one function.—*Rose Inn*

⅋Set aside a time to plan the menu for your guests. Indicate on the menu the recipe book and page number for each recipe. Paper clip any recipe cards to the menu page. Then go through the menu, recipe by recipe, and make your shopping list. Check your staples at this time, too. Don't assume you have that light corn syrup, etc.

Shop at a warehouse grocery store once every two or three months and stock up so that you save yourself time. The added bonus is that you are always prepared for unexpected guests.—*The Inn at 410*

⅋While the adage to keep entertaining simple is true, it shouldn't deter you totally from cooking up an intricate dish that you really want to serve. The trick is to then be sure that all the other dishes you are planning to serve are easy.—*Shellmont B&B*

⅋Always use fresh-squeezed orange juice; it tastes much better and fizzes especially nicely with champagne.—*La Maison*

⅋A warming stone really does keep breads warm for at least one hour. Place the stone in a pretty basket and top with your breads—morning or evening.—*Doanleigh Wallagh B&B*

⅋Although it is easy to find a way to keep food at its proper serving temperature, it is not that easy to make it look nice at the same time. One day we experimented. We took a thick crystal bowl and baked it in the oven in a water bath. We added the entree and found the way to keep the dish warm throughout our guests' meal. Now we put all of our individual crystal bowls into the oven waterbath before serving.—*Wellington B&B*

After the coffeepot goes on, the first thing to do to prepare for guests is to set—or as the English say, lay—the table. That way, if a guest arrives before you are completely finished with details, he or she can sit down, have coffee, and read the paper or talk to you. If the table is set, guests know that you were expecting them, and they feel welcomed.—*Betsy's B&B*

Music is the single most important element to consider when entertaining guests. The music one plays sets the mood for the entire experience at your home. There is nothing quite so stark as a totally quiet room where conversations pierce the air as if in competition with one another. Music masks these conversations quite nicely so as to preserve a sense of intimacy among small groups of guests.

Chamber music seems to work most effectively both in setting the mood and in creating the proper background, though light "cocktail" piano or small-jazz-combo music can be equally pleasant. The hosts, however, must pay particular attention not to allow the volume of the music to be so high so as to cause guests to raise their voices in competition. Just a pleasant, soft approach will go a long way in promoting the same in guests, who soon will be complimenting the hosts for the mood that they have created. —*The Birchwood Inn*

Don't wait for the day of arrival to get out your serving pieces. If you have not used them in a long time, you may have too many more essential preparations going on to be able to take the time for washing or polishing utensils.

A warm touch is to have small gifts on the table for each guest. They can be simple things, perhaps a wrapped floating candle or a kitchen magnet.—*Shellmont B&B*

Grocery shopping for a large crowd of household guests can be laborious and confusing. It's easy to forget items, even though they're on your shopping list. Although some of the food for the splendid breakfasts here comes from the farm where we raise chickens, keep bees, and harvest a large crop of raspberries, there is still plenty of supermarket shopping to do.

To make shopping more efficient, we prepared a list of all the things we normally purchase, putting them under subtitles like produce and dairy. Then we made fifty copies to be kept on file. Before our grocery excursion, we fill one of these out, including cleaning items and odds and ends. Providing you don't leave the list home, it's a big help and saves time, because you aren't writing everything down each week.—*Barley Sheaf Farm*

A LOVINGLY TENDED TABLE

❧We are very fortunate to have several sets of china, crystal, and flatware at the inn. Most are quite old and were my mother's and aunt's. Setting the table has been one of my favorite tasks since we opened our B&B, and although the table always looked wonderful, the guests were only able to enjoy it for a fleeting moment. We wanted them to savor the inviting appearance of a carefully set table, so now I set the entire table for breakfast before the guests are to arrive for an overnight stay at the inn (usually check-in time). They see the table and know that something very special is going to be served to them. They have something wonderful to wake up to.—*The English Manor*

CENTERPIECES

❧Your table can set the mood. An old-fashioned atmosphere can be created by placing antique greeting cards as the center-pieces, flanking them with oranges studded with whole cloves and scattering them with dried rose petals. Another attractive and useful centerpiece is a bowl full of fruit on top of a pretty doily. Then, depending on the season, I scatter flower petals around the bowl and on the doily and intermingle satin ribbons with the petals.—*Bluff Creek Inn*

❧An array of glass candlesticks of differing heights makes an interesting centerpiece. Add spring flowers, fall foliage, or Christmas greenery.—*Inn at Buckeystown*

❧The four seasons are celebrated in a hearty and earthy style on our dining-room table. Small potted plants, such as ivy or violets, flank the rim of an antique washbowl. Inside the bowl is a potted plant, changed according to the time of year: poinsettia for Christmas, tulips or daffodils in the spring, and fresh flowers from the garden during the summer and fall.—*Ash Mill Farm*

❧A collection of antique eggcups serves as a centerpiece for less formal meal times. —*The Chatelaine B&B*

❧We try to use whatever flowers the land has to offer. But many of these wildflowers have weak stems. No problem. Use clear drinking straws to make the stems sturdier. Simply slip the stem into the straw and treat it as any other cut flower.—*Neil Creek House*

❧Interesting centerpieces can be made by using what you have on hand. For example, foliage from your yard or simple leafless branches tied with a ribbon. A pyramid-shaped cheese grater can have flowers and twigs poked through its holes.—*Lanaux House*

❧Centerpieces consist of plants that grow in our area, including hedge apples, horse chestnuts (buckeyes), and pinecones with fir and boxwood greenery in the fall; peonies, lilacs, and roses in the spring. A simple bowl of nuts in their shells with a nutcracker makes a good decoration and keeps guests occupied.—*Boydville The Inn at Martinsburg*

❧A lovely centerpiece that matches the theme of your dinner or party can be suspended over the dining-room table. This will provide more room on the table and won't

"Do unto others as you would have them do unto you." Treat guests as you would like to be treated; then embellish it!
—The Inn at Merridun

be in anyone's way. Suspend the centerpiece from the ceiling, using clear fishing line. —*Victorian B&B*

Gail's Touch: Centerpieces give the table a focal point. There is nothing worse, however, than a centerpiece that blocks the line of view between people sitting across from one another. In addition to the solution given by The Victorian B&B, you can also choose to place the centerpiece at one of the corners of the table, if it is too tall and cumbersome for the center.

❧Make your entire dining table a centerpiece! Have a piece of glass cut to your table size. During foliage season place drifts of colored leaves under the glass. Develop your own themes: woodland garden, colonial garden, herb garden. Press plants all summer; then use them under glass all winter. (Use blotting paper between the table and plants with succulent foliage or flowers.)—*Bungay Jar*

❧Pinecones and greens, miniature pumpkins, a large wicker basket full of freshly dug moss, and violets announce the various seasons when I place them on the table as centerpieces.—*Sage Cottage*

We try to use everything fresh at hand for centerpieces. My favorite is persimmons stacked on a cake pedestal. The effect is a delight to the eye. You can stack almost any fruit or vegetable and add a little greenery or other garnish.—*Old Pioneer Garden Inn*

If you do use fresh flowers for a centerpiece, use floral preservative in the water (available at florist-supply places). Also, soda water instead of tap water seems to help flowers last longer, due to the carbon dioxide in the water.—*Eastlake Inn*

To add color to fresh-flower arrangements, fill a clear vase with complementary food coloring.—*Garnet Hill Lodge*

Colorful marble chips in the bottom of a vase hold fresh flowers nicely for a centerpiece.—*Reluctant Panther*

Small potted plants, like violets, are easier to keep up and last longer than flowers, and they are just as pretty. They add color to any table.—*The Inn at Maplewood Farm*

Gail's Touch: My mother loved African violets and would have agreed with the tutorial by The Inn at Maplewood Farm. She would have added, "Plant the violets in polygonal ceramic pots with angled sides. Every few days, turn the pots so that the plants get different exposures from the light."

CANDLES

Lighting is a main ingredient of a good table setting. Lighting your dining area with plenty of candles and kerosene lamps really adds to the atmosphere. You might get your guests involved in lighting the candles. That's a nice way to make them feel a part of your entertaining.—*Bluff Creek Inn*

Although they are more expensive, it's best to buy dripless candles. They won't mess your candle holders or tablecloth, and besides, they last longer than nondripless ones.

If your conventional candles drip, remove wax from candle holders by putting them in the refrigerator to cool. Then carefully remove the wax with your fingernails. Wash off the residue with hot, soapy water.
—*Beal House*

Votive candles burning on the table and in different parts of the house are an elegant welcome for dinner guests. Put several along the mantel, along windowsills, above doorsills, on plate rails, and on the counter in the powder room. Be sure to place them safely and away from fabrics and other flammables. They give even an informal beach house that inviting glow of formality.—*Spring Bank Inn*

All our rooms have candles in them. Since we use so many of them, we have found that using household emergency utility candles works well. They are less expensive than decorator candles and look just as good on the table or anywhere. They usually can be found in any grocery or hardware store. —*Little River Inn*

Gail's Touch: Keep a scented candle burning in the powder room during a dinner party as another welcome sign.

Candles burn more slowly if they are stored in closed boxes in the refrigerator. We store them in our cool wine cellar. We have also found that melted candle stubs poured into punch cups, with a wick inserted, make glowing candle lights for window sills.—*Rabbit Hill Inn*

PLACE CARDS

Since we seat our guests at large harvest tables for breakfast, we put name cards out. Then the guests have an assigned seat and don't feel awkward deciding where to sit. This is a good idea for your own guests, even those you know well.—*Barley Sheaf Farm*

Gail's Touch: For an interesting place card, arrange a small bunch of dried flowers that coordinate with your table-setting colors and tie it with a bow. Slip in a color-coordinated card with the guest's name. The bouquet goes home with the guest. Flowering herbs also work nicely.

Make place cards with cookies or cupcakes by writing the name of the guest on top of the sweet.—*Clauser's B&B*

You can use seashells as place cards. Write the name of your guest on the shell and set it down beside the fork or at the bottom of a long-stemmed glass.—*Laurel Hill Plantation*

Porcelain place cards work well, as you can write on them with felt-tip pens and clean them off with water. Determining the evening's seating arrangement is a daily job. One night, a large group of local residents came for dinner. We put names of famous people (presidents, movie stars, athletes, etc.) on the place cards. Everyone got to pick who they wanted to be for the evening. Pope John Paul and Saddam Hussein had a rousing conversation. The ladies had a good time deciding who looked most like Dolly Parton or Princess Diana (or wished she did).—*Glacier Bay Country Inn*

TABLECLOTHS

✍Some bolt fabrics make beautiful tablecloths. I cut to shape and hem polyester/cotton/rayon—blend fabric in beautiful plaids (60 inches wide). The tablecloths wash beautifully and need little ironing. We often serve fresh steamed crab with lots of melted butter for dinner. After an entire season of use, the tablecloths show no stains and still look great!—*Glacier Bay Country Inn*

Gail's Touch: Many times you shy away from buying an antique or other tablecloth you really like because it isn't large enough for your table. But you don't have to cover the entire top. Try turning the tablecloth until you get a corner at each of the four

place settings for a small table and just center it for a large table. This provides the right coverage and still shows off the wood of the table.

✍If you use an old quilt to cover a buffet table, spray on a protective fabric coating to guard against any spills. Usually, you won't have much of a problem with food spills. But beware of dripping candles. They will stain the quilt.—*Inn at Weathersfield*

✍I have a smaller lace tablecloth over the bottom one, tied on the ends with a ribbon and a flower stuck through the ribbon. It's a pretty effect. Any tablecloth that hangs well over the table can be gathered at the four corners and tied with a pretty ribbon. It looks nice and stays out of your guest's way. —*Eton House*

✍If you have round tablecloths and no round table, use them on your large, rectangular dining-room table over rectangular cloths. We even use a card-table or luncheon cloth as an accent for the center of the table.—*Victorian B&B*

✍Sheets, plain or printed, make excellent tablecloths. Drape one or two together, and top with a lace cloth to make a very romantic table.—*Palmer House*

❦Black makes an elegant statement for a tabletop. Simply use a brand-new, flat bed sheet, which, for example, works nicely on an oval table for a seating of six.—*Clauser's B&B*

❦To make an interesting table covering, take a sheet and bunch it up to form a pouf in the middle. Tie a ribbon around the base of the pouf and use the middle portion for a basket of rolls or a pretty centerpiece. Tuck dried flowers into the excess fabric. —*Holden House*

❦We have cut down on our linen-storage problem by putting as many as four table-cloths on the table at once. The bulk serves as padding as well as keeping them from getting creased in folds in a drawer.—*Victorian B&B*

PLACE MATS

❦Our place mats are made of the dining-room wallpaper. You can buy plastic covers just for making your own place mats. Cut the wallpaper to size and insert.—*Eton House*

❦Place mats are better to use if there are only two guests at the table. Our table is meant to seat eight, and using two place mats provides a more intimate feeling than would be possible with a large expanse of, say, white linen.—*White House*

❦To add color to the table and cut down on laundering, place a paper-lace place mat over a solid-colored, ruffled fabric place mat. For example, a cranberry-colored fabric mat is topped with a white paper mat and a color-ful, kelly green cloth napkin. The paper keeps the mat clean.—*Chestnut Hill on the Delaware*

Gail's Touch: I enjoy buying linen towels with a design printed on them, especially as souvenirs from places I've visited. When you have enough of them, use them as place mats. Iron them flat and place them two-thirds on the table and the other one-third off the table. They look attractive and will instigate conversation if they are all from dif-ferent places. For example, one of mine is from Williamsburg, Virginia. There are dates on the cloth and sketches of some of the buildings at Williamsburg. It's always an eye-catcher that prompts guests to get into a dis-cussion of travel.

FOR MORE INFORMATION ON INNS LISTED IN THIS BOOK, SEE THE DIRECTORY BEGINNING ON PAGE 203.

❧Have a glass top made for your dining-room table. Place lace doilies underneath as place mats. Your dishes go directly onto the glass. The cleanup is easy, and the table stays in good shape.—*Widow Kip's*

❧Mirrored place mats help the table sparkle. Also, mirrors, especially those with unusual frames, can be very showy serving platters, particularly for a buffet. Nice for fruits, cheeses, desserts.—*Palmer House*

❧We use finger towels for place mats and napkins. They launder easily and come in an array of colors to coordinate with your decor.—*Captain Stannard House*

❧Use Scotchgard spray on new place mats. This way, you can clean them with a damp cloth instead of putting them through a lot of wear and tear in the washing machine. This way, too, they will keep their shape and newness. Respray place mats every so often as needed.—*Twin Gates B&B*

Gail's Touch: The use of fingerbowls is a charming custom that makes a great deal of sense for today. Why not keep small bowls of water on your table? Traditionally, these bowls were filled with tepid water and set before each guest just before dessert. I think the bowls can be placed on the table at the beginning of the meal and used by dinner guests to clean their hands between courses. You can add a slice of lemon to the bowl for color and added cleanliness. It can be placed on a flat plate on a doily, with a fresh napkin beside it. The hostess should quickly use the fingerbowl first, in case a guest is unfamiliar or uncomfortable with the procedure.

NAPKINS AND NAPKIN RINGS

❧Make your own fabric napkins out of permanent-press fabric. This avoids the hassle of ironing, especially before large dinner parties, and saves a little time for your own simple pleasures, like putting on lipstick. —*Victorian Oaks B&B*

Gail's Touch: Did early man wipe his mouth with animal skin, his hand, or a dried leaf? We may never know for sure. We have traced the use of napkins to early Rome, however, where guests even brought their own wiping cloths to a friend's feast. Sometimes, they carried leftover vittles home, wrapped in the cloth. During the Middle Ages only the aristocracy used nap-

🦋 Portraits of Inn-spiration 🦋

Since the first year we opened the inn, one particular couple have been regular guests. They were in their thirties and both divorced at the time they started coming to the inn.

Bill called me one day and asked, "You know that barn at the end of your road? Do you know the owner?" I told him that I did know him. "Well," said Bill, "do you think he'd let me paint MARRY ME SUE on the barn wall?" Bill wanted to surprise Sue with his proposal on their way to the inn. I told him that it was doubtful, but perhaps he might agree to a banner instead. So I walked down the road to talk to my neighbor.

I broached the subject cautiously, based on my last conversation with this crusty Yankee. I had given him a ride, and as he left the car, he told me I was a pretty good driver, for a woman. I told him what Bill wanted to do. "Maybe a banner could be hung?" I asked politely. My neighbor looked at me with a twinkle in his eye and said, "Hell, why doesn't he just paint it up there?"

So the sign painter came and did his job, with my neighbor supervising his every move.

Loving every romantic minute, I made sure the local newspaper and television station knew what was going on and right on time. At noon on Saturday, Bill and Sue pulled into the drive. She was shocked, surprised, and thrilled! and, yes, she accepted.

I had prepared a champagne picnic, so after all the hullabaloo, we left them to their lunch by the barn.

To this day, the proposal remains painted on the barn. Bill and Sue are now happily married and return to our inn often.

The Half Penney Inn

kins. And it is believed to be during this era that finer napkins were made for dining and wiping. Noblemen wore large collars, so the napkins were tied around their necks to shield the ruffles. This was a difficult maneuver, as the ruche was quite cumbersome. Hence, we get the expression "to make both ends meet." Fancy napkin folding in geometric shapes began to take place, and by the 1600s it became an art form. The rich competed for the best napkin displays.

Much effort ensures success.
—The Shelburne Inn

❧An easy cloth-napkin design is to fold the napkin once, then make 1 1/2-inch accordion folds. Pull it through a napkin ring for a nice fan shape.—*Greenhurst Inn*

❧We use richly colored washcloths and brightly striped dishcloths for breakfast napkins. Guests enjoy the creative use of these cloths and find them more absorbent. They also launder better than regular fabric napkins.—*Summerport B&B*

❧Most of us think of cloth napkins as a lot of work these days, and so we tend to use paper ones most of the time. But cloth napkins can be so inexpensive and easy to launder that you can use them daily. Here at the inn, we make our own (15-by-18-inches with a very small, rolled hem) from a cotton/polyester blend, so they can be easily washed, dried, and folded. They really do dress up a table and are very little work.—*Hill Farm Inn*

❧I have a collection of more than 200 antique handkerchiefs. The beautiful colors and embroidery on these inspired me to use them as napkins. They look beautiful on the table, and I'm making good use of antiques that otherwise might sit in a trunk somewhere and turn yellow.—*Victorian House*

❧A quick and easy way to set a place for breakfast with a cloth napkin is to tuck the napkin through the handle of a coffee mug and fluff it out.—*Ilverthorpe Cottage*

❧Napkin rings initially had a utilitarian rather than decorative purpose. The napkins were large and required intricate laundry care, so they were used for more than one meal. The ring was inscribed with the regular user's name. Ring and napkin were put aside until they were used by the same person at the next meal.—*Conyers House*

We use tole-painted napkin rings. Each ring has a distinguishing design. Guests store their napkin in their ring and use it for a couple of breakfasts. This saves on laundry and napkin wear and tear, and it keeps a tradition going. You can do the same in your own home. If you don't paint, use some other identifying method. Being able to hold onto a cloth napkin that is hardly soiled may encourage more people to use them more often.—*Laurel Hill Plantation*

Napkins are in rings on our table. We arrange the napkin so that the top fluffs out around the base of the goblet.—*Red House*

Cookie cutters make wonderful rings for thinner napkins.—*Benner House*

We use napkin rings made from fabric that matches our wallpaper. To make the rings, cut strips of fabric and stiffen them with fabric stiffener, following the manufacturer's directions. Form a ring for the napkin to go through, using one of the strips. Form a bow with streamers, using three stiffened strips. When the bow is completely dry, hot-glue the bow to the ring. You can also use holiday fabric to make these for seasonal table settings.—*Kingsley House*

Artificial flowers can be used as napkin rings. Simply bend the stems in a circle and slip the cloth napkin through the circle. —*Clauser's B&B*

If you are entertaining a large crowd and don't have enough napkin rings, use decorative ribbons tied in a bow. They are inexpensive and can be reused.—*Holden House*

Gail's Touch: Having a party for youngsters or children in their early teens? Set the table with paper napkins fed through a medium-to-large, hard and edible pretzel. This may be the introduction to napkin rings for some of your young party-goers.

Small wicker mats make very nice napkin holders. Double the mats and sew them together at the tops. Weave lace through the wicker, and trim with a bow.—*Heritage Inn*

Cloth napkins are a must—even for breakfast!—*Covered Bridge Inn*

UNCOMMON TOUCHES

We use old books for handing out our menus. Place the menu in the center of a book and hold it in place with a gold, elastic string wrapped around the binding and knotted. Bring a book to each guest. The books are great conversation starters and at home you can match the book to your guests' interests.—*Pine Knob Inn*

❧To work more efficiently, always use a tray for serving and clearing the table. It will save time and steps.—*The Mellon Patch Inn*

❧Scoop out the shell of an orange and place your intermezzo or sherbet into it. Garnish with orange curls. Use half a melon for ice-cream sundaes.—*John Palmer House*

❧Don't be afraid to let your imagination run wild when thinking about ways to dress a table. I love using extraordinary containers for serving and display. For example, I have a few fan-shaped vases. I don't use them just for flowers. I put sauces into them. They look pretty on the table, encourage conversation, and work really well for pouring.

An antique tin, opened to show any inside labeling on the lid, also makes a wonderful container. Place a colorful napkin inside the tin and add fresh-baked muffins or cookies. Top with a piece of baby's breath.

Unmatched china and crystal that you can buy inexpensively from garage sales provide an interesting array at the table.—*Bluff Creek Inn*

Gail's Touch: Old or new eggcups can serve as decorative and conversational pieces while holding table necessities, including pats of butter and toothpicks.

❧Use antique butter-pat dishes as receptacles on the table for dipped, wet teabags. —*Rose Manor*

❧Make use of seashells by using them as servers on a table where seafood is being served. You can even clean them in the dishwasher. We live on the coast and can gather large clam or scallop shells (4 or 5 inches in size). If such shells are unavailable to you, they can be purchased.—*Laurel Hill Plantation*

❧We use marble and terra-cotta tile samples to keep trays of food warm on the serving table. They can be heated in the oven while the food bakes, then placed on top of hot pads under trays. They continue to keep food warm for about one hour.—*Red Castle Inn*

❧Children's plastic pails make excellent ice buckets for porch or patio tables. The shovels are novel servers.—*Palmer House*

❧Old half-pint milk bottles are used for individual servings of maple syrup.—*Inn on Golden Pond*

❧Silver goblets for orange juice seem to keep the juice colder and make the entire table sparkle. Unexpected and elegant, they make everyone feel special. And why not? If you've got them, use them for heaven's sake.—*Tyler Hill B&B*

❧Cover the tops of milk, syrup, water, or juice pitchers with a lace doily instead of plastic wrap when displaying them on a buffet or, for that matter, any time you are serving in pitchers, large or small. The doilies look pretty and keep out anything undesirable.—*Château du Sureau*

❧Halved coconuts make interesting ice-cream dishes for any informal summer luau.—*Shire Inn*

❧Frequently during summer we serve chilled soups in frosted sherbet glasses. It's always a big hit.—*Victorian B&B*

❧During summer we serve lemonade with ice made from freezing pink lemonade and cherries in the ice-cube tray. The effect is soothing and pleasing to the eye.—*Chicago Pike Inn*

❧Clay flowerpots rubbed with oil and lined with aluminum foil make great containers for chicken pot pie. Fill the pot with the hot pie filling, top with a circle of pastry (fluting the edges), and bake. Serve in the plant pot.—*Glacier Bay Country Inn*

❧Our entire meal-serving philosophy is to treat our cookery as art, from plate presentation to table setting and right down to the flower we set upon each guest's dinner napkin.—*Blueberry Hill*

❧We use clear glass dishes in our place settings. They make very pleasing settings, whatever your color of napkins or tablecloths. You can place a doily or even a pressed leaf or dried flower underneath the clear dish.—*Hamilton House*

❧Use 12-inch serving plates as the underlining to your entree dish.—*Conyers House*

❧An antique breadboard is a nice server for cookies and snacks.—*Captain's House*

FOR MORE INFORMATION ON INNS LISTED IN THIS BOOK, SEE THE DIRECTORY BEGINNING ON PAGE 203.

Gail's Touch: Use old brick molds as serving trays. Fill each section with dips, crackers, vegetables, and even napkins.

❧Instead of traditional shakers, we provide a salt grinder and two pepper grinders—one for white pepper and one for black. We point these out, along with telling our guests that we are conscious of not oversalting the food we prepare.—*Shire Inn*

❧Relishes, served in our dining room, come off an antique wooden sausage stuffer. We added legs.—*Birchwood Inn*

❧Wicker baskets can become colorful servers for muffins or rolls if you add a fabric liner of washable material.—*Heritage Inn*

❧Fresh herbs in clay pots, baskets of dried herbs, and an assortment of calico napkins and interesting place mats help keep you from getting bored when you set the table every morning.—*Sage Cottage*

❧If you need more room at the table after you've used your leaf extensions, go to the lumberyard and have a rectangular piece of plywood cut at least half again as long as your table. Place a protective cloth over your table, and put the plywood on top. Decorate with a tablecloth. This is great to keep handy, especially for parties and holidays when you have large groups. Store the plywood in a dry place to prevent warping.—*Two Brooks*

Gail's Touch: An attractive and interesting way to get more serving space is to use a stepladder. Place an open one adjacent to the table. Pretty plates and bowls can be placed on each rung. Paint the ladder. Stencil it. Do whatever pleases your taste to make the ladder complement your decor and style. It is prettiest when each rung has something on it. Decorate with green plants or flowers if you have the space.

❧Since ours is a traditional inn with no television sets in the bedrooms, we supply the one vital piece of information we feel all guests want to tune in to—the weather report. As part of our breakfast preparation, we add an index card to the table with the day's forecast.—*The Elms B&B*

❧For a buffet use stacks of pretty books to build height for placement of some of your buffet food items.—*The Arcadian Inn*

Gail's Touch: For a country buffet think

about using an antique wheelbarrow filled with hay. Place your food in country dishes on top of the hay and let guests help themselves.

❧ When preparing a salad for a buffet table, instead of placing the washed and dried greens into a bowl, place them in a gathering basket, reminding your guests that these greens have just come out of the garden. —*Highland Lake Inn*

❧ Serving foods on a covered glass pedestal cake plate adds elegance to the table, and its height offers definition and drama. —*Riversbend B&B*

❧ Guests come to enjoy your company and may feel uncomfortable and distracted if you are spending too much time working. Serve buffet style to relieve some of your work load. Have food stations at various spots in the room; for example, salad and bread at one station, main entree at another, pasta at another, and dessert in its own corner.—*Isaiah Hall B&B Inn*

❧ We take time setting up the buffet to ensure that it works out well later. We start early in the day by putting out proxy plates where the actual food will go. Using paper plates, each dish is labeled so that when it is time to put the real thing out, the buffet is all set up and arranged—no last-minute figuring. This method also keeps you from forgetting about the salad or condiment you made but were preserving in the refrigerator—sight unseen until after the party! —*Crystal Rose Inn*

GARNISHES

❧ Use that zucchini that grew into a monster overnight to make a Viking ship for your veggie salad. Cut the zucchini in half lengthwise. Scoop out enough insides to make room for the salad. A bamboo skewer makes a good mast. Decorate a paper sail to fit the occasion. Tongue depressors make great oars, with a little bit of unskilled whittling.—*Robins Nest*

❧ For our salads we use cookie cutters to cut out hearts from turnips. Just add them to the bowl.—*Old Broad Bay Inn*

❧ Our garnishes include a tomato rose on the side of Spanish scrambled eggs to add the *olé*. We make tomato roses two ways. Either take a cherry tomato, cut off the stem top, and then make two interesting cuts almost all the way through. Then turn it upside down and spread it out to look like petals. Or peel the skin from a tomato in a continuous circle and roll it up like a rose.

The Aztec mushroom is made by taking a medium-to-large mushroom cap and starting in the center with the tip of a sharp knife and making little indentations in the mushroom as you work around in circles. We use it on our quiche. It also looks good on top of a steak. —*Williams House*

❧ We often use Swiss chard to line trays of food instead of doilies.

We buy a huge purple or savoy cabbage, pull out the center, and pour dip into the cabbage cavity. Sometimes we stand a large basket on one end and prop the cabbage up next to it for a dramatic effect. Then we fill the area in with raw vegetables to dip, including radishes and baby ears of corn (from a can).—*Eastlake Inn*

❧ No entree or bread will be ignored by your guests when it is presented with a special touch. Any type of garnish will give your dish pizzazz. When accenting with flowers, it's nice to tell your guests what the flowers are and, of course, which ones are edible.—*Ilverthorpe Cottage*

❧ "Tussie mussies" are our way of making small bouquets to garnish the plate. Just pick small bunches of herbs from the garden and tie them with chive stalks. —*Clifton Country Inn*

❧ Everyone knows parsley makes a great garnish. But fresh parsley is great on breakfast dishes, not just at dinner. We have a window box of the herb growing outside the kitchen door, providing us with a steady supply of parsley all summer. We freeze our fall crop to be used in our dishes all winter.—*Palmer House*

Our favorite quote is the Irish Blessing that hangs in our inn: "May the road rise to meet you May the wind be always at your back May the sun shine warm upon your face May the rains fall soft upon your fields And until we meet again May God hold you in the palm of His hand." (author unkown) —Shelmont B&B

❧ Herbs make great garnishes. You can put them on butter pats or on the main course.—*Edge of Thyme*

❧ Garnishings don't have to be exotic or elaborate to make an eye-appealing dish. A simple slice of orange on a plate of French toast or a strawberry on celery leaves brightens the morning and shouts in its sunny voice you care enough to try.—*Tyler Hill B&B*

❧ This is a cute garnish that can be added to a fruit tray or decorative centerpiece. It's a mouse made from a pear: Slice a pear in half lengthwise so that it lies flat, leaving the stem intact. Add two whole cloves for eyes. From the sliced-off section, cut two small pieces for ears. Carve a small hole above the clove and attach each ear with a toothpick. Add a toothpick as a tail, covering it with a fresh chive stem.—*Ilverthorpe Cottage*

❧ Strawberries—cut into thin slices and fanned out on a plate—make an easy and pretty food topping.—*Inn at Starlight Lake*

EDIBLE FLOWERS

❧Edible scented geranium leaves make a dramatic addition to recipes. For example, you can infuse them in a bread or cake preparation. Line the sides of a greased and floured baking dish with cleaned geranium leaves. Pour the batter into the pan carefully, so as not to disturb the leaves. After baking, remove the bread or cake from the pan, peeling away any leaves that may have stuck to the creation. Discard the pretty leaves and serve the recipe with the imprint of the leaves on top. The scent from the oil in the geraniums will impart a fresh taste of whatever edible geranium you are using. It's nice to use complementary scents such as lemon geraniums for lemon breads or cakes, for example, or pineapple geraniums, with their strong flavors, to enhance plain coffee cakes.—*The Lovelander Inn*

❧Edible flowers should be picked first thing in the morning when the dew is still on them. Foods in bloom look great on the table, but here is a list of flowers and help in determining how to use them in cooking:

❧ Borage: flourishes in ordinary soil, very easily grown, and honey/cucumber in taste; delicious in salads

❧ Chrysanthemum: best in soups and salads

❧ Gardenia: soft, delicate white flowers

with a vivid, sweet fragrance; good for making candied flowers (see below)

❧ Gladiolus: similar to lettuce in flavor; great in salads and stunning as a garnish

❧ Marigolds: mildly pleasant peppery flavor; great in soups and vegetable side dishes

❧ Nasturtiums: light, peppery flavor, similar to watercress; good for salads and garnishes

❧ Pansies: no distinctive flavor but very colorful in crepes and as a garnish

❧ Roses: petals are high in vitamin C; good for teas, candy, salads, and as a garnish

❧ Violets: readily give up color and flavor when boiled; high in vitamin C; good in salads and teas.—*Turtleback Farm Inn*

❧Candied flowers are especially pretty as a garnish for desserts. They taste good, too. Here is a recipe for making candied flowers. The vodka in the recipe helps the flowers to dry quickly:

1 egg white, beaten to a froth

2 tablespoons vodka

1/2 cup or more, as needed, superfine white sugar pansies (or other flowers to be candied— borage, scented geraniums, or violets)

small artist's paintbrush

Mix together the egg white and the vodka. Set aside. Place the sugar into a wide-mouthed bowl. Cover a wire rack with parchment paper.

Dip the paintbrush into the egg mixture and paint each flower, coating all surfaces and getting in between the flower petals. Sprinkle the sugar overtop the flower. Place the coated flower face down on the parchment and coat the other side with sugar.

When you have covered all the flowers you wish, place the rack in a cool, dry, well-ventilated area where they can dry completely.

When the flowers are dry, carefully put them into a heavy-duty plastic freezer container, layered no more than three flowers deep, separated by a sheet of parchment between layers. Keep them in the freezer for up to one year or use immediately. Do not store the flowers at room temperature as humidity can creep in and cause them to turn into mush in a few short months.—*Heritage Park Inn*

❧Fresh fruits and flowers are my kind of garnishes. Also, golden oregano with nasturtiums, dwarf sage with calendulas, and borage with purple basil all give lift to summer palates. In winter thyme is useful with grapes and oranges.—*Sage Cottage*

At the level of the soul, we are all the same.

—Willow Brook Inn

When pansies are in season, we place one flower on each guest's morning melon. It adds wonderful color and a delicate touch.—*Brafferton Inn*

A nice idea for ice water on the table: Place one edible flower in each ice-cube pocket before freezing. When the cubes are frozen, place several in a glass and pour in the water. Bring to the table to the oohs and ahhs of your guests.—*1830 Inn on the Green*

If you want to put flower garnishes on your guests' plates, but they are not in abundance, take a few petals instead of the entire flower. Make sure you know your flowers. Some of them, such as lilies of the valley and begonias, are poisonous.—*Ujjala's B&B*

Many types of edible flowers can be used as garnishes. Here are a few: mustard flower, chrysanthemum, honeysuckle, tulip, squash blossom, rose, fennel, chive, gladiola, forget-me-not, day lilies, and jasmine.
—*Governors' Inn*

White flowers make great garnishes. Watch for creepie-crawlies hidden between petals and leaves. Wash your flowers very well.—*Conyers House*

In addition to using edible flowers as a garnish, they may also be used in cooking, such as in a crêpe batter. Edibles are colorful and add interest to the plate.—*Settlers Inn*

Chapter 6

KEEPING THE ROMANCE IN COOKING

ARTFUL WAYS TO SPEND TIME IN THE KITCHEN

You may have noticed on your travels to inns in recent years that innkeepers are serving more low-fat, heart-healthier dishes whether for breakfast or dinner. That is because innkeepers care about their guests even though they are virtual strangers. As one innkeeper, Mary Lynn Tucker of The Manor at Taylor's Store, in Sweet Mountain Lake, Virginia, put it in her cookbook, *Hearth Healthy Hospitality,* "When we first opened in 1986 . . . some guests expected the traditional southern breakfast of bacon, eggs, grits, biscuits, gravy, and extra butter. Neither Lee nor I could, in clear conscience, feed people we cared so much about like that."

I really cannot think of anything more romantic than that attitude, and Mary Lynn has managed to develop recipes that are still healthy and yet pleasing to the palate and the soul. Innkeepers, like Mary Lynn, began to take a hard look at their menus and started making changes, but to everyone's relief, the care-for-your diet has not become a religious movement at inns.

Here is how it is. Visitors such as you and I are so busy during the week stressing ourselves out with exercise, work, and personal responsibilities—which also include keeping on top of watching what we eat—that we need a break. Striving hard to maintain a quality diet is indeed a magnanimous enterprise. Everyone should be concerned with over-fatting and over-taxing their body. However, when it comes time for a vacation, a night out, or just a quiet, special dinner at home, we want to at least unburden ourselves for awhile and forget the stresses of the daily grind.

Most people are staying at an inn to immerse themselves in romantic surroundings, entertainment, and glorious cuisine. Sumptuous breakfasts and dinners are part of the attractions of an inn. It's the same at home. Someone invited to your place for dinner is in anticipation of a delicious meal, not one in which they have to try to swallow down hard-and-slow and force a smile.

The result is the serving and/or receiving of what I call low-fat luxury cuisine—a way to blend a sensitivity for eating healthier food but not at the price of it being tasteless, dispassionate, or forlorn. The recipes that follow are thoroughly romantic and enjoyable and I think you will see are not overly taxed with fatty ingredients. I think you will also find that these recipes are very simple to prepare. There is nothing more unromantic than an evening in your dining room with friends where you are huffing and puffing, out-of-breath with the heavy load of cooking you need to do. When entertaining, select recipes that you can make in advance or get outside help in your kitchen that night. Perhaps a top cooking student would like to get some experience and help you out at the same time.

Enjoying a special meal at home is a romantic, sensual experience to begin with. To keep that feeling going, you must complement the table with good things for you and your loved ones and guests—dishes that are also cooked with lots of amoré.

GATEWAY TO A BEAUTIFUL DAY: BREAKFAST

Overripe pears, peaches, apples, kiwis, strawberries, and other overripe fruits can be placed in a blender with ice, milk, and fruit juice to make a delicious and nourishing drink. Here's one example of a favorite beverage.

ORANGE FRAPPÉ
4 cups freshly squeezed orange juice
Juice of 1 lemon
1 large banana
6 strawberries, fresh or frozen
1/4 cup whipping cream
6 ice cubes
Fresh mint leaves for garnish

Blend all the ingredients but the mint on high for 1 minute. Serve in frosted, stemmed goblets, garnished with fresh mint. Yield: 6 servings.—*Grant Corner Inn*

We make all our morning juice, including apple, grape, and tomato juice. Good culinary shops sell automatic juicers. You don't need an expensive one. You can freeze or can some of the juices. We use empty plastic, one-liter bottles to freeze the juice.—*Robins Nest*

To keep our juice cold throughout breakfast, we place juice containers inside a freezer's ice-storage bucket. On either side of the containers, we insert small, rigid freeze packs like those used for picnics. They keep the juice cold and eliminate wetness and inconvenience for guests.—*Inn on Golden Pond*

Gail's Touch: A refreshing breakfast beverage or cocktail we make at our house is Cranberry Juice Sparkler. Mix two-thirds cranberry juice to one-third club soda. Add ice and rub a wedge of lime around the glass rim, squeeze remaining lime juice into the glass and serve.

HOT CURRIED FRUIT
1 16-ounce can pears
1 16-ounce can peaches
1 16-ounce can pineapple chunks
1 16-ounce can pitted sweet cherries
1/3 cup loosely packed brown sugar
4 tablespoons butter, melted
1 1/2 teaspoons curry powder

Preheat oven to 325 degrees. Drain fruit and place in a buttered 2-quart casserole. Mix brown sugar, butter, and curry powder. Pour mixture over fruit. Bake for 30 minutes. Yield: 12–14 servings.—*The Summer Cottage*

When fresh fruit is in abundance, we combine fruits such as black raspberries with nectarine chunks and blueberries, and stir in blueberry, raspberry, or vanilla yogurt for a breakfast, snack, or lunch dish.

We also provide a special breakfast treat on warm summer mornings by serving frozen fruit salad, a nice make-ahead dish. Line muffin tins with paper muffin cups. Fill with fruit and freeze. When frozen, remove from muffin tins and store in plastic bags. Serve frozen.—*The Decoy*

The addition of a paper doily underneath a fruit cup makes it special.—*Benner House*

"I was hungry and you gave me food. I was thirsty and you gave me drink. I was a stranger and you took me in." (Matthew 25:35)
—Mansion Inn

To freeze berries, place them on a flat cookie sheet. Freeze and then place in plastic bags. Label each bag.—*Hannah's House*

Pineapple is an acid fruit. Place chunks of it into a fresh fruit mixture, and it will prevent the other fruits from turning brown.

To cut a pineapple, first twist the top off. Cut the fruit in half lengthwise, and then quarter each half. Remove the middle core. Cut away from the skin into chunks, and place the chunks back on the skin for serving.—*Haikuleana*

BREAKFAST PARFAIT

Fill parfait glass in this order:

2–3 tablespoons granola
2–3 tablespoons flavored yogurt
2–3 tablespoons fresh fruit of the season

Repeat, ending with fresh fruit at the top of the glass.—*Churchtown Inn*

HOMEMADE GRANOLA

3 cups old-fashioned rolled oats
1 cup chopped walnuts
1 cup wheat germ
1/4 cup brown sugar
1/4 cup whole-wheat flour
1/4 cup honey
1/4 cup molasses
1/2 cup vegetable oil
1/4 cup water
1 tablespoon vanilla extract
1 cup raisins
1 cup shredded coconut

Preheat oven to 325 degrees. Combine all the ingredients with the exception of the raisins and coconut. Spread on a well-greased baking sheet. Bake for 30 minutes, or until browned, stirring occasionally. Remove from oven. Add raisins and coconut. The granola crisps as it cools. Yield: 6–8 servings. —*Captain's House*

YOGURT POPPY SEED COFFEE CAKE

1 2-ounce package poppy seeds
1 cup plain yogurt
1 cup margarine
1 1/2 cups sugar
2 cups plus 2 tablespoons all-purpose flour
2 teaspoons vanilla extract
2 teaspoons baking soda
4 eggs, separated

Grease a tube pan. Preheat oven to 375 degrees.

Soak the poppy seeds in the yogurt. Meanwhile, cream together the margarine and the sugar. Blend into the yogurt mixture.

In a separate bowl, beat the egg yolks and add them to the yogurt mixture. Stir in the vanilla, flour and baking soda.

In another bowl, beat the egg whites until stiff. Fold them into the yogurt mixture. Pour into the pan and bake for 45 minutes or until the cake springs back when touched. (Do not open the oven door while baking.) Yield: 1 cake.— *Teton Tree House*

❧ APPLE MUFFINS

This is the absolute favorite recipe at The Lord Proprietors' Inn

1 1/2 cups firmly packed brown sugar
2/3 cup oil
1 egg
1 cup buttermilk
1 teaspoon salt
1 teaspoon baking soda
1 teaspoon vanilla extract
2 cups flour
1 1/2 cups chopped Granny Smith apples
1/2 cup chopped nuts

Preheat oven to 350 degrees. Mix together brown sugar, oil, and egg. In a 2-cup measure, mix the buttermilk, salt, baking soda, and vanilla. Stir. Mix thoroughly into egg mixture. Add the flour all at once, and fold in the apples and nuts. Pour into greased muffin cups. Bake for 30 minutes. Yield: 12 muffins.

FOR MORE INFORMATION ON INNS LISTED IN THIS BOOK, SEE THE DIRECTORY BEGINNING ON PAGE 203.

❧ BUTTERMILK AND BANANA BRAN MUFFINS

2 1/2 cups unprocessed bran
1 1/3 cups whole-wheat flour
2 1/2 teaspoons baking soda
1/2 teaspoon salt
1 cup raisins
1 cup shredded unsweetened coconut
2 eggs
1/2 cup buttermilk
1/2 cup vegetable oil
1 cup mashed ripe bananas
1/2 cup honey

Preheat oven to 375 degrees. Combine bran, flour, soda, salt, raisins, and coconut. In another bowl beat eggs; then add remaining ingredients. Combine the two mixtures until blended. Spoon into greased muffin cups. Bake for 20–25 minutes. Yield: 18–24 muffins.— *Forsyth Park Inn*

❧ PINEAPPLE MUFFINS

1/2 cup butter
2 eggs
1 1/8 cups sugar
3 cups flour
3 teaspoons baking powder
1/2 teaspoon salt
1/8 teaspoon baking soda
1 cup milk
1 teaspoon vanilla extract

1 16-ounce can crushed pineapple

Preheat oven to 400 degrees. Cream together butter, eggs, and sugar. Combine dry ingredients in a separate bowl. Add vanilla to milk. Add flour mixture to the butter mixture, alternately with the milk. Add pineapple. Spoon into muffin tins. Bake for 15–20 minutes. Yield: 18–24 muffins.
—*Forsyth Park Inn*

Morning Glory Muffins

2 cups flour
1 1/4 cups sugar
2 teaspoons baking soda
2 teaspoons cinnamon
3 eggs, beaten
1 cup vegetable oil
2 teaspoons vanilla extract
2 cups grated carrots
1 apple, grated
1/2 cup raisins
1/2 cup chopped pecans
1/2 cup shredded unsweetened coconut

Preheat oven to 375 degrees. Grease muffin cups and areas between cups. In a large bowl mix first 4 ingredients. Set aside. In a small bowl mix together eggs, oil, and vanilla. Add to flour mixture. Stir until moist. Fold in carrots, apple, raisins, pecans, and coconut. Spoon into the muffin cups, filling

each one to the rim. Bake for 25 minutes. Yield: 12 muffins.—*Partridge Brook Inn*

Quick Raisin and Bran Muffin Mix

This mix keeps for six weeks in the refrigerator. It's nice to have it made up in advance and then bake the muffins when you're ready. There's nothing better in the morning than muffins cooking in the oven.

4 beaten eggs
2 cups sugar
1 cup salad oil
1 quart buttermilk
5 teaspoons baking soda
2 teaspoons salt
5 cups flour
1 15-ounce box raisin bran cereal

Mix together. Add to this mix whatever you like, such as nuts, coconut, or fruits. Refrigerate. Take out the amount you need when ready to bake. Pour batter into greased muffin tins. Bake muffins in a 400-degree oven for 20–25 minutes. Yield: About 3 dozen.—*Folkestone B&B*

Leave out milk or water in muffin recipes, and substitute a flavorful and moist applesauce.—*The Decoy*

For more information on inns listed in this book, see the directory Beginning on page 203.

❧ COFFEE MUG BREAD

A favorite with our guests is breakfast in a coffee mug. Grease the inside of a coffee mug, preferably one with a pedestal base. partially thaw a loaf of frozen bread dough. Cut the loaf in half crosswise. Then divide each half into 4 strips. Roll each strip between the palms of your hand, and then dredge it in a mixture of cinnamon sugar and chopped walnuts. Twist 2 strips together, divide in half, and place in a spiral fashion into 2 mugs. Let the dough rise until double in bulk. The dough will extend beyond the top of the mug and resemble a swirl of whipped cream topping. Bake about 15 minutes in a 350-degree oven. Garnish with a cinnamon stick, and serve immediately, right in the mug!—*Ilverthorpe Cottage*

❧Since it's difficult enough for a hostess to have company—expected or otherwise—anything that can be done in advance eases the stress of entertaining. We manage to serve home-baked goodies—even on short notice—by employing our muffin trick. Here's how to make muffins in advance, so they will still taste as though you just made them.

> *"A customer (guest) is not an interruption of our work . . . he is the purpose of it. We are not doing him a favor by serving him . . . he is doing us a favor by giving us the opportunity to do so." (from an L.L. Bean customer)*
> —The Maine Stay

Grease your muffin cups (we use the very tiny ones, but this works with any size) with a non-stick spray. Make muffin batter, one batch at a time. Fill each muffin cup half full, and immediately place the pan in the freezer. Caution: Do not allow the batter to begin to rise before you pop the pan into the freezer. The dough must be allowed to rise only in the oven.

When the muffin batter is frozen, pop the muffins out of the pan and place in a plastic bag, marking the bag with the type of muffin. Repeat until you have several different muffins, such as cranberry, blueberry, date, lemon, and pumpkin.

Store the plastic bags in the freezer until you're ready to serve. Simply prepare the muffin cups again, pop the frozen muffins back into them, and bake at 350 degrees for about 25 minutes for smaller muffins and 35 minutes for larger muffins.—*Governor's Inn (Vermont)*

✎Prepare muffin batter ahead of time and freeze it in muffin tins. When ready to bake, take them directly from the freezer to the oven. Bake frozen and uncovered 5 minutes longer than the recipe indicates. This yields a far superior muffin than if you were to freeze the cooked muffins.—*Main Street B&B*

Gail's Touch: During the Victorian era (1837–1901), muffins were sold in the streets by vendors, who carried trays of them around their necks, ringing a handbell to attract attention to their tasty treats. I guess that's where the little childhood jingle, "I wish I were the muffin man" came from.

✎Popovers at breakfast are a tradition at the Beal House. Guests exclaim how they have never seen such large, puffy popovers (known as Yorkshire Pudding in England). Here's how to make your popovers burst with pride:

First, make your batter the night before. Leave the batter to rest at room temperature (near a cooler place in very hot weather). In

I only drink champagne when I'm alone. When I have company, I consider it obligatory. I trifle with it when I'm hungry and drink it when I am. Otherwise I never touch it— unless I'm thirsty.

—Trojan Horse Inn

the morning preheat the oven to 400 degrees. Place the popover pan into the oven for 15 minutes. Remove the pan and spray cooking oil into each cup. Whisk the batter slightly and pour, filling each cup to the brim. Cook for 45 minutes. Make sure the oven is at 400 degrees. Use an inexpensive thermometer to test that your oven temperature is accurate. This is very important.—*Beal House*

✎If you don't feel like making muffins and you have over-ripe bananas, throw whole bunches into the freezer for later. They turn black and are mushy when you defrost them, but that makes them easier to use when you do make muffins or quick bread.—*Boydville The Inn at Martinsburg*

✎If we have fruit that is overly ripe, rather than throw it out, we puree it, add softened butter and confectioner's sugar, and blend well. We then have fruit butter to serve with muffins in the morning. These butters can be frozen for up to one month.—*Palmer House*

We make our own butter because it's healthier, plus we enjoy keeping the old method alive. We can make certain that there are no chemicals or additives in our butter by churning our own. Churned butter is lighter and sweeter, and we don't add any salt. Sometimes we add herbs or a fruity liqueur.

You can buy wooden or pottery churns, new or antique. If you buy an old wooden one, here's one way to clean it before using: Clean with a mixture of water, detergent, and baking soda. Wash well. Then fill the churn with fresh water and keep rinsing it well. Let sit one-half hour to dry.

We prefer a tabletop or hand-held churn, typical of those used in an eighteenth-century kitchen. Ours is a red-glazed pottery churn. The best way to churn butter is with heavy cream that comes directly from a farm that has been authorized by the health department to supply such cream. It is the cream skimmed off the top of raw milk. Using this, it takes only twenty minutes to get butter. You also can use goat's milk or heavy cream in churning butter. If you use regular milk, you'll wonder if it will ever churn; it takes much longer to work.

Leave the cream out on the counter the night before, preferably near a window where it can be kept cool. The cream will thicken in a cool area. Next morning, pour the cream into the churn. Place the churn between your legs (if it's a hand-held one), and use an upward motion to make your butter.
—*Inn at Weathersfield*

This is good at breakfast or brunch. Microwave unsalted butter until softened. Mix in brown sugar and cinnamon to taste. Using a pastry tube with a star tip, pipe into individual serving dishes. Chill until firm. Tastes good and looks attractive.
—*Kedron Valley Inn*

Use small candy molds to make interestingly shaped butter pats. Make them ahead and freeze them until needed.
—*Victorian House*

An easy and attractive effect is accomplished by cutting butter and making crisscrossing lines with a fork to resemble a pineapple's skin. It looks nice on the table.
—*Wisconsin House*

Butter can take on all kinds of shapes when you press cookie cutters into very cold butter.—*Bluff Creek Inn*

FOR MORE INFORMATION ON INNS LISTED IN THIS BOOK, SEE THE DIRECTORY BEGINNING ON PAGE **203**.

❧Apricot Glaze French Toast

4 eggs, beaten
1/2 cup heavy cream
1/4 cup light cream
1 teaspoon vanilla extract
1/2 teaspoon cinnamon
1 8-ounce package whipped cream cheese, softened
12 3/4-to-1-inch slices French bread
Butter
12 ounces apricot preserves, heated
Banana slices for garnish

Combine eggs, cream, vanilla, and cinnamon. Let stand. Spread cream cheese on 6 slices of bread, and put 1 slice on top of each one making a sandwich. Do not overfill near the edge of the bread. Dip sandwich into egg mixture for 10 minutes. Turn. Let stand another 10 minutes. Fry on a buttered grill at 250–300 degrees for about 5 minutes per side or until golden brown. Pour heated preserves over the top of the sandwich. Garnish with banana slices. Yield: 6 sandwiches.
—*Churchtown Inn*

❧Baked French Toast

No butter or syrup is needed for this moist and flavorful French toast. This is a make-ahead dish.

1 cup packed light or dark brown sugar
1/2 cup butter
2 tablespoons light or dark corn syrup
1 loaf French bread, cut in 3/4-inch slices (estimate 2 slices per person, plus a few more for hearty eaters)
5 eggs
1 1/2 cups milk
1 teaspoon vanilla extract

In a medium saucepan over medium-low heat, mix and melt brown sugar, butter, and corn syrup. Meanwhile, spray a baking dish with nonstick vegetable oil. Pour the butter and sugar mixture into a 9-by-13-inch baking dish. In a blender mix eggs, milk, and vanilla. Arrange bread slices in baking dish. Pour egg mixture over bread slices, not missing any areas, and using all of the mixture. The excess will be absorbed by the bread slices.

Cover the baking dish and refrigerate overnight. The next morning, preheat oven to 350 degrees. Uncover the baking dish and bake for 30 minutes. Serve directly from the baking dish. Yield: about 8 servings.
—*Little River Inn*

❧My favorite cooking shortcut is to eliminate separating the eggs when making a waffle recipe. Simply place the proper number of whole eggs and milk into a bowl. Let your mixer run on high while the rest of the ingredients are being prepared. By the time you're ready to add the dry ingredients, the egg mixture is light and fluffy.—*Sunning Hill*

❧Keep sourdough starter on hand to be added to prepared mixes or pancakes, waffles, and breads. It adds an interesting flavor. —*Old Yacht Club Inn*

❧Baked Apple Pancakes
4–5 red Delicious or Granny Smith apples,
    peeled, cored, and thinly sliced
1/2 cup unsalted butter
1/2 cup sugar
1/2 teaspoon cinnamon
6 eggs
1 cup flour
Scant cup milk

Preheat oven to 375 degrees. In an 8-inch cast-iron skillet, melt butter. Sauté apples. Sprinkle with sugar and cinnamon. Cook until sugar is melted and apples have begun to soften. Mix together eggs, flour, and milk, and pour over apples. Bake for 20–30 minutes or until puffed and done in the center. Serve warm with maple syrup. Yield: at least 6 servings.—*Bramble Inn*

❧To soften hard brown sugar, put it in a pan with a little water and heat gradually. Serve as syrup on pancakes or use as called for in recipes.—*Mayhurst B&B*

❧Want to make pancakes lighter than air? Use low-fat milk instead of whole milk. —*Shire Inn*

❧Banana Pancakes
This recipe yields a crêpelike pancake.
1 1/2 cups flour
2 tablespoons sugar
2 1/2 teaspoons baking powder
1/2 teaspoon salt
2 eggs
1 1/4 cups milk
3 tablespoons oil or melted butter
2 medium-sized, overripe bananas, mashed

Mix together flour, sugar, baking powder, and salt. In another bowl mix together eggs, milk, and oil or butter. Combine this with the dry ingredients. Add mashed bananas. Heat griddle and pour batter to desired pancake size. Yield: 4–6 servings. —*Thomas Huckins House*

❧Stuffed Fruit Toast
Cut a large slice of Italian bread and slit the center. Stuff it with fresh fruit. Make a dipping batter of egg, flour, brown sugar to taste, and milk. Dip the stuffed bread into

the batter and then deep-fry. Cover with powdered sugar.—*Doubleday Inn*

❧Quick Fruit Crisp

1 29-ounce can sliced peaches, apples, or
    pears, undrained
1 18 1/2-ounce box yellow cake mix
1/2 cup melted butter
1 cup shredded unsweetened coconut
    (optional)
1 cup chopped pecans
Cinnamon to sprinkle on top
Whipped cream

Preheat oven to 325 degrees. Place ingredients in the order listed (except the whipped cream) into a 9-by-13-inch ungreased baking dish. Bake approximately 50 minutes. Serve warm with a dash of whipped cream. Yield: 12 small servings.—*Churchtown Inn*

❧Glazed Sausage and Apples

This is a nice side dish.

2 pounds precooked sausage links
1/3 cup water
1/4 cup loosely packed brown sugar
2 large tart apples, sliced
1 large onion, chopped

Brown sausages in large skillet. Remove sausages, drain on paper towels, and add remaining ingredients to same skillet. Cook 8 to 10 minutes until tender, then stir sausages into mixture, and continue cooking about 10 minutes longer. Yield: 6 servings. —*The Summer Cottage*

Gail's Touch:

❧Individual Sausage-and-Egg Vegetable Tarts

1/2 pound ground sweet or breakfast
    sausage
2 large eggs, beaten
1/2 cup milk
1/2 cup all-purpose flour
1/2 teaspoon oregano
1/2 teaspoon white pepper
1/4 cup chopped green onion
1/4 cup shredded cheddar, Swiss, or
    Gruyère cheese
1/2 cup coarsely chopped fresh tomatoes
1/2 cup sour cream, for garnish

Preheat oven to 425 degrees. Cook the sausage in a medium skillet over medium-high heat until browned. Remove from the heat and drain.

In a medium bowl, combine the eggs, milk, flour, oregano, and pepper until smooth.

Coat 4 4 1/2-inch tart pans with non-stick coating. Pour in the egg-and-milk mixture. Add the sausage and the onions.

Sprinkle with the tomatoes and bake in the oven for 10 to 12 minutes or until the tarts are puffy and golden brown. Sprinkle the cheese overtop and return to the oven for another minute or so until the cheese is melted. Top with a dollop of sour cream. Yield: 4 tarts.

❧ Breakfast Egg Casserole

1 pound bulk breakfast sausage
4–5 slices of bread, cubed
1/3 pound mild cheddar cheese, cubed
6 eggs
2 cups milk
1 teaspoon salt (optional)
1 teaspoon dry mustard

Grease a 9-by-13-inch pan. In a medium skillet brown sausage. Remove and drain. Place the bread cubes in pan; then add the sausage meat. Arrange cheese cubes over meat. In a small bowl beat eggs, milk, salt, and mustard. Pour egg mixture over the cheese cubes. Refrigerate overnight. In the morning preheat oven to 350 degrees. Bake the casserole for 45 minutes. Yield: about 8 servings.—*Winters Creek Inn*

❧ Poached Eggs with Herbal Stuffing

1 cup herb-seasoned croutons
1 tablespoon butter, melted
1/3 cup hot water
1 tablespoon mixed dried herbs, if desired
2 eggs
1 tablespoon Parmesan cheese
1 teaspoon chopped green onions or chives

Layer the bread in 1 1/2-cup to cup ramekins. Keep the dishes warm.

Poach 2 eggs and place them on top of the stuffing. Sprinkle with the cheese and the onions and serve immediately. Yield: 1 serving. —*Doanleigh Wallagh Inn*

❧ When a recipe calls for beating egg whites separately, the tiniest bit of yolk will keep them from whipping fully. The best way to remove a speck of yolk (or even a piece of eggshell) is to use another piece of eggshell to scoop it out.—*Out-the-Inn-Door*

❧ Shaw House Egg for One

Slice miniature sausages or cocktail hot dogs in half, and sauté in butter in a skillet. Cover the bottom of a ramekin (or any individual baking dish) with the sausage or hot dogs. Spoon in 3 tablespoons of your favorite white sauce. Crack an egg on top. Cover with grated cheese. Bake for 8 minutes in a 325-degree oven.—*Shaw House*

For more information on inns listed in this book, see the directory Beginning on page 203.

✄ Freeze egg whites or yolks in tightly sealed containers. Thaw at room temperature.—*Britt House*

✄ Place eggs in the refrigerator with large ends up, as this keeps the yolks centered. Eggs will remain unspoiled in the refrigerator for up to one month. Since eggshells are porous, eggs may absorb odors from other foods in the refrigerator. Keep strong-smelling foods tightly covered and as far as possible from the eggs.—*Britt House*

✄ To save time, cook poached eggs in advance and refrigerate. They store beautifully and can be used in recipes or reheated. —*Carter House*

✄ Serving a soft-boiled egg in an eggcup brings back Grandma's house or European travel memories. It makes a plain egg an event!—*Bluebelle House*

✄ We serve our eggs in glass hen dishes. The eggs keep warm, and the dishes really look great.—*Beal House*

Gail's Touch:

❧ BRUNCH VEGETABLE PIZZA
Cream cheese in this pizza pie makes it a lighter version, suitable for early in the day, or serve this pizza as an appetizer. Note that The White Oak Inn suggests three possible vegetable toppings. As an editor's note, whenever I use a Boboli brand shell, I find it makes a crispier crust if you bake on an oven rack for a few minutes.

PIZZA:
1 large pizza shell, such as Boboli brand,
    baked light golden brown
2 8-ounce packages cream cheese
3 tablespoons mayonnaise
1 clove garlic, minced

TOPPING CHOICES:
a) 3 cups diced fresh tomatoes mixed with
    1 tablespoon olive oil, 2 tablespoons
    chopped scallions, 1 teaspoon oregano
b) 3-cup mixture of sliced mushrooms,
    onions, and yellow bell pepper,
    diced and lightly sautéed in a lit-
    tle olive oil
c) 3-cup mixture of broccoli and diced
    carrots, steamed for 3 minutes and
    then mixed with 1/2 cup grated
    Swiss cheese

GARNISHING:
1/4 cup fresh basil, coarsely chopped
Lemon pepper
Parmesan cheese

Preheat oven to 350 degrees. Mix

together the cream cheese, mayonnaise, and garlic. Set aside. Mix together a choice of vegetable topping. Spread the cream cheese mixture over the pizza crust. Sprinkle the vegetable mixture overtop and sprinkle with the basil and lemon pepper and the Parmesan cheese as desired.

Bake for 5 to 10 minutes or until warmed through and cheeses are melted and bubbly. Yield: 1 pizza.

❧ CRAB BRUNCH SQUARES WITH RED-PEPPER CREAM SAUCE

4 eggs
2 2/3 cups milk
3/4 teaspoon Dijon-style mustard
6 ounces Brie, rind removed, cut in
    1/4 inch cubes
1/2 cup sliced black olives
1 small onion, finely chopped
2 tablespoons finely chopped parsley
1 teaspoon worcestershire sauce
3 1/2 cups cooked rice
1 pound fresh, frozen, or canned lump
    crabmeat, picked through for shells

Preheat oven to 325 degrees. In mixing bowl beat eggs, milk, and mustard until blended. Stir in remaining ingredients. Pour into greased 9-by-13-inch baking pan. Bake for 40–45 minutes, or until knife inserted at center comes out clean. Serve with Red-Pepper Cream Sauce.

RED-PEPPER CREAM SAUCE:
4 tablespoons unsalted butter
1 large ripe red pepper, seeded and cut in
    1/4-inch dice
1/4 cup thinly sliced green onion
1/4 cup flour
1/4 teaspoon salt
1/4 teaspoon white pepper
1 3/4 cups milk
3 teaspoons lemon juice
Fresh snipped chives for garnish

Melt butter in small, heavy saucepan. Sauté red pepper and green onion for 2 minutes. Add flour and sauté on low heat 3 minutes. Blend in salt and pepper, then gradually whisk in milk and lemon juice. Cook for 1 minute, then transfer to blender container. Blend on high for 2 minutes, or until pepper and onion are pureed. Spoon over brunch squares and garnish with chives. Yield: 10 servings.—*Grant Corner Inn*

❧ It can be a pain to peel eggs when you're making deviled or hard-boiled eggs. Two tips: First, try to buy your eggs five or six days before you need them, especially farm-fresh eggs. Fresh eggs are very hard to peel. Second, put one-half cup of salt into the

water with the eggs. Cook as you usually do. Then, place five or six eggs at a time into a colander and shake them rapidly while running under water. They peel themselves.
—*The Decoy*

PORTABLE FEASTS

🍃 For something different, pack a picnic breakfast for your guests. Our picnic hamper often includes French toast in pottery dishes to keep it warm on the way to a nearby park. Padded place mats further protect the food from getting cold. A thermos is filled with coffee.—*Glenborough Inn*

🍃 Gourmet picnics are prepared for guests upon request. Here's what we put into our picnic hampers. You can do something similar for yours. We fill a wooden basket with an elegant four-course meal. A detailed menu of what's inside is handwritten. There are linen napkins and silverware tied with ribbon. One hamper might start picnickers with a chilled *potage* of fresh tomato-and-lemon cream and nut bread with cream cheese. A sandwich of smoked baby clams with cucumbers and dill dressing might follow, all topped off with a pleasing bottle of French wine.

We offer the inn's collection of recipes for our guests. They can prepare some of the dishes at home and make up their own picnic baskets so that they can remember a special day in Vermont. The linen, wine glasses, and basket are for guests to keep.
—*The Governor's Inn (Vermont)*

INDULGENT INTERLUDES: APPETIZERS, SNACKS, BEVERAGES

🍃 SESAME CHEESE STICKS
1 cup flour, sifted
1/2 teaspoon salt
1/2 teaspoon ground ginger
1 cup grated sharp cheese
1/4 cup toasted sesame seeds
1 egg yolk, beaten
1/3 cup butter, melted
1 tablespoon water
1/2 teaspoon worcestershire sauce

Preheat oven to 350 degrees. Sift together dry ingredients. Stir in cheese and sesame seeds. Combine remaining ingredients; then add them to first mixture and stir to form a ball. Roll out on slightly floured board to 1/4-inch thickness. Cut into 1-by-3-inch strips. Bake on ungreased baking sheet for 10–15 minutes. Yield: 4 dozen.
—*The Summer Cottage*

❧ HOT ARTICHOKE DIP

1 12-ounce can unmarinated artichokes,
broken up
1/2 cup mayonnaise
2 ounces chopped green chilies
1 cup Parmesan cheese

Preheat oven to 350 degrees. Mix all ingredients and bake in a 4-cup shallow bowl for 15 minutes. Serve with crackers.
—*Glenborough Inn*

❧ THE GOVERNOR'S INN MUSHROOM STRUDEL

This is our most-requested recipe.

6 cups minced mushrooms, caps and stems
1 teaspoon salt
1/4 teaspoon curry powder
6 tablespoons sherry
4 tablespoons chopped shallots
1/4 cup sweet butter
1 cup sour cream
1 cup plus 3 tablespoons dry bread crumbs
1 package frozen phyllo dough, thawed
1/2 cup sweet butter, melted
Sour cream
Fresh parsley

Sauté mushrooms with seasonings, sherry, and shallots in the butter until mushrooms are wilted and liquid is gone (about 20 minutes on low heat). Cool. Add sour cream and 3 tablespoons dry bread crumbs. Refrigerate overnight.

Preheat oven to 375 degrees. Unwrap phyllo dough carefully. Place a sheet of dough on a large breadboard. Brush with melted butter and sprinkle with bread crumbs. Repeat until you have 4 layers. Spoon half the mushroom mixture onto the narrow end of the dough. Turn long sides of dough in about 1 inch to seal filling. Roll up dough like a jelly roll. Brush top of the roll with butter, and sprinkle with a few more crumbs. Place on a lightly greased cookie sheet. Score dough with a sharp knife for 8 equal slices. Make a second roll, using remaining mushroom filling. Bake for 40 minutes. Garnish with dollop of sour cream and chopped parsley. Serve hot. Yield: 16 slices.—*The Governor's Inn (Vermont)*

❧ GREEK HUMMUS DIP

This is great with crackers or triangles of pita bread.

1 15 1/2-ounce can garbanzo beans, drained
2 lemons, juiced
2 garlic cloves, pressed
1/2 cup tahini
Olive oil
Paprika
Green or black Greek olives

In a blender combine beans, lemon juice, garlic, and tahini. Add more lemon juice, salt, or garlic to taste. Spread the dip on a plate, dribble olive oil over it, sprinkle with paprika, and dot with green or black Greek olives. Yield: 8–10 servings.—*Eastlake Inn*

❧ HOT RYES
1 cup finely grated Swiss cheese
1/4 cup crumbled cooked bacon
1 4 1/2-ounce can ripe olives, chopped
1/4 cup minced green onions or chives
1 teaspoon worcestershire sauce
1/4 cup mayonnaise
Party rye bread

Preheat oven to 375 degrees. Mix first 6 ingredients together. Spread 1 tablespoon on each slice of bread. Bake for 10–15 minutes. May be frozen after baking and reheated. Yield: 36 servings.—*Inn of the Arts*

❧ PORTRAITS OF INN-SPIRATION ❧

Several years ago some guests, on their way back from a funeral, were caught in an ice storm and stayed in our Sunday Room. They had their deceased aunt's ashes with them and decided to scatter the ashes in our Victorian garden. A very nice eulogy was written about "Aunt Pearl" in our guest book.

As the years went by, different guests have joined in and have written about Aunt Pearl in the book. One guest had this to say: ". . . the sound of her wedding gown blowing in the breeze woke me in the night. . . ."

We now have a "picture" of Aunt Pearl hanging above the mantel of our fireplace. She even plays a part in our Murder Mystery Weekends. As each guest writes about her, the tale gets taller and taller.

The legend, begun by her nephew, lives on!

McKay House

⌘ To keep cheese from drying out, dip a linen cloth or cheesecloth in wine. Squeeze out the excess wine and wrap the cheese in the cloth. The cheese is not only kept moist, but its flavor is improved.—*Cliff House*

⌘ Cheese also can be kept fresh by covering it with a cloth moistened with vinegar. —*Pride House*

❧ SHRIMP SPREAD

1 6-ounce can tiny shrimp, drained and mashed
1 teaspoon lemon juice
2 tablespoons mayonnaise
1 tablespoon grated onion
Salt (optional)

Mix ingredients together, adding a dash of salt if desired. Chill, then serve with crackers. —*Graham's B&B Inn*

❧ SHRIMP APPETIZER

2 6 1/2-ounce cans medium deveined shrimp, drained
2 8-ounce packages cream cheese
1/2 large onion, chopped
Juice of 1/2 lemon
1/8 teaspoon worcestershire sauce

Preheat oven to 350 degrees. Mix ingredients. Pour into soufflé dish and bake for 30 minutes. Serve with crackers.—*Inn of the Arts*

❧ MEXICAN ROLL-UPS

1 4-ounce can black olives, chopped
8 ounces cream cheese, softened
1/8 teaspoon tabasco sauce
2 medium-size flour tortillas
Medium-hot salsa

Fold olives into softened cream cheese. Add tabasco sauce. Mix. Divide the mixture in half. Fill each tortilla with half of the cream-cheese filling. Roll the tortillas to form cylinders. Cut into 3/4-inch slices. Hold each roll-up together with a decorative toothpick. Place salsa in a bowl as a dip for the roll-ups.—*Locust Hill*

❧ CLAM SPREAD

1 tablespoon light cream (add more if needed)
8 ounces cream cheese, softened
1 bunch green onions, chopped (tops too)
1/2 teaspoon garlic powder
2–3 grinds fresh black pepper
1 6 1/2-ounce can chopped clams

Mix cream into cream cheese. Add onions, garlic powder, and pepper. Mix. Stir in clams. Chill at least 2 hours; best when chilled overnight. Serve with crackers or toast points.—*Wanek's Lodge*

❧ HOT BUTTERED WEDGWOOD

2 ounces almond liqueur
1 cup hot tea, cider, or apple juice
1 tablespoon whipped unsalted butter
1/8 teaspoon of orange peel
1 cinnamon stick

Pour the almond liqueur into a mug. Fill with the hot tea, cider, or juice. Add the butter and orange peel. Garnish with a cinnamon stick. Yield: 1 serving.—*Wedgwood Inn*

❧ HOMEMADE COFFEE LIQUEUR

2 cups boiling water
2 ounces powdered instant coffee
3 cups sugar
1 fifth brandy or vodka
1 vanilla bean, cut in sections

Pour boiling water over coffee. Stir to dissolve. Stir in sugar until dissolved. Cool. Add brandy or vodka. Pour into desired number of sterilized, dark-brown bottles. Add a section of vanilla bean to each bottle. Place each bottle in a brown bag. Store for 1 month, shaking weekly. Yield: about 1 quart. —*Britt House*

❧ FIRESIDE QUENCHER

Although this is a great summer refresher, it can quench your thirst any time of the year. Fill a tall glass with ice. Add 2 teaspoons of bitters and 1 1/2–2 ounces of lime juice. Fill with sparkling mineral water. Add a dash of dark rum for a little kick.—*Tulip Tree Inn*

❧ CRANBERRY CORDIAL

1 pound cranberries, washed and picked
over
1 pound sugar
1 fifth of gin

Dry and punch a hole through each cranberry. In a half-gallon jar place berries, sugar, and gin. Seal the jar and store it for 6 weeks, shaking it at least once a day. Strain and place in a nice decanter with a tight-fitting stopper. —*Folkestone B&B*

❧ AMARETTO CORDIAL

6 cups sugar
1 quart water
3 ounces almond extract
2 quarts vodka

Combine sugar and water. Bring to a boil and simmer for 5 minutes. Add almond extract and vodka. Store in a dark bottle. Yield: 18–20 servings.—*Folkestone B&B*

❧ WASSAIL

1 gallon apple juice
1 quart cranberry juice
1 cup sugar

3 cinnamon sticks

1 tablespoon whole allspice

3 small oranges studded with whole cloves

1 1/2–2 cups dark rum

Combine ingredients. Heat gently. Simmer for 1/2 hour. Serve warm. Yield: 18–20 servings.—*Churchtown Inn*

Fill a bundt pan with water and add fruit, tiny flowers, and greenery. Freeze. When ready for ice in the punch bowl, remove the bundt ice sculpture from the pan. (Dip the pan in hot water to help remove the sculpture.) This is beautiful when floating in the punch.—*Garnet Hill Lodge*

COUNTRY CORN AND CHEESE BREAD

1 1/2 cups cornmeal

1/2 cup flour

1/2 teaspoon baking soda

1/2 teaspoon salt

1 cup whole milk

2 large eggs, beaten

2 tablespoons vegetable oil

2 cups grated Vermont cheddar cheese

1 8-ounce can cream-style corn

1 pound lean, good-quality bacon, cooked, drained, and crumbled

Preheat oven to 350 degrees. Combine first 4 ingredients and mix well. Add milk, eggs, and vegetable oil, stirring well. Stir in remaining ingredients. Pour into a greased tube pan. Bake for 45 minutes or until lightly browned. Cool for 10 minutes before removing from pan. Serve slightly warm. Yield: 6–8 servings.—*The Governor's Inn (Vermont)*

Gail's Touch:

DILL AND CHEESE BREAD

1 1/2 cups cottage cheese

1/4 cup water

2 tablespoons sugar

2 tablespoons minced onion

1 tablespoon butter

3 teaspoons dill seeds

1 teaspoon salt

1/4 teaspoon baking soda

1 egg

2 1/4–2 1/2 cups flour

1 package yeast dissolved in 1/4 cup warm water

Softened butter

Heat cottage cheese to lukewarm in a pan and then add 1/4 cup water. Pour remaining ingredients, except softened yeast mixture and flour, into large bowl. Add softened yeast mixture. Then add flour to form a stiff dough, beating as flour is added. Cover dough. Let rise in warm place (85–90 degrees), until light and doubled in size,

❧ PORTRAITS OF INN-SPIRATION ❧

A couple celebrating their tenth wedding anniversary were checking in for an overnight stay. As her husband did the paperwork, the woman meandered around the inn. She returned to our front-foyer area and excitedly inquired about the baby grand piano in our living room: Where had we purchased it? When?

We gave her the name of the piano company from whom we had made the purchase and told her that the piano had recently been refinished.

Very emphatically, the woman told us that the piano once belonged to her! In fact, she had played the very same piano for her husband when they were courting. It had been in her parents' home. After her father had remarried, her stepmother decided to sell a few items—including the piano—without notifying her stepdaughter. The lost piano has been a missing link for the woman all these years.

That evening we were expecting a large birthday celebration. The birthday party had hired an excellent pianist for the cocktail portion of the celebration, but my husband and I hired him for an additional hour. Knowing the piano's history, we sat our anniversary couple in the dining room for dinner, then in the living room for a romantic dessert with the pianist.

In appreciation for all that had transpired during her short stay, the woman placed the beautiful bouquet of flowers that her husband had sent to her room, on the piano for other guests to enjoy.

Creating memories is what innkeeping is all about . . . and one never knows what form it will take.

The Inn at Olde New Berlin

out of the rind around the edges, leaving rind between each V, so that you have almost a pinwheel effect.—*Corner Cupboard Inn*

Interested in a more salt-free diet? Add caraway seeds or garlic in your cooking instead of salt.   —*Shire Inn*

Gail's Touch: Save the leaves of fresh radishes to add extra-peppery zing to any dish, including stir-fried vegetables.

To freeze fresh vegetables, blanch them in boiling water two to three minutes. Then run them under cold water to stop the cooking process. Place in plastic bags and freeze.—*Emersons' Guest House*

Tired of your lobster curling up while being boiled? Tie the tasty crustacean to a wooden board first; then cook.—*Shire Inn*

Lemon yogurt is great as a topping for fish, and maple yogurt goes well over old-fashioned oatmeal.—*Knoll Farm Country Inn*

Unfortunately, ginger root tends to get stringy. Thus it's difficult to grate finely when a recipe calls for the ingredient in nonsolid form. Our chef accidentally discovered that by freezing ginger you can grate it as finely as you do Parmesan cheese. Also, it can be frozen again with no harm to the flavor. —*Pilgrim's Inn*

SWEET ENDINGS

WHITE CHOCOLATE FRUIT CORDIAL

A gourmet dessert for a special night in front of the fireplace.

1 8-ounce package cream cheese, room temperature
1 1/2 cups whipping cream
3/4 cup powdered sugar, sifted
3 ounces white chocolate, melted and slightly cooled
1 12-ounce bag frozen unsweetened raspberries, thawed
1/3 cup sugar
1 8-ounce can unsweetened apricots, drained
Amaretto liqueur
fresh mint leaves

Line 6 1/2-cup ramekins or custard cups with double thickness of dampened cheesecloth, extending beyond edges to enclose filling completely. Using an electric mixer, beat cream cheese with 1/4 cup of the cream and the powdered sugar in a large bowl until fluffy. Add white chocolate and beat until smooth, about 2 minutes. In another bowl whip 1 cup cream to stiff peaks. Gently fold whipped cream into cream-cheese mixture. Spoon 1/2 cup cheese mixture into each prepared mold. Fold cheesecloth over tops. Place molds on a rack set over a pan. Refrigerate for at least 8 hours or overnight.

Drain raspberries, reserving juice. Purée berries with 1/3 cup sugar in processor. Press through fine sieve into a medium-sized bowl to remove seeds. Add just enough reserved juice to thin puree to sauce consistency. Cover and refrigerate.

Puree apricots in food processor. Add amaretto to taste. Transfer to small bowl. Cover and refrigerate. (Sauces may be prepared 3 hours ahead.)

Whip remaining 1/4 cup cream to stiff peaks. Spoon into pastry bag fitted with star tip. Pull back cheesecloth. Pour 3 tablespoons raspberry sauce on left side of the plate. Spoon 1 tablespoon apricot sauce in center of raspberry sauce. Draw knife through center of apricot circle, forming heart pattern. Repeat with remaining molds and sauces. Pipe rosettes of cream onto each plate, and garnish with mint leaves. Yield: 6 servings.—*Bramble Inn*

FOR MORE INFORMATION ON INNS LISTED IN THIS BOOK, SEE THE DIRECTORY BEGINNING ON PAGE 203.

❧ OLD FASHIONED BROWNIES

1 1/4 cups graham cracker crumbs
1 14-ounce can sweetened condensed milk
1 cup chocolate chips
3/4 cup chopped walnuts
Powdered sugar

Preheat oven to 325 degrees. Grease and flour 8-inch-square baking pan. Mix the ingredients and spread evenly in the pan. Bake approximately 25 minutes. Cut while still warm into 2-by-4-inch squares. Dust with powdered sugar before serving. Yield: 8 servings.—*Benner House*

❧ PRIZE-WINNING SPICE CAKE

2 cups flour
1 teaspoon cinnamon
1 teaspoon ground cloves
1 teaspoon allspice
1/2 teaspoon salt
1 teaspoon baking soda
2 teaspoons baking powder
2 eggs, beaten until lemon colored
1 cup sugar
2 tablespoons molasses
1 cup buttermilk
2/3 cup oil

Preheat oven to 375 degrees. Stir together flour, cinnamon, cloves, allspice, salt, baking soda, and baking powder. Set aside. Beat eggs and gradually add sugar and molasses. Beat well. Add dry ingredients to the egg mixture, alternately with the buttermilk. Gently add the oil. Pour into 2 greased loaf pans, and bake for 25 minutes. Serve with a favorite cream-cheese topping. Yield: 2 loaves.—*Britt House*

❧ CHOCOLATE TRUFFLE CHEESECAKE WITH RASPBERRY SAUCE

You will need to prepare this cake a day ahead.

CRUST:
2 1/2 cups chocolate wafer crumbs
1/3 cup butter, melted
1/2 cup sugar
FILLING:
1 8-ounce package semisweet chocolate squares, cut into 1/2-inch cubes
1/4 cup strong, hot coffee
3 8-ounce packages cream cheese, cut into 1-inch cubes
1 cup sour cream
1 cup sugar
2 eggs
2 tablespoons whipping cream
1 teaspoon vanilla extract
1/4 cup Chambord liqueur
SAUCE:
1 10-ounce package frozen raspberries, thawed

2 teaspoons cornstarch

Preheat oven to 375 degrees.

Prepare the crust. Blend together the chocolate crumbs, butter, and 1/2 cup only of the sugar. Press into the bottom and 1 1/2-inches up the sides of a greased 9-inch springform pan. Set aside.

Prepare the filling. Process the chocolate cubes in a food processor until finely ground. While running, pour in the hot coffee. Process until the chocolate is melted. Add the cream cheese, sour cream, sugar, eggs, whipping cream, vanilla, and Chambord. Process until smooth, a few minutes. Stop to scrape the sides when needed.

Pour the mixture into the prepared pan and bake for 55 minutes. The center should still be soft. Let cool at room temperature. Cover and chill at least 8 hours.

When about ready to serve, prepare the raspberry sauce.

Drain the raspberries, reserving the juice. Combine the juice with the cornstarch in a small saucepan and cool over medium heat, stirring until smooth and thickened. Cool. Place a pool of sauce onto a serving plate and add a slice of cake and serve.—*Rowell's Inn*

❧ AMARETTO BREAD PUDDING

6 thin bread slices, buttered

3 eggs
2 egg yolks
1/2 cup sugar
1/8 teaspoon salt
1 1/4 cups milk
1 1/2 cups light cream
1 1/2 teaspoons vanilla
1 1/2 teaspoons amaretto liqueur
1/8 teaspoon nutmeg
1/8 teaspoon cinnamon

Preheat oven to 325 degrees. Cover the bottom of a 9-by-13-inch baking pan with the buttered bread. Mix together all the remaining ingredients. Pour mixture over the bread. Bake for 55 minutes. Cut into squares. Serve each piece with a dollop of whipped cream and the desired amount of amaretto poured on top. Yield: 8–10 servings.

—*Academy Street B&B*

❧ Chocolate Bread Pudding with Brandied Apricots and Pears

1 tablespoon butter
2 cups half-and-half
6 ounces semisweet chocolate chips
1/2 loaf day-old French bread, cut into
    1/2-inch cubes
3/4 cup brandy
1/3 cup chopped dried apricots
2 pears, peeled and sliced

1 cup heavy cream, whipped
3 large eggs
3/4 cup sugar
1 teaspoon vanilla extract

Preheat oven to 350 degrees.

Butter a 7-by-11-inch baking pan. In a saucepan heat half-and-half. Remove, and stir in chocolate chips until smooth. Place bread cubes in a large bowl, stir in chocolate mixture, and let stand 45 minutes.

Heat brandy and apricots. Remove from heat and stir in pear slices. Cool and drain, adding some of the liquid to the whipped cream.

Whisk together eggs, sugar, and vanilla. Stir into chocolate-bread mixture along with the brandied fruit. Pour into prepared pan and bake 1 hour or until golden brown. Serve warm with the brandied whipped cream. Yield: 10–12 servings.—*Trillium House*

❧ Torte Turnaround

Change that ordinary chocolate cake mix into an exciting torte. Buy a top-quality cake mix. Bake according to package directions. Split layers in half. Spread raspberry preserves between layers. Drizzle with raspberry liqueur. Assemble the torte, and pipe thick whipped cream as frosting. Decorate with raspberries and more drizzled liqueur.

—*Inn at Buckeystown*

❦ SWEET-AND-SPICY POACHED PEARS

1 1/2 cups water or enough to cover the
pears
1 cup dry white wine
1 cinnamon stick
1 teaspoon vanilla extract
1/4 cup raspberry or strawberry preserves
Zest of 1 small lemon
6 ripe but firm medium-sized pears,
peeled, stems intact
Freshly grated nutmeg

In a large saucepan, combine all of the ingredients except the pears and the nutmeg. Bring the liquid to a boil and cook over medium high heat for 15 minutes. Reduce the heat to a simmer. Add the pears and cook covered for 15 minutes or until the pears are tender. Remove the pan from the heat and let the pears cool in the liquid.

Serve warm or chilled with a little extract liquid spooned over each and a sprinkling of freshly grated nutmeg to top each serving. Yield: 6 servings.

Here's a recipe on how to make your own vanilla extract: Place two to three pieces of vanilla bean in a small jar. Add some vodka. Let it stand for a few months. Replenish with vodka. Makes a great Christmas present.—*Old Broad Bay Inn*

Make your own homemade chocolate mints. Crush peppermint candies into melted chocolate. Pour into candy molds and let harden.—*Briar Rose*

Plastic squeeze bottles make great instruments for sauces. One of ours, for example, holds our chocolate sauce. It makes it easy to decorate desserts on top. One of the patterns we use is a spiderweb made by the squeeze of the plastic container. —*The Bramble Inn*

Allspice makes a tasty addition to whipped cream. Serve atop a *caffè latte.* —*Shire Inn*

❦ GINGER MUFFINS

3/4 cup butter
1/2 cup sugar
2 eggs
1/8 teaspoon cinnamon
1 teaspoon ginger
1/2 teaspoon allspice
1/2 cup buttermilk
1 teaspoon baking soda
1/2 cup dark molasses
1/2 cup chopped nuts
1/2 cup raisins
2 cups flour

Preheat oven to 400 degrees. Mix ingredients in order given. Grease 12 to 16 muffin cups or use cupcake liners. Fill each cup 3/4 full. Bake for 10 minutes. Yield: 12–16 muffins.—*Butternut Inn*

❧ CRANBERRY AND WALNUT MUFFINS

2 cups flour
2 teaspoons baking powder
1/2 tablespoon salt
1/2 cup butter
1 cup sugar
2 large eggs
1 teaspoon vanilla extract
1 teaspoon butter-vanilla extract
2 large tablespoons sour cream (or 3 large tablespoons cream cheese)
3 ounces canned whole cranberries
1/2 cup milk
1/2 cup walnuts, chopped (optional)
TOPPING:
1 tablespoon sugar
1/4 teaspoon nutmeg
1/4 teaspoon cinnamon

Preheat oven to 375 degrees. Grease 12 to 16 muffin cups and the areas between the cups. Sift together flour, baking powder, and salt. In a mixing bowl cream butter and sugar until fluffy. Beat in eggs, vanillas, and sour cream. Stir butter and sugar mixture into flour mixture. Fold in cranberries. Add walnuts. Spoon batter into muffin cups, filling to the top.

Mix together topping ingredients. Sprinkle a little topping over each muffin. Bake 25 minutes until golden. Cool 10–15 minutes before removing. Yield: 12–16 moist cakelike muffins.—*Audrie's Cranbury Corner*

❧ DUTCH APPLE MUFFINS

1 egg
3/4 cup milk
1/2 cup vegetable oil
1 medium apple, peeled and chopped
2 cups flour
1/3 cup firmly packed brown sugar
3 teaspoons baking powder
1 teaspoon salt
1/2 teaspoon cinnamon
TOPPING:
1/4 cup packed brown sugar
1/4 cup chopped nuts
1/2 teaspoon cinnamon

Preheat oven to 400 degrees. Grease 8 large muffin cups. Beat egg in medium bowl; stir in milk, oil, and apple. Stir in remaining muffin ingredients all at once, stirring just until moistened. Fill muffin cups and sprinkle with the topping. Bake about 25 minutes. Yield: 8 large muffins.—*Main Street B&B*

❧ ORANGE MUFFINS

1 whole orange
1/3 cup orange juice
3/4 stick butter
1 egg
1/2 cup raisins
1 1/2 cups sifted flour
3/4 cup sugar
1 teaspoon baking powder
1 teaspoon baking soda
1 teaspoon salt

Preheat oven to 400 degrees. Grate the rind from the orange. Discard the pith. Quarter and seed the orange. In a blender mix the rind, quarters, orange juice, butter, and egg. Add raisins. Blend for 5 seconds. Transfer to a large bowl. Sift the flour, sugar, baking powder, baking soda, and salt. Stir flour mixture into orange mixture until combined. Divide batter into 16 buttered and floured muffin cups or 8 large ones. Bake for 15–20 minutes. Yield: 8–16 muffins.

—Maidstone Arms

❧ PEACH COBBLER MUFFINS

1 egg
1/2 cup sour cream
1/2 cup milk
1 teaspoon vanilla extract
4 tablespoons vegetable oil
3 large peaches, peeled and diced
2 cups flour
1/2 cup sugar
1 tablespoon baking powder
1/4 teaspoon baking soda
1/4 teaspoon salt
TOPPING:
1/4 cup flour
1/4 cup sugar
1/4 teaspoon ground cinnamon
2 tablespoons butter

Preheat oven to 400 degrees. Grease 8 large muffin cups. In a medium-sized bowl combine egg, sour cream, milk, vanilla, and oil. Stir in the peaches. In a large bowl combine flour, sugar, baking powder, baking soda, and salt. Pour in the peach mixture and stir until just moistened. Fill muffin cups. Prepare topping, using a pastry blender. Sprinkle the batter with topping. Bake 30–35 minutes. Yield: 8 large muffins.

—Main Street B&B

THE MAGIC OF MUFFIN-MAKING

❧The trick to making most muffins is in the wrist. Once the wet ingredients hit the dry ingredients, you have only a few minutes to get those muffins into the oven to ensure they will rise high. If you spend too much

time, the gases will be released, and you'll have only little mounds instead of nice and hearty, eye-opening breads.
—*Chetwynd House*

❧Be careful when blending muffin batter. You don't want it to be smooth. Leaving lumps yields a high-rising, light muffin.
—*Spring Bank Inn*

❧Sprinkling some cinnamon sugar on top of muffins will not only add flavor, but also will make them crispier on top.—*Holden House*

❧The seasons can help you decide what type of bread to bake for your guests. Whatever fruit is in season can be baked into a bread when it is plentiful, at its best, and least expensive.—*Captain Dexter House*

❧Use a quality ice-cream scoop (one with a good spring) to put muffin batter into pans. It makes filling the pan quick and easy, and the muffins cook uniformly. Our scoop is one quarter of a cup, but you should adjust according to your pans.—*Nauset House*

❧To soften hard raisins, put them into a plastic bag and then place bag in warm water.—*Mayhurst B&B*

❧Rinse a pan with cold water before scalding milk to prevent sticking.
—*Pride House*

Chapter 7

IT'S TEA TIME

BREWING FRIENDLY CHATS AND LEAVES THAT TALK

Taking tea immediately bestirs feelings of tranquility. The very word suggests calm and peace. Tea is truly one of life's simple pleasures, and it is so accessible. The leaves from the *Camellia sinensis* bush are easily at hand, whether loose or in a small paper sack, and, of course, a teacup and hot water are never far away.

Tea means much more than what we have been taught about the beverage over the years. Tea does stand on ceremony; however, you don't always need to be ceremonious to enjoy the benefits of this ancient beverage. Whether pouring the traditional "proper cup" or just sinking a teabag into a mug full of hot water, tea has restorative powers, and this holds true whether you are enjoying it alone or with someone.

Inns offer tea time to their guests in a variety of ways. First of all there are always the welcome teas. A tea and buffet are often the first of an inn's culinary charms that await check-in guests. "There's nothing more comforting to newcomers of the inn than having tea out on our wooden cart for arriving guests," notes Nancy Helsper of Heritage Park Bed-and-Breakfast in San Diego, California. In fact, like Heritage Park, many inns keep hot water out for tea all day long.

Some inns really do it up for afternoon tea, not only with houseguests; they have tearooms that are open to the general public, just as England has its independent tea shops. Freshly baked hot scones are usually available, with mountains of clotted cream and sweet preserves; small finger sandwiches and other savories; and a host of mouth-watering sweet cakes. It remains my belief that tea is served at small inns more than anywhere else in this country, and that these inns play a major role in the proliferation of afternoon tea time. Tea's lingering effects go home with us where we want to repeat the feeling over and over again.

Tea is so popular at The Governor's Inn in Ludlow, Vermont, that it has become the inn's trademark. The inn has glossy, blank note cards of its spectacular teacup collection, which it uses for letter writing, greetings, invitations, and promotions. Guests have formed favorite alliances with certain cups that they insist on drinking from upon return visits to the inn.

Tea is a beverage that most people universally like. Whereas coffee is always popular, not everyone enjoys coffee. Rarely do you hear someone say no to a cup of tea, and that is because tea has a romantic, soothing connotation, somewhat akin to grabbing a security blanket.

Innkeepers are the equivalent of the ancient Asian tea masters. They set the scene and coax the environment for friendly exchanges to take place among strangers as well as friends. At home a tea party is the perfect event for making entertaining easy on you and for making guests feel relaxed.

Tea can take you on a magical journey to places you have never been before because the satisfying leaves tempt you to cosset your inner feelings and make you happy inside. Your mind opens up, and you have time to listen and chat with someone, gaining insight from what they have to say. To me, tea is a ceremony, no matter where or how you take it, because it always affords the opportunity to think about what is essential in your life and it never fails to invite beauty and simplicity—if even for a moment—into your heart and mind.

When you take a teacup in hand, you are easily cajoled into moving and thinking gracefully. You cannot help but repose. Any moment with tea in hand is a reason for celebrating the joys of life.

Tea is a gift that you can lavish on yourself. After going to an inn and being reminded of how wonderful tea every day can be, you are likely to want to get involved in taking tea. Start a teapot collection and

> *"You gotta find reason to laugh, or you're not getting your money's worth for the price of admission to this life."*
> —Langdon House

have them all over the house—bedrooms, kitchen, family room, even in the office. Their bright colors and different shapes will never fail to bring a smile to your face.

I set aside a cloth-lined basket with all my different tea flavors. Tea offers us a chance to shift moods or to choose a flavor based on how we are feeling. I have loose and bagged tea. Truly, the loose tea is the most delicious and worth the effort, but I never want to miss out on a cup when I am very busy, so tea bags are always plentiful in my pantry. Besides, if you like loose tea but don't want to fuss, there is a new appliance out that I highly recommend. The makers of Mr. Coffee™ have developed Mrs. Tea.™ Just like the coffee maker, you use filters that hold the tea leaves. The tea is brewed automatically and easily, and you only have the one pot to fuss with—no teakettle. It's all done in one ceramic, Brown-Betty style pot that also accommodates tea bags, so there's really no excuse anymore for not using loose tea.

I think if I have any advice for serving tea it would be that when you do serve a tea party, you really commit to the affair. Create a conducive milieu; go all out. One of my favorite afternoon teas is at The Gingerbread Mansion in Ferndale, California. An antique Victorian sideboard is set with lace and dainty teacups and lovely silverware. Two teapots coddle two different-flavored teas—raspberry is a favorite at this inn. On a small table beside the sideboard are tiers of sweets and savories, all bite-sized foods and decadent chocolates, handmade at the inn. The sun streams through lace curtains, and, I assure you, it is something out of a movie in which you feel you are the star.

Whether you are at an inn or at home or at a friend's place, tea requires your attention. It is not a beverage that you sip unmindfully. When you take tea, you are on your way to serenity, living the country inn life and your own life more meaningfully than ever.

A POT FULL OF MEMORIES

Fill your teakettle with cold water and bring it to a boil. Meanwhile, fill a thermal pot with hot tap water. When the water is just about to boil, pour out the tap water from your thermal pot and put in loose tea. (Don't use tea bags. The paper bags cut some of the characteristic edge from the tea by filtering out some of the tannin.)

Bring the warmed pot with the loose tea to the stove, and pour the boiling water over the leaves. Don't let the water boil long, for oxygen is lost from the water as it boils, and this affects the tea's flavor.

Cap the thermal pot and let it sit for five minutes. Meanwhile, heat your china teapot by filling it with hot tap water. (The best pot is called a Brown Betty, and the glaze looks like that on a bean pot. Iron is baked into the clay or the glaze, and this helps retain heat.) Pour the water out of the teapot; then strain the tea from the thermal pot, through a small mesh metal strainer, into the teapot.

—*Britt House*

❧Aubrey Franklin, a nationally pro-claimed tea ambassador, told us how to make the perfect cup:

The boiling and brewing are the impor-tant factors in the perfect cup. With so many world-famous blends available today, here is the correct tea drill:

1. Rinse the kettle of its contents and start with fresh, cold tap water.

2. The trick is to bring the water to its first rolling boil. Never overboil. Overboiling takes the oxygen out of the water, which in turn creates a flat beverage. Turn the heat down.

3. Take the teapot to the kettle, and rinse out the pot with the hot water from the ket-tle. Never take the kettle to the teapot, as you lose one degree of heat per second, and hot

water for tea must be 212 degrees.

4. Use one tea bag or teaspoon of loose tea per cup. Leaves enter the warm pot, and the infusion starts as the leaves start to open up.

5. Pour hot water gently over the leaves. (Never bruise the leaves.)

6. Allow the tea to brew for a minimum of three to five minutes, according to the blend of tea and how you like your tea.

—*Hannah Marie Country Inn*

❧Place six regular tea bags in the filter basket of your coffee brewer, tags and all, and water for 12 cups in the water well. Start the automatic drip. This makes wonderful tea.

—*The Decoy*

❧One way to flavor tea is to put a drop or two of extract into it. This, however, is not the tea purist's method of doing things. Personally, I feel there are so many good blends of flavored teas out there to enjoy that you can get flavor from the tea itself.

You can actually have a blend of tea made up to offer the best complement to your tap water. Send a sample of your water to Fortnum & Mason Ltd. in Piccadilly, England. They will put together a blend that goes with the makeup of your water. Your library will have information about the company and how to send the water sample. —*Marlborough Inn*

Make certain that none of the herbs and flowers you plan to use in making tea have been sprayed with insecticides. Collect red clover blossoms. Wash them thoroughly and place them in a pot with water. Add ripped mint leaves (ripping allows the release of mint flavor), and bring the water to a boil. Add other packaged tea blends (such as black teas) and let the tea steep for twenty minutes. Strain and serve. Add lemon or orange zest, cinnamon stick or cloves. This also makes an excellent iced tea.—*Rabbit Hill Inn*

Milk, not cream, is what is added to tea. Cream is too heavy, and many tea drinkers wouldn't put either one in their cup. —*Marlborough Inn*

Once tea is refrigerated it usually becomes cloudy. Remove the haze by running it through the microwave until clear. Add ice.—*Clayton Country Inn*

We make iced tea by the gallon, using loose tea covered with boiling water. Straining the tea leaves is quick and easy when you use a drip filter attachment and filter—the ones made for coffee makers. —*Glacier Bay Country Inn*

PORTRAITS OF INN-SPIRATION

One morning, a couple celebrating their thirtieth wedding anniversary were enjoying breakfast in front of the fireplace in our tearoom. The mantel once belonged to a Methodist minister in Chicago. The surprised couple thought the mantel looked familiar. Thirty years ago they were married in front of the very same fireplace, halfway across the country, in Chicago Heights, Illinois.

Seal Beach Inn

Gail's Touch: The general rule of measuring loose tea is to add one tablespoon per cup. I don't know why, but the old saying "And add one for the pot" no longer holds true.

❧In summer we serve iced tea in our kitchen from an antique ceramic crock. They seem to go together in an old-fashioned way.—*Captain Lord Mansion*

❧To add delicious flavors to cold tea, add flavored gelatins to regular iced tea. Pour in slowly to desired taste.—*Summerport B&B*

BESTOWING THE BEVERAGE

❧Hosting a tea is a very social occasion where you can introduce a number of guests in your home in a nonthreatening manner. Tea is a cultural way of having a cocktail party. People have something to do with their hands, sipping from teacups and munching on finger sandwiches and assorted sweets. A tea offers your guests an uplifting time due to the caffeine and sugar served.

At Britt House we offer a strong English tea from 4:00 to 6:00 p.m. Bed-and-breakfast started in Great Britain, and tea was important to the people there. This is one of the reasons we decided to incorporate the tradition at the inn.

Our setup for tea includes a large, oak, mission-style table dressed with a lace cloth or a crisply ironed linen cloth, topped by a big bouquet of fresh flowers. To add interest to the table, we vary the size and shapes of the foods. For example, we might have a bundt cake with fluffy icing for texture, served on a pedestal for height. To vary the flavors, we serve something not so sweet, such as Irish soda bread and scones. There is usually a fresh pie mixed among all of this, and the sandwiches sometimes include cucumber and egg salad, plus eggplant dip for the health-conscious.

Carmel and Basil Luck, our English friends, taught us how to make the tea we use at Britt House. We use a strong Irish black tea (Ceylon and Golden Assam). The English drink their tea stronger than we do, so we modified the amounts they gave us, but our tea does have a "presence."—*Britt House*

❧Use only china teapots when serving tea. The thicker the pottery, the less heat you get in the cup.—*Gingerbread House*

For more information on inns listed in this book, see the directory beginning on page 203.

We have a teapot collection and enjoy serving tea in the pots with a tea cozy over them to keep them hot.—*Glacier Bay Country Inn*

Gail's Touch: Tea cozies can be appropriate, but be careful when making fresh tea that you don't leave the leaves in the pot too long with a cozy on top. The tea can become bitter.

An interesting assortment of teas fills a large basket on the dining-room table. Our guests root through the basket in search of a tea they've never tried before.
—*Annie Horan's*

We often serve individual bouquets of herbs with our herb teas in the afternoon. The herb teas allow guests to experiment with flavors. Sometimes we send guests home with small packages of herbs.—*Bungay Jar*

Our tea is served informally in the main-floor parlor. It includes finger foods, shortbread confections, cookies, fork foods, cakes, pies, and tarts. The service is arranged on a teacart, using silver compotes for visual appeal. In summer we serve iced tea. Lemon-mint leaves from the garden are garnish.
—*Red Castle Inn*

During wintertime we serve tea in the common area. In addition to beverages, we provide foot warmers. They are antique, British porcelain warmers that are filled with hot water. We bring them out on a tray, and each guest takes one if they desire. They remove their shoes and place their feet on top of the warmer. It's an old tradition we enjoy rekindling here.—*Jefferson Inn*

Tea in the winter includes the provision of hot soup. The soup is heated in a cast-iron pot on top of a wood-burning stove and is served right from the pot. Bowls, spoons, and ladles are kept on a table. The hot soup is very popular with skiers who need something to hold them until dinner.
—*Mill Brook B&B*

For a pretty tea plate, dig up a violet from the yard and put it in a little crock on the plate with the tea treats. The plants survive nicely in the house for several days and can then be replanted in the garden.
—*Sage Cottage*

Teapots are in every guest room. Four o'clock tea is available, complete with a tea cozy. Delicate teacups are a must. They seem to make the tea tastier. A tea set in your guest room makes a friend or relative feel immediately welcome and warm.—*Ujjala's B&B*

☙Afternoon tea at The Gingerbread Mansion is served in one of the four parlors between 4:00 and 6:00 P.M. Items are attractively displayed on three glass-covered trays and placed on an elegantly carved sideboard. The trays protect the sideboard from hot beverages, any spilled cream, and/or sticky cake.

One tray holds the old-fashioned electric coffeepot and the pot of tea. Each sits on a wicker trivet. Included on a second tray is a small bowl for spoons that have been used.

Cups and saucers are all different, so guests may choose one that suits their whim.—*Gingerbread Mansion*

ENCHANTING TEAS

Gail's Touch: If you're looking for an interesting way to shower a bride, a tea is a perfect type of party and a nice way to introduce a young bride to the tradition of taking tea.

And why not a tea tasting, the same way people hold wine tastings? Ask each of your guests to bring two varieties of loose or bagged tea and a teapot. Serve tea in demitasse cups and spoons so that your guests taste only a small amount at one time. Provide each guest with paper and pen so they can make personal comments about each tea they taste. Later they will know which ones they want to go out and buy for their own supply. Be sure to have a large bowl on the table so that guests can pour any remaining tea from their cup as they go on to the next flavor. Also have each guest bring a tea tip such as this one: To rid your kettle of those ugly white deposits of calcium or lime, pour in about one-quarter cup of vinegar and one quart of water. Bring to a boil and allow to boil for ten minutes. Empty the pot. Wash and rinse thoroughly.

☙We have a tea for my daughter and her friends. We set a child-sized table and chairs with a fine linen cloth. A cocoa set and teapots that have been in our family are placed on the table along with demitasse spoons. Sandwiches are served, but the children cut their own with a cookie cutter of their choice. They reach into an old tin for the 1-inch-high tin cutters in many various shapes. Something sweet is also served. Sometimes they have tea, but most often, apple juice is poured out of the teakettle. Usually they select something to read from a stack of old books, and they also choose which stuffed friends will take tea with them. Our nursery tea usually includes children four to ten years old.—*Main Street B&B*

❧Have a picnic tea. Hot water carries well in a thermos. Pack your china teacups, napkins, silverware, tea, sweets, and sandwiches. What a romantic way to spend a quiet afternoon.

For another special tea bring out all your old family pictures and set them on the tea table. It sets the mood for relaxing and opens the way to the past for your tea guests.

Children can also enjoy a tea. Since they love to dress up, have them arrive in their parents' old clothes or provide them upon arrival with vintage hats, gloves, jewelry, and scarves.

A Mad Hatter Tea is fun for the young at heart of any age. We put out dolls from the story along with the book itself. Tea foods become quite special. Among our treats are whimsical butter shapes we make from molds such as one that represents the Cheshire Cat. We also make meringue mushrooms (see page 141). Remember to tell your guests to guard their thoughts when eating them, or they may grow larger or smaller. For this tea

If you don't ask, the answer is no. If you do ask, you have a fifty/fifty chance it will be yes.

—Crystal Rose Inn

you can also serve a cake cut into 1 1/2-by-2 1/2-inch pieces; pipe onto the top of each piece the words "Eat Me," as per the story.

Serve cherry or strawberry tarts. Add a few birthday candles and wish everyone an "unbirthday." Remind your guests that they have 364 unbirthdays.

When planning a Mad Hatter Tea, let your imagination run wild. Reread the wonderful story to get your own ideas.—*Hannah Marie Country Inn*

❧My favorite tea is served to a Brownie troop and their moms. This high tea would make an occasion full of fun as well as providing a learning experience for any grouping of youngsters.

Containers of coffee as well as regular, decaffeinated, and flavored teas are placed where everyone can help themselves. As they are seated on the lawn under a cooling tree or around a warm fire in winter, several small sandwiches and sweets are served. The ingredients are named and described to all.

As seems appropriate, we tell them about the origins of the tea custom, events like the Boston Tea Party, and then discuss where other high teas are held today in their area.

We then take a tour of Spring Bank. Each girl signs the guest book and takes home lavender soap as a souvenir from the inn.—*Spring Bank Inn*

❧Chocolate pastry teas were popular during the Victorian era. To encourage the theme here, look through chocolate cookbooks and chocolate magazines for recipes. Try to introduce the flavor of chocolate in recipes where your guests wouldn't ordinarily expect it. Try adding chocolate to butter, for example.

Early Wednesday evenings, we serve high tea, the supper tea of the northern countrysides of England and Scotland. This most substantial of the tea meals has food that is both satisfying and alluring: savory pasties (filled with beef, potatoes, carrots, and onions), Scotch eggs, cakes, and an apple-and-cheese flan that is a hallmark British dessert. This is not a dainty affair. It's a cheerful, noisy gathering of guests after a day's work.

A nice idea for a shower gift, anniversary, birthday, or you name it, is a tea basket. Into a basket tuck recipes for muffins or scones, a mix of tea biscuits, a few blends of tea, a tea

"Wherever there is a human being, there is an opportunity for kindness." (Benjamin DeJong)
—Victorian Rose Garden

strainer, perhaps a cup and saucer, and it's ready for a favorite friend. Actually you can fill the basket with anything you wish, according to your budget.—*Hannah Marie Country Inn*

❧Have a picnic tea for someone special. I went with a young friend for one of her chemotherapy treatments and decided that a picnic with tea would cheer her up. Into a picnic basket I took along some mint tea to make her feel better; sweets and savories, including sliced pear and cheese; a hot-water thermos and a ceramic teapot; cups and saucers; linen napkins; a breakfast tray with a pretty fabric covering; and even a CD player. I spread the picnic out in the treatment office, and my friend was able to smile for three hours during the treatment. A very uncomfortable time was made bearable. I did the same for my mother-in-law who is in a nursing home.

A friend of mine keeps a three-legged table, two folding chairs, and a basket of tableware in the trunk of her car. She takes tea parties with friends to scenic sites. —*Garratt Mansion*

Gail's Touch: Some other ideas are:

Oriental tea with a variety of teas and dim sum.

Hold a poetry reading during a tea.

A garden tea is nice in warm weather.

Hold a mother-daughter tea with friends and neighbors.

Sometimes, the theme is there without trying to create it. For example, at Sweetwater Farm in Glen Mills, Pennsylvania, tea is appropriately served from the farmhouse kitchen with all home-baked goods served on country ware such as yellow ware and antique blue-and-white dishes native to the inn's area.

TIMELESS BREWS

❧ FIRE-AND-ICE VICTORIAN TEA

1 cup water
2 tablespoons sugar
3 whole cloves
1 cinnamon stick
2 orange Pekoe tea bags
2 cups apricot nectar
2 tablespoons frozen orange juice concentrate
Club soda
Light rum
Orange-flavored liqueur, such as Grand Marnier

Orange slices and ripe strawberries

Combine water, sugar, cloves, cinnamon, and tea bags in a saucepan. Simmer for 5 minutes; then allow to stand for 15 minutes. Strain into a glass container. Add apricot nectar and orange juice concentrate. Stir. Allow to cool and then refrigerate. When ready to serve, pour over ice in a brandy snifter and add club soda to each glass. Add 1 ounce light rum and a splash of Grand Marnier to each. Garnish with a fresh orange slice and a plump, ripe strawberry, stem and all. Also wonderful without the rum and Grand Marnier. Yield: about 1 quart, or 8 servings.
—*The Governor's Inn*

❧ GREEN ICED TEA

A handful of bee balm and sweet cicely steeped in 6 cups of boiling water for 8 minutes makes a beautiful green blend for iced tea. The taste is a combination of mint and licorice. A bee-balm leaf in each glass, with a violet or even a dandelion blossom, makes a drink fit for the fanciest spring tea. Yield: 6 servings.—*Sage Cottage*

❧ ROSEMARY TEA

When winter comes, my favorite is rosemary tea. Since rosemary has to spend the winter indoors in our climate, we just pick a sprig or two and add about 2 cups boiling water, cover, steep for 5 minutes, and then sit back and enjoy the fragrance of a sunny summer's day. Yield: 2 cups.—*Sage Cottage*

❧ CHURCHTOWN'S MINT TEA

About 5–6 shoots each of peppermint and spearmint, fresh from the garden, are placed in a tall metal pot (such as one for cooking spaghetti). Add boiling water to cover. Let steep for a couple of hours. Makes a delightful aroma throughout the house. Yield: 24 servings.

❧ SUN TEA

Fill a gallon jar with water. Add 8 regular-flavored tea bags and 2 of a flavored tea such as black currant. Let sit in the sun for 3–4 hours. The black currant gives the tea a great flavor. Yield: about 24 servings.
—*Little River Inn*

❧ FRESHLY SQUEEZED LEMONADE

This is a refreshing drink to serve during teatime on hot days.

2 cups sugar
1 cup water
Rind of 1 lemon
1/8 teaspoon of salt
8–10 lemons

1 gallon water
Lemon slices

On stove top mix sugar, 1 cup water, lemon rind, and salt. Heat to dissolve sugar. Do not boil. This is your syrup. Let it cool to room temperature.

Squeeze lemons to give you 2 cups of lemon juice. Mix your syrup, lemon juice, and 1 gallon of water. Remove lemon rind. Chill and garnish with lemon slices. Yield: about 24 servings.—*Little River Inn*

❧ CHOCOLATE LEMONADE

Use a 12-ounce can of frozen lemonade concentrate. Mix with water according to directions, and add about 1/4 cup of chocolate syrup or chocolate to taste. Our guests love this beverage. Yield: about 1/2 gallon.
—*Hannah Marie Country Inn*

❧ VIENNESE MOCHA

Just in case a tea guest prefers coffee.

1/4 cup half-and-half
3/4 cup milk
2 tablespoons sugar
2 teaspoons Dutch-process cocoa
3/4 cup freshly brewed strong coffee
1/4 cup whipped cream
Cinnamon

In small saucepan over medium heat, stir

together half-and-half, milk, sugar, and cocoa until blended. Bring mixture to a boil; then add coffee. Pour mocha into mugs or cups and top with whipped cream and sprinkled cinnamon. Yield: 2 servings.—*Grant Corner Inn*

SCONES, TEA CAKES, AND BREADS

❧ TEA SCONES

The word *scone* is actually from the Dutch *schoonbrot*, meaning beautiful bread.

2 cups sifted flour
2 tablespoons sugar
3 teaspoons baking powder
1/2 teaspoon salt
1/3 cup butter
1 egg, beaten
3/4 cup milk (approximately)

Preheat oven to 425 degrees. Sift together flour, sugar, baking powder, and salt. Cut in the butter with a pastry blender until the flour-coated particles of butter are the size of coarse cornmeal. Add the egg and most of the milk, reserving some milk. Stir quickly and lightly, only until no flour shows. Add more milk if needed to make a soft dough.

Turn the dough out on a floured surface and knead gently, about 15 times. Cut the dough in half. Shape each half into a ball, press each half down into a round about 1/2-inch thick, and cut it into 8 wedges like a pie. Place the wedges on a greased cookie sheet, without allowing the sides to touch. Glaze, if desired, with lightly beaten egg. Bake until deep-golden brown, about 12 minutes. (Uncooked scones may be frozen on the cookie sheet and dropped in a plastic bag for baking later.) Serve hot with whipped cream or butter, marmalade, and a good blend of tea. Yield: 8 servings.
—*Mayhurst B&B*

❧ CLOTTED CREAM

Add 1 1/2 tablespoons of buttermilk to 1 cup of heavy cream. Let it sit out, covered, for 12 hours. Then store in the refrigerator.
—*The Decoy*

❧ PINEAPPLE SPICE SCONES

This scone recipe is used for teatime for Brownie troops at Spring Bank Inn. It is a particularly appealing scone for all ages, but the addition of the pineapple makes it most appropriate for introducing young people to the traditional teatime treat.

3 cups flour
1/3 cup sugar
2 1/2 teaspoons baking powder

1/2 teaspoon salt

3/4 cup margarine or butter

1 8-ounce can crushed pineapple (juice pack)

Light cream or milk

3 tablespoons chopped macadamia nuts or almonds

1 tablespoon sugar

1/2 teaspoon cinnamon

Preheat oven to 425 degrees. In a mixing bowl stir together flour, sugar, baking powder, and salt. Cut in margarine until mixture resembles coarse crumbs. Make a well in center. Stir in undrained pineapple until dry ingredients are just moistened (dough will be sticky). On lightly floured surface knead gently 10 to 12 times; roll dough to 1/4-inch thickness. Cut with floured 2 1/2-inch biscuit cutter. Place dough circles on ungreased baking sheet. Brush tops with cream or milk. For topping combine nuts, 1 tablespoon sugar, and cinnamon. Sprinkle about 1 teaspoon of mixture over the top of each scone. Bake about 15 minutes. Serve warm. Yield: 20.
—*Spring Bank Inn*

Clotted cream is traditionally served with scones in England, and at our inn, we also serve the real thing. Our guests always want to know what clotted cream is. The cream we use is imported. It is produced by the Jersey cow, which, in England, eats lush green grass. When the cow produces its milk, cream rises and clots at the top. Unlike whipped cream, clotted cream is slightly sour rather than sugary.—*Gingerbread House*

Coconut Tea Cakes

3 1/2 cups flour

2 cups sugar

1 1/2 tablespoons baking powder

3 cups sweetened flaked or shredded coconut

3 sticks butter, melted

2 cups milk, room temperature

2 tablespoons cream of coconut

5 eggs, room temperature

1 cup egg whites (about 5)

Preheat oven to 375 degrees. Into medium bowl sift flour, sugar, and baking powder. Mix in coconut and set aside. In another bowl whisk together butter, milk, cream of coconut, and whole eggs. Set aside. In a small bowl beat egg whites until stiff but not dry. Pour butter mixture into flour mixture. Stir well to blend. Fold in beaten egg whites. Fill paper-lined muffin cups two-thirds full. Bake for 15–20 minutes, or until golden brown. Yield: 24 muffins.—*Grant Corner Inn*

FOR MORE INFORMATION ON INNS LISTED IN THIS BOOK, SEE THE DIRECTORY BEGINNING ON PAGE 203.

FRENCH TEA CAKES

2 eggs
1 cup sugar
1 cup sifted cake flour
3/4 cup melted and cooled butter
1 tablespoon rum
1 teaspoon vanilla extract
1 teaspoon lemon rind

Preheat oven to 450 degrees. Heat the eggs and sugar in a double boiler until lukewarm, stirring constantly. Remove from heat and beat until thick but light and creamy. When cool, gradually add the flour. Add the melted and cooled butter, rum, vanilla, and lemon rind. Pour into greased madeleine pans or small muffin tins. Bake for 15 minutes. Yield: 16 cakes.—*The Summer Cottage*

STRAWBERRY TEA CAKES

1 3/4 cups flour
1 teaspoon baking soda
1/4 teaspoon salt
1 cup sugar
1/2 cup unsweetened flaked or shredded
    coconut
2 eggs
1/2 cup oil
1 1/2 cups strawberries, hulled and halved
    lengthwise

Preheat oven to 350 degrees. Stir together flour, soda, salt, and sugar. Stir in coconut. In separate bowl combine eggs and oil. Add berries and stir gently. Gently add flour mixture to berry mixture and stir to blend. Pour into greased muffin cups, filling each cup half full. Bake for 20–30 minutes. You may top with whipped cream. Yield: 18 cakes.
—*Britt House*

LEMON CASHEW BREAD

1 1/2 cups flour
3/4 cup sugar
2 tablespoons grated lemon rind
1 teaspoon baking powder
1/2 teaspoon salt
1/2 cup unsalted cashews, toasted and
    chopped
1/4 cup milk
1/4 cup fresh lemon juice
6 tablespoons vegetable oil
2 eggs
GLAZE:
1/2 cup sugar
2 tablespoons lemon juice

Preheat oven to 350 degrees. Grease an 8 1/2-by-4-inch loaf pan. In medium-sized mixing bowl combine ingredients in order given (except glaze ingredients). Pour into prepared pan and bake for 1 hour. Cool 15 minutes. Remove from pan. Poke holes in top

of loaf with a toothpick. Mix sugar and lemon juice. Brush over top and sides of loaf, with special attention to the top. Let stand until glaze hardens before slicing. Yield: 1 loaf.
—*Grant Corner Inn*

❧ LEMON YOGURT BREAD

3 cups flour
1 teaspoon salt
1 teaspoon baking soda
1/2 teaspoon baking powder
1 cup sesame or poppy seeds
3 eggs
1 cup oil
1 cup sugar
2 cups lemon yogurt
2 tablespoons fresh-squeezed lemon juice

Preheat oven to 325 degrees. Sift together flour, salt, baking soda, and baking powder. Stir in seeds. In a large bowl beat eggs. Add oil and sugar. Cream well. Mix in yogurt and lemon juice until combined. Spoon into 2 greased loaf pans or 1 large bundt pan. Bake for 1 hour.—*Wedgwood Inn*

❧ TROPICAL TEA BREAD

2/3 cup butter
1 1/3 cups honey
4 eggs
4 tablespoons milk
1 teaspoon vanilla extract
2 tablespoons vegetable oil
4 cups sifted flour
1 teaspoon salt
1 3/4 teaspoons baking powder
1 teaspoon baking soda
2 cups toasted coconut
2 1/4 cups mashed bananas
4 teaspoons grated lemon rind
2 teaspoons fresh lemon juice

Preheat oven to 350 degrees. Grease and flour two 9-by-5-inch loaf pans. Cream butter until fluffy; add honey in thin stream. Beat in eggs; stir in milk, vanilla, and oil. Sift dry ingredients into a medium-sized bowl. Stir in toasted coconut and set aside. In small bowl blend bananas, lemon rind, and lemon juice. Add dry ingredients to creamed mixture alternately with banana mixture, blending only until moistened. Spoon into pans. Bake for 55 minutes. Cool in pans 5 minutes. Remove and cool thoroughly before slicing. Yield: 2 loaves.—*Grant Corner Inn*

❧ PUMPKIN-RAISIN BUNDT BREAD

3 eggs
1 1/2 cups sugar
1 1/2 cups pumpkin puree
1 cup plus 2 tablespoons vegetable oil
2 teaspoons vanilla extract

2 1/4 cups flour
1 1/2 teaspoons baking soda
1 1/2 teaspoons baking powder
1 1/2 teaspoons salt
2 teaspoons pumpkin pie spice
1/2 cup coarsely chopped pecans
1 cup raisins

Preheat oven to 350 degrees. In medium-sized mixing bowl beat eggs and sugar until well blended. Add pumpkin, oil, and vanilla, mixing well. Set aside. Sift flour, soda, baking powder, salt, and pie spice. Add to pumpkin mixture and beat. Add pecans and raisins, stirring to blend. Pour into nonstick bundt pan. Bake for 1 hour, until a toothpick inserted at center comes out clean. Yield: 12 servings. —*Grant Corner Inn*

❧ WHOLE-WHEAT WILD MAINE BLUEBERRY BREAD

3/4 cup butter
1 1/2 cups sugar
3 eggs
1 1/2 teaspoons vanilla extract
2 cups unbleached white flour
1 cup whole wheat flour
1 1/2 teaspoons baking soda
1 1/2 teaspoons baking powder
1/4 teaspoon salt
1 1/2 cups sour cream

1 15-ounce can wild Maine blueberries, drained

Preheat oven to 350 degrees. Grease two 8 1/2-by-4 1/2-by-2 3/4-inch pans. Combine butter, sugar, eggs, and vanilla. Beat at medium speed for 2 minutes. Combine the flours, baking soda, baking powder, and salt. Add the flour mixture to the butter and sugar mixture, alternately with the sour cream. Stir in the blueberries. Bake 55–60 minutes or until tester comes out clean. Cool before taking out of the pan. Yield: 2 loaves.—*Silver Maple Lodge*

❧ STRAWBERRY BREAD

3 cups flour
2 cups sugar
1 teaspoon baking soda
1 teaspoon salt
1 teaspoon cinnamon
4 eggs, beaten
1 1/4 cups vegetable oil
2 10-ounce packages frozen strawberries, thawed and chopped

Preheat oven to 350 degrees. In a large mixing bowl combine flour, sugar, baking soda, salt, and cinnamon. Make a well in the center of the mixture. Combine remaining ingredients and add to dry ingredients, stirring until well mixed. Spoon mixture into 2 greased and floured 9-by-5-by-3-inch loaf pans. Bake for 1 hour. Cool 10 minutes and then remove from pan.—*Brass Bed B&B*

PIES, CAKES, AND SWEETS

❧ SOUR CREAM (OR YOGURT) RAISIN PIE

Pastry dough for a 9-inch pie:

2 eggs

1 cup sugar

1 cup lemon yogurt plus 1 tablespoon lemon juice

1 cup raisins

Pinch salt

1/4 teaspoon nutmeg

Beat eggs. Add sugar and beat until light. Fold yogurt and lemon juice into the egg mixture. Add the raisins, salt, and nutmeg, and mix thoroughly. Line a pie pan with pastry dough and pour in mixture. Cover with a top crust and bake in 350-degree oven for 30 minutes. Yield: 8–10 servings.—*Britt House*

❧ GRAND MARNIER TRIFLE

A trifle is really the British way of using bits and pieces of desserts and ending up with a most impressive teatime delicacy.

1 pound leftover cake (orange, banana, white pound, walnut, yellow, but not chocolate)

Custard

Raspberry jam

Bananas, strawberries, pears, and/or peaches

Sherry or orange-flavored liqueur such as Grand Marnier

Mint leaves

Cut cake into slabs 1-inch thick. Place in loaf pan. Top with a layer of custard, a layer of jam, a layer of fruit, a layer of whipped cream, and a drizzle of liqueur. Then start the process over until the pan is full, ending with whipped cream. Chill thoroughly. Garnish with fruit and mint leaves. Yield: about 8 servings.—*Britt House*

❧ RAISIN HARVEST COFFEE CAKE

1 1/2 cups sifted flour

3 3/4 teaspoons baking powder

1/4 teaspoon salt

3/4 cup sugar

3/4 cup butter

2 cups peeled and finely chopped cooking apples

1 1/2 cups dark seedless raisins

2 large eggs, well-beaten

1 tablespoon milk

Sugar for topping

Preheat oven to 350 degrees. Into a large bowl resift flour with baking powder, salt,

and sugar. Add butter and mix until mixture resembles fine bread crumbs. Stir in apples, raisins, eggs, and milk. Batter will be stiff. Spread in well-greased 9-inch square pan and sprinkle generously with sugar. Bake for 55–60 minutes. Allow to cool slightly before cutting. Serve warm. This may be made ahead and frozen. Yield: 4–6 servings.
—*Red Willow Farm*

❧ANISE CAKES
2 tablespoons brown sugar
3/4 cup flour
1/4 teaspoon baking powder
1/4 cup margarine
1 large egg
1/2 teaspoon crushed anise seeds
1 cup rolled oats

Preheat oven to 375 degrees. Combine sugar, flour, baking powder, and margarine in a bowl. Mix together until well combined and light. Add the egg and anise seeds and beat lightly. Stir in oats. Drop by tiny spoonfuls onto a lightly greased cookie sheet. Bake 8 minutes or until lightly browned. Yield: 3 dozen.—*Sage Cottage*

❧SQUIRE TARBOX INN POUND CAKE
1 cup (1/2 pound) soft cream cheese
1 1/2 cups (3 sticks) softened butter
2 cups sugar
1/8 teaspoon salt
1 1/2 teaspoons lemon or vanilla extract
6 eggs, room temperature
3 cups unsifted flour

Preheat oven to 325 degrees. Blend cheese and butter in an electric mixer. With the speed on high, beat in the sugar, salt, and extract until light. Add eggs one at a time and beat until the batter is very light and fluffy. With the mixer on low speed, add flour and blend only until mixed. Turn into a buttered and floured 10-inch tube pan and bake 1 hour and 15 minutes. Cool for 5 minutes. Invert on a rack to cool thoroughly. Yield: 16 servings.

❧CRANBERRY CHEESECAKE BARS

This is a family recipe that we serve at teatime. It is especially festive during the Christmas season.

CRUST:
2 1/2 cups flour
1 cup butter, softened
2/3 cup sugar
2 eggs, beaten
1/2 cup chopped pecans

Preheat oven to 350 degrees. In a large bowl combine all ingredients except nuts. Mix at low speed until crumbly. Add pecans.

Press into a 9-by-13-inch pan. Bake for 8–10 minutes.

TOPPING:

8 ounces cream cheese, softened

1/4 cup powdered sugar

1 teaspoon vanilla extract

1 egg

1 16-ounce can whole-berry cranberry
    sauce

1/4 teaspoon nutmeg

Combine cheese, powdered sugar, vanilla, and egg. Beat until smooth. Pour cream cheese mixture over baked crust. Add nutmeg to cranberry sauce. Blend well. Spoon cranberry sauce in 3 lengthwise rows over the cream cheese mixture. Pull a knife through the mixture to swirl. Bake in the 350-degree oven for 30–40 minutes or until set. Cool completely. Cut into bars. Yield: about 24 servings.—The *Summer Cottage*

SPICED JAM BARS

1/2 cup sugar

1/2 cup margarine, softened

1 teaspoon vanilla

1 egg

1 cup flour

1/2 cup chopped walnuts

1/2 cup quick-cooking oats

1/2 teaspoon baking powder

1/2 teaspoon cinnamon

1/4 teaspoon salt

1/4 teaspoon ground cloves

1/2 cup strawberry jam

Preheat oven to 350 degrees. Cream sugar, margarine, vanilla, and egg. Stir in remaining ingredients except jam until well mixed. Spread half the mixture into a greased 8-inch-square baking pan. Spread jam evenly over the top of the dough; then drop teaspoonfuls of remaining dough over the jam. Bake for 25–30 minutes, until lightly browned. Cool. Cut into bars. Yield: 2 dozen.—*The Summer Cottage*

SWISS APPLE FLAN

CRUST:

10 ounces finely chopped walnuts

2 sticks unsalted butter, softened

1/3 cup sugar

3 cups all-purpose flour

1 egg, beaten

1 teaspoon almond extract

Grease a 9-inch springform tart pan. Mix together all the ingredients until well-blended. Press into the tart pan. Chill 30 minutes in the refrigerator before adding the filling.

FILLING:

3 teaspoons white sugar

3 teaspoons brown sugar

1 egg
1/4 cup flour
1/4 cup whipping cream
2 tablespoons rum
3/4 cup shredded Swiss cheese
4 medium-tart apples, peeled and sliced
3/4 teaspoon cinnamon
1/3 cup brown sugar

Preheat oven to 400 degrees. Beat the 6 teaspoons of sugars and egg until thick. Add flour and mix. Add whipping cream and rum. Stir until mixed. Pour mixture into unbaked nut crust. Sprinkle the shredded Swiss cheese evenly over the egg-sugar mixture. Place the apple slices in a circular pattern on top of the Swiss cheese. With a flat hand press the apple slices gently down into the cheese and egg mixture. Sprinkle the cinnamon and 1/3 cup brown sugar on top. Bake for 40 minutes. Yield: about 8 servings.

—*Hannah Marie Country Inn*

❧ BLACKBERRY COBBLER

PASTRY:
2 cups sifted, unbleached flour
1/4 teaspoon salt
1/2 teaspoon baking soda
2 teaspoons baking powder
6 tablespoons butter
1/2 cup sugar
2/3 cup buttermilk
Cream

FILLING:
5 cups blackberries
3/4 cup sugar
2 teaspoons cornstarch
4 tablespoons butter, in small pieces

NUTMEG SAUCE:
2/3 cup sugar
1/4 teaspoon grated nutmeg
2 teaspoons cornstarch
Pinch of salt
1 cup boiling water
3 tablespoons orange juice or peach brandy

Make the pastry. Sift the flour, salt, soda, and baking powder into a mixing bowl. Cut butter into the flour mixture with two knives of pastry blender. Add sugar. Blend mixture until it is coarse. Sprinkle in the milk, and mix with a spatula or wooden spoon. Shape dough into a ball, and place it on a lightly floured surface. Knead for a minute or two, giving quick punches into the dough. Cut ball in half. Roll out one half to 1/2-to 1/4-inch thickness and lay it in an 8-by-8-by-2-inch baking pan. Cover with wax paper and let it cool in the refrigerator. Refrigerate the other half of dough, too.

When ready to make cobbler, remove dough from the refrigerator. Preheat oven to

450 degrees. Make filling: Sprinkle a small amount of the sugar over the pastry. Fill it with berries. Sprinkle remaining sugar, the cornstarch, and butter over the berries. Roll out second half of dough and place on top of berries. Make steam holes in top. Brush top with the cream and sprinkle a little sugar on top. Place the pan in the preheated oven. Once you shut the oven door, turn temperature to 425 degrees and bake 45 minutes. Remove from oven and let cool on rack a bit before serving. Serve with thick and creamy nutmeg sauce.

To make sauce: Place sugar, nutmeg, cornstarch, and salt in a 1-quart saucepan. Stir well. Pour in the boiling water, stirring as you pour. Set over medium heat to boil gently for 10 minutes. Set aside until ready to serve. Reheat without boiling, and add orange juice or brandy. Yield: about 8–10 servings.—*Sleepy Hollow Farm*

❧ Walnut Pie

3 well-beaten eggs
1 cup sugar
1 cup crushed graham crackers
1/2 cup chopped walnuts

Preheat oven to 350 degrees. Add dry ingredients to eggs and turn into a well-greased 8-inch or 9-inch glass pie plate. Bake

for 20–25 minutes. Serve at room temperature or cold, with or without whipped cream or ice cream. Yield: 8 servings.—*Red Castle Inn*

❧ English Lemon Curd

Use this as a filling for small pastry-tart shells for teatime or as a spread for muffins and sweet breads.

4 eggs, beaten
2 1/2 tablespoons lemon rind
8 tablespoons lemon juice
1 cup sugar
1 cup butter or margarine
1/8 teaspoon salt

Combine all ingredients in top of double boiler. Cook over boiling water until thickened, about 20 minutes. Place in clean jars. Seal and store in refrigerator. Yield: 1 1/2 pints.—*Balcony Downs*

❧ Cappuccino Cheesecake

CHOCOLATE CRUST:
1 cup flour
1 tablespoon sugar
3 tablespoons cocoa
1 egg yolk
3 tablespoons ice water
*3/4 stick unsalted butter, chilled and cut
      into 6 pieces*

Preheat oven to 400 degrees. Put all

ingredients in a work bowl of food processor. Process until the mass forms a ball of dough. Line a flan pan (removable ring) with the dough. Bake for 10 minutes. Set aside.

FILLING:

8 ounces cream cheese, softened
1 teaspoon cinnamon
1 cup sugar
3 eggs
1/4 cup sour cream
1/2 cup extra-strong espresso

Blend all the ingredients in food processor. Pour into crust. Bake in the 400-degree oven for 30–40 minutes. Yield: 8–10 servings.—*Bramble Inn*

❧ ALMOND SNOWBALLS

We like to serve these cookies during the Christmas season.

1 cup butter
1 cup powdered sugar, plus more for
  rolling cookies
1 tablespoon vanilla extract
1 tablespoon amaretto liqueur
2 cups all-purpose flour
1 cup finely chopped almonds (best done
  in food processor to coarse-powder
  consistency)

Cream together butter and 1 cup sugar. Add vanilla and liqueur. Beat until well blended. Gradually add flour, then almonds. Chill dough for 1 hour.

Preheat oven to 325 degrees. Break off pieces of dough with a melon-ball maker and place on a cookie sheet. Bake for 13–15 minutes. While still hot, roll in powdered sugar. (These cookies do not freeze well but will last several weeks in an airtight container.) Yield: about 3–4 dozen cookies.—*Alexander's Inn (New Jersey)*

SUMPTUOUS SAVORIES

❧ SQUIRE TARBOX NUT LOAF

6 tablespoons butter
3 cups chopped celery
3 cups chopped onions
1 cup cooked long-grain rice
1 cup ground almonds
2 cups chopped walnuts
2 cups toasted cashews
1/4 cup rolled oats
1/2 cup sesame seeds
1/4 cup sunflower seeds
2 pounds soft goat cheese (or cottage cheese)
2 teaspoons salt
2 teaspoons pepper
1 teaspoon blended herbs (basil, oregano)
6 beaten eggs

Preheat oven to 400 degrees. Melt butter

in a large skillet and sauté celery and onions until tender. Combine them in a large bowl with the rice, almonds, walnuts, cashews, rolled oats, sesame seeds, sunflower seeds, soft cheese, salt, pepper, and herbs. Blend in the beaten eggs and pour the batter into three 9-by-5-by-3-inch buttered loaf pans. Bake for 1 hour or until quite dark on top. Serve warm. Yield: 3 loaves.

❧ SPRING BISCUIT TREATS

1 cup flour
3 tablespoons margarine
1 1/2 teaspoons baking powder
1/4 teaspoon grated lemon peel or 1 table-
    spoon minced lemon balm
3 ounces skim milk
Violet blossoms
1 egg white, broken up with a fork

Preheat oven to 425 degrees. Combine flour, margarine, baking powder, and lemon peel or lemon balm in a small bowl. Cut margarine into flour with a pastry cutter or two knives until the shortening is the size of peas. Stir milk in lightly. Turn out onto lightly floured board or pastry cloth and pat gently into a 3-inch square. Fold in half and repeat twice more (for a light, flakier biscuit). Cut with small flower-shaped cutters. Place biscuits close together on baking sheet. Dip violet blossoms in egg white and place one on each biscuit. Bake for 10–12 minutes. Yield: 12 biscuits.—*Sage Cottage*

❧ SPRING BANK INN SANDWICH

We make this sandwich for Brownies at high tea: Mix together 1 cup peanut butter, 1 tablespoon each milk powder and marmalade, and 1/2 cup each raisins and mashed banana. Spread on toast quarters. Sprinkle with wheat germ.

❧ DEVILS ON HORSEBACK

What a curious name! Our supper tea (high tea) guests love them.

1/4 cup raisins soaked overnight in 1 tea-
    spoon dark rum and water just to cover
1/4 cup cream cheese
16 large prunes
1 cup dry red wine
8 bacon slices

Preheat oven to 375 degrees. Drain raisins and discard rum and water. Puree raisins and cream cheese in a small blender or mix with a fork, mashing the raisins. Simmer the prunes in wine about 10 minutes. Cool. Fill the prunes with the raisin and cream cheese mixture (1/2 to 1 teaspoonful, depending on the size of the prunes). Don't overstuff, as cream cheese mixture will run out the sides. Wrap half of a slice of bacon around each stuffed prune and secure with a toothpick. Stand on one of the open ends in a baking pan with sides. Bake until the bacon is brown and crisp, about 12 minutes. Drain on paper towels. Serve warm. Yield: 16 "little devils."—*Hannah Marie Country Inn*

❦ CUCUMBER SANDWICHES

Hothouse cucumbers, while more expensive, have fewer seeds and thus are more desirable.

> *Crustless bread, thinly sliced and cut into*
> *3-inch squares*
> *Cream cheese*
> *1 cucumber, peeled and thinly sliced into*
> *rounds*

Cut bread 1/8-inch thick, if possible. Spread with cream cheese. Top with a thin slice of cucumber.—*Britt House*

❦ BEEF PASTIES

Our pasties take many forms and are served during high tea. Use your favorite pie-pastry recipe for the crust. Cut circles of the pastry to the size you'd like your pasties to be. We cut ours in 6-inch circles, the size for fruit pies.

> *2 pounds beef round steak*
> *2 tablespoons oil*
> *1 large onion, chopped*
> *1 cup carrots, peeled and thinly sliced*
> *2 cups peeled, cooked, and diced potatoes*
> *(1/2-inch squares)*
> *3 cups beef broth*
> *1/2 teaspoon salt*
> *1/2 teaspoon pepper*
> *2 tablespoons cornstarch*
> *2/3 cup red wine*

Trim the fat from the steak and cut the meat into 1/2-inch pieces. Brown meat in oil in a large skillet. Remove meat and set aside. Add the onion, carrots, and potatoes to the pan, and cook until onions are limp. Add the meat broth, salt, and pepper. Bring to a boil, cover, and simmer for 1 hour until the meat is tender. Add the cornstarch mixed with the wine.

Preheat oven to 400 degrees. Place equal amounts of filling on each pastry round. Using a dampened finger quickly smooth the edges of the pastry, folding half the pastry over the filling. Use a fork to seal the edges and crimp the pastry. Make holes in the pastry with the fork to release steam. Bake about 30 minutes, or until lightly browned. Yield: 24 or more servings.—*Hannah Marie Country Inn*

❦ MERINGUE MUSHROOMS

We serve these at our Mad Hatter Tea, as in the mushroom episode from *Alice in*

Wonderland. We dress as King and Queen of Hearts and pass around the mushrooms, daring all to take a bite. They're easy to make and are a good way to use up your egg whites.

> *2 egg whites from large eggs*
> *1/2 cup sugar*
> *1/4 teaspoon vanilla*

Preheat oven to 200 degrees. Oil the surface of a cookie sheet or baking pan lightly with oil. Dust with flour.

Beat egg whites until stiff peaks are formed. Add 1/4 cup sugar and vanilla. Continue beating until the egg whites are glossy. Using a spatula, fold the remaining 1/4 cup sugar into the egg whites. Prepare a pastry bag, using a plain tip to form the mushrooms. Select the tip size according to how small or large you want to make the mushrooms. Pipe the meringue mixture in the shape of a mushroom onto prepared baking pan. Bake for 2 hours. When cool, put them on a doily-lined plate.

—*Hannah Marie Country Inn*

✿Cookie cutters make great designer shapes for sandwiches.

Nasturtium leaves make lovely tea sand-

Everybody should have his own bed . . . and breakfast every day. (Habitat for Humanity)
—The Chatelaine

wiches. Just add mayonnaise.—*Rabbit Hill Inn*

Gail's Touch: Make a checkerboard of sandwiches by using alternating squares of white and brown bread. Serve with a "game" in progress—top a few of the slices with halved cherry tomatoes as the checkers.

Trim the crust off breads for tea after filling the sandwich. It's easier that way.

Use only thin breads filled with thinly sliced or finely minced fillings.

Spread each sandwich with unsalted butter before filling. The butter acts as a protector, preventing the bread from soaking up moisture from the filling.

If filling with cucumber, use cucumber varieties that have fewer seeds. Peel and slice cucumbers. Place on a dish and lightly salt the slices. Place a weighted dish over the cucumbers and let sit for a while. This will help drain moisture from them.

To enhance your presentation, have three or four different types of sandwiches, but place each type on a different plate.

Have some of the sandwiches on each plate or platter facing upward so that the type of filling shows.

To keep sandwiches fresh, cover them with dried lettuce leaves and then a dampened cloth until you are ready to serve.

COFFEE PERKS

Scents of cinnamon drift through the house when the coffee brews at Ash Mill Farm. One-quarter of a teaspoon of the spice is added to a ten-quart pot of coffee. This gives the coffee a nice flavor and cuts down on the bitterness. All our guests think the coffee is a special blend. Add your own amount of cinnamon, according to taste. —*Ash Mill Farm*

Dried orange peel takes away bitterness in coffee.—*Boydville The Inn at Martinsburg*

When serving coffee in ceramic or silver serving pots, fill them first with very hot water. Warming the pot helps thermalize the coffee so that it stays hot.—*Chicago Pike Inn*

In Sandwich we're lucky enough to have a natural spring that gives us wonderfully clean drinking water. We use this water in coffee makers. Not only does the coffee taste better, but the coffee maker remains clean without much mineral deposit. The same can be accomplished with bottled spring water. —*Six Water Street B&B*

Invest in a small *cappuccino* or *espresso* maker. Your guests at home will love this extra touch, as ours do at the inn.

Use oversized coffee cups or mugs with whatever you serve. We use nine-ounce cups. Even if people don't finish everything (but they usually do), it shows that you are generous. Suggest to them that they drink only what they can.—*La Maison*

There are now coffee carafes that keep coffee hot for up to twenty-four hours. This way, you can make the coffee before going to bed and have it waiting for early-rising guests.—*The Manor House*

We have a coffee-mug rack. Our guests help themselves to whichever mug they want for their morning coffee or afternoon tea. The mugs are conversation pieces. The rack is a nice way for displaying a mug collection at home and makes guests feel comfortable to reach for a cup of something at any time.—*October Country Inn*

FOR MORE INFORMATION ON INNS LISTED IN THIS BOOK, SEE THE DIRECTORY BEGINNING ON PAGE 203.

WINE WISDOM

Being in the wine country, we have found the absolute best way to chill champagne (especially if you're in a hurry): Add water to the ice in an ice bucket. Then submerge the bottle three-fourths of the way into the bucket. You'll have ice-cold bubbly in just fifteen minutes.—*Beazley House*

Up here in Vermont we have lots of snow, so we use some of it in ice buckets for chilling wine and champagne. The snow does a better job of cooling and looks much nicer than ice. —*Tulip Tree Inn*

The 1819 Red Brick Inn houses a small winery in the basement, where the innkeepers make a sparkling wine for sale to guests and passersby. Inn rooms are named after wine varieties. For example, the Bordeaux Room has a carpet in a color reminiscent of the essence of that type of wine, stenciling of grapes as a border along the walls, a grapevine wreath, and posters by local artists of area vineyards.

Innkeeper Raymond Spencer believes

Being thoughtful, just as being thoughtless, will be remembered for a long time. How do you want to be remembered?"

—Willow Brook Inn

that wine serving shouldn't be stuffy. No one should feel intimidated. He offers these tips on wine for your own entertaining:

Ideally, wine should be stored in a room that is kept at a temperature of 50° to 60° F. At home, this is not always possible. Besides, there is a misconception about wine storage. The point is not so much to maintain a lower temperature but to store wine where the temperature is consistent. This means it can be a closet in a modern, ranch-style home, as long as the closet does not reach temperatures of more than ninety degrees in summer and sixty in winter. The fluctuation of temperatures can cause a cloudiness of the wine. Or if the wine is kept too cold, it can develop nitrate crystals.

If you're just starting to try wines, find a local wine merchant. Ask him for a recommendation, but don't buy anything expensive yet. Wait until you try his suggestion. If you don't like his choice, find another wine merchant.

Head out to a winery to sample a number of wines. Here, too, you can examine the cleanliness of the preparation rooms. Sanitation is important.

The older a wine is, the longer it should be opened prior to serving. Think of it as a room closed up for twenty years. Open the bottle and let it breathe to freshen it up—an hour or so, on average.

Avoid too much ceremony when serving wine. You don't want to inhibit your dinner guests, who may not know much about wines. Instead, help your guests enjoy it just as much as they will enjoy your food. When the wine is first opened, someone should smell it and taste it for obvious off characteristics of flavor or aroma.

It is better to serve red wine in a glass with a wide-mouthed bowl, since red wine releases more aroma. White wines can be poured into a tulip glass that has a large bowl at the bottom and a narrower mouth so that you can capture and concentrate the aroma. Champagne needs to be served in fluted glasses, contrary to the traditionally wide and not very deep glasses. The narrow glasses allow for the vision of stringy bubbles that will last longer.—*1819 Red Brick Inn*

Gail's Touch: To keep an open bottle of champagne bubbly until the next day, just place the straight end of a metal spoon in the neck and store the bottle in your refrigerator.

For a simple gathering or an intimate dinner, a standard 750-ml bottle will give you about five to six glasses of wine. For a large party you can figure on seventy-five glasses of wine per case.

Chapter 8

THE JOY OF DECORATING

CREATING ADVENTUROUS AND PEACEABLE PLACES

"Always have something beautiful in sight even if it's just a daisy in a jelly glass," tutors H. Jackson Brown, author of the famed *Life's Little Instruction Book*. I'm not sure I need to say anything more, as Brown says it simply. What vision. What integrity. What a message in a short sentence. To me this modern-day soothsayer of all things possible has put his finger on what makes a room—any room—a cameo of your hopes and dreams.

A room must have lovely things in it. One should be surrounded by personal pleasures and should not be intimidated if the decorating isn't, in the eyes of the decorators, perfect. The idea is to have the room contain things that are true and real.

Decorating does not have to follow rules or guidelines. Decorating is making your individualized space your own whether colors match or mismatch or textures seemingly collide. Decorating is another of life's simple pleasures. A room should be filled with beauty and should be a repository for your passions whether it's the bathroom, the family room or the bedroom. The idea is to make it look nice—"beautiful" as Brown describes—for you, not for someone else.

I only have one rule of decorating; that is, to commit to it. For me everything in a room has to exude beauty, whether beauty of its own or beauty because it does match or it does complement other details in the room. I like rooms with character, brimming with color and interest. I see a photograph in everything I set up in a room. I approach decorating as though I were styling a picture. The balance that is found in nature makes it into every one of my rooms. I am looking to create images: whisperings of history, with antiques and traditional accents; practicalities of everyday life, but with country airs; and personal treasures that are my promises of tomorrow.

For some people, pulling together all these elements may seem a bit difficult. But it's rather easy if first, you look inside yourself when planning a decorating scheme. What do you wish to get out of the room every day you visit there? Ask this of yourself rather than what you think someone else needs to get out of the room. Only take that into consideration if the room is shared with someone; then, make a joint canvas of two or more hearts and souls. Kids can be great at helping you with decorating. They are spontaneous, innocent, and quick to know what they like and don't like. Ask your children for some assistance. You will be surprised by the good ideas they have.

Once you have established the essence of what you want from a room, there are some considerations that can help you put that feeling together. The innkeepers are indeed masters at the art of decorating. They have so many rooms to decorate. Each room tends to be entirely different from the next, woven with individualism and the sighings and delights of the innkeepers. The rooms they create become kaleidoscopes faceted with optimistic and halcyon moods, well harvested with amenities that tease and awaken all the senses.

The message here is that a room must be alive. You should be able to experience its presence—it should have a presence—and it should offer you adventure as well as peace. This wonderful space ought to stimulate your imagination and, at the same time, make you comfortable. If you need assistance to get you going or to foster your confidence, the following pages will do all of that for you and more. Then, as long as you put yourself into the picture, the rest will flow. Remember, all it takes is a "daisy in a jelly glass," so to speak.

TIMELESS POINTS OF VIEW

First, regard the whole prospect of decorating with enthusiasm. While the details can seem daunting at first, it is one of the most creative things you can do in your home and one of the most satisfying.

Start your planning by considering the uses of each area you are decorating.

Consider that you will need to take different approaches in your planning. Kitchen and dining rooms need to be functional yet give off an energetic decor, whereas bedrooms must be restful.

Don't be afraid to mix decor with caution. Be eclectic, if you wish. A good rule to follow is that when you are mixing period furnishings and those from different countries, touch on each period or country in each room so that you maintain harmony throughout.

Here are a few quick, basic rules:

Don't skimp. Cheap fabrics wear out fast.

Always line curtains, as they hang better and last longer. The lining takes the brunt of the sunlight.

Lamps are the jewels of a room. Choose them carefully, making sure that their size is appropriate.—*Inn on the Common*

When decorating a room, avoid all the clichés—typical bric-a-brac items that you will get tired of quickly. Invest in a few fine pieces that speak volumes.

Do things for the unexpected look, like pairing modern fabric with an antique to create pleasant tension—a light and airy mood.—*The Seal Beach Inn*

Keep your decor simple. Simplicity gives an eloquence to many of the things we do. Don't use two or three when one is enough.—*Captain Swift Inn*

We have added a bit of the unexpected at our inn—a way to think through your decorating at home.

The Mackinac Island guest room holds a porch swing for two. The Venetian room has

---

🌺 PORTRAITS OF INN-SPIRATION 🌺

A real conversation stopper occurred once when a new bride came downstairs to the dining room one morning wearing only her nightgown. We tried to carry on normally with breakfast, but. . . .

Captain Ezra Nye House

an 1800s tapestry with Venetian gondolas. Athens has Greek columns and faux-cracked walls, with Greek capitals for nightstands. Bavaria has an alpine scene that looks like a view from a window and a sleigh bed with a feather mattress, symbolic of the snowy Alps. The Africa room has mosquito netting over the bed and a safari helmet—very romantic, like the film *Out of Africa.*
—*The Mockingbird Inn*

🪶Make a scrapbook when you do any decorating. In it keep swatches of wallpaper, fabrics, paint chips, and other pertinent information, such as what book the wallpaper came from and the design number. This will be a useful resource later when you need to identify fabric and other textures for replacement and redecorating.—*Chestnut Hill on the Delaware*

🪶When decorating a room, keep in mind the goal to make it a warm environment. You do this with colors, fabrics, and accent pieces. Candles in the room, for example, create a soft and romantic feeling.

Today we need our own comfortable nurturing spot to retreat to. Your house or apartment needs to be your home for the mind and spirit as well as for the body. Don't let your life-style or financial situation be an issue in making a home. Remember to make it a place that suits your personality, allowing yourself to use your senses (of color, shape, texture, and aroma) as directional signals. These components will help you and your family and friends relax. Home is where the heart is, and that heart is you!—*Ujjala's B&B*

🪶Consider what's outside your window when you plan your decorating. Bring the outside in, if you like the view. For example, we have a weathered barn outside our living room. Therefore, we decided not to hang curtains and to work with the barn's shades of brown and all the greenery from the outside in decorating the inside. We selected a light beige for the walls and upholstered pieces and a small red oriental carpet.—*White Goose Inn*

🪶Keep your rooms cheerful. Avoid depressing, dark colors, even if they are authentic. Generally, if your room's windows face north, decorate in light, airy colors. If

> *Every job is a self-portrait of the person who does it. Autograph your work with excellence.*
> —Sassafras Inn

they face east or west, beware of any fabrics or rugs that may fade from direct sun. But should your room's windows face south, let your imagination run wild.—*Doubleday Inn*

❧When decorating, don't overlook catalogs for ideas as well as for goods, including linens, curtains, and accessories. Our curtains, mostly lace, draw rave reviews from guests, who love their old-world charm. Although they look as if they were bought in Europe, they actually came from an American department-store catalog. With catalogs you can shop at your leisure, and, most of the time, you can depend on the merchandise to be delivered to your door in a matter of days.—*Quill and Quilt*

❧We try to keep everything within the time frame of 1908 or before. When you decorate your home, stick to the same decor throughout, or at least don't mix and match within the same room. Of course, there is a certain amount of mixing that can be done. An eclectic blend of modern and antique pieces can work if you can strike the right balance; however, not all mixtures work. Georgian and country get confusing, for example.—*Edge of Thyme*

❧Never be timid when using color, and never worry about what anyone else will think of your ideas. Be true to your tastes, and you'll find a consistency throughout your home. Follow your instincts, and you will surprise yourself at the continuity your ideas will present. The only time you fail at home decorating is when you begin to worry if others will like it!—*Hutchinson House*

SWEET PARTNERSHIPS

❧Decorating can be fun when you take a situation and work to complement it. Look at a room closely, and think about what will suit it best. Each room is an individual. For example, we have a dormer in one room that resembles a sharply angled pup tent. A theme for the room suddenly emerged. The window is at the end of the room, so we designed curtains to look like the tent flap was open on both sides. We chose burlap material and a muslin lining. The window overlooks a creek, which adds to the campfire theme. We named the room the Nevada Suite. Kerosene-style electric lanterns—similar to those used in tents—hang from a ceiling beam. Room accents include a Western wallpaper border, a large cactus, and colorful, striped rugs and blanket.—*Winters Creek Inn*

❧Develop an overall motif when decorating a room, a theme that suits you as an individual. Build on your interest. Is it sailing? Have a nautical corner. Our interest is antiques appropriate to gardening and old barns. Our B&B was built from an old barn, so we collect old gardening implements. Choose things that have meaning to you, and your house will develop a sense of place, a certain effect that no decorator can achieve for you.—*Bungay Jar*

❧Choosing a theme helps your decorating scheme. Included in our theme are hearts. We use them quite a bit but feel we have the right balance. We carry the theme right down to the heart-shaped butter mints we make and heart-shaped flower beds out front.—*Sweet Adeline's*

❧Before we opened the inn, we decided that each guest room would have a theme based on one of our collections. One room holds our nautical objects, including seafaring paintings as well as old lobster traps, which we use as luggage racks.

Bill comes from a musical family, so he had collected a lot of old instruments. In our Music Room, we have an old organ and an old violin that we made into a lamp.

❧Since train collecting and collecting old bottles are hobbies of ours, we decorated two rooms in those motifs.—*Birchwood Inn*

❧Each of our guest rooms reflects a different kind of turn-of-the-century travel. The Airplane Room has an antique propeller above the bed instead of a headboard. The bathroom-mirror frame in the Steamship Room is a brass porthole. A chair in the Buggy Room is an antique buggy seat, and old hubcaps are above the bed in the Automobile Room.—*Robins Nest*

FRESH IMAGINATION WITH PAPER

❧We use wallpaper everywhere. It gives rooms individual personalities.

A wallpaper border can be placed a little more than halfway down the wall to act as a chair rail.

When decorating a bedroom, select your bedspread first and decorate around it. If you choose curtains or wallpaper first, it can be a real problem to find an attractive bedspread.—*Inn on Golden Pond*

❧Use leftover room fabrics or wallpaper as backdrops in picture frames.—*Rabbit Hill Inn*

Carpet and wallpaper the closets to match the bedroom. This gives the feel of a special effort on your part.—*The Manor House*

Consider covering with wallpaper any steam pipes that run up the walls in rooms. It's a nice effect.—*Shire Inn*

Gail's Touch: Use a room's wallpaper or a coordinated one to make book covers for old books whose covers are badly worn. Stacked unevenly on a bookcase, blanket chest, or dresser, they make an interesting accent. Don't actually paste the wallpaper onto the book. Just fold and tape it.

Wallpaper with other materials besides the real thing. We used topographical maps of the area to cover one of our walls. You apply these with wallpaper paste. Be sure to lay out the paper carefully, knowing what will go where. Sketch out on paper as to how the sections will fit. Finish with a clear varnish to protect the paper.—*Window on the Winds*

Decorative wallpaper borders can simulate a headboard for a bed. Simply adhere the border to the wall, above the bed, and between the two posts of the bed.
—*Middlebury Inn*

To remove wallpaper, prepare a fifty-fifty solution of water and vinegar. Apply it with a sponge. As the paper loosens, peel it off the wall.—*Zachariah Foss Guest House*

Fabric can be used in the same way wallpaper border is used. Cut the fabric to the desired width. Use wallpaper paste to adhere the fabric to the wall. Cover it with polyurethane. Paste a lace border along the upper and lower edges.—*Victorian House*

We've covered some of our walls with burlap for a rustic appearance. Buy the burlap by the yard. Cut it to fit the wall, and staple it in the corners.—*Park House*

PAINTED IMPRESSIONS

Gail's Touch: The art of stenciling proliferated in the 1800s when decorating walls with wallpaper became desirable in Europe but too expensive to do in America. Itinerant artists, such as Moses Eaton, Jr., traveled to homes in New England, looking for work. Today we tend to think of the art as only fitting in homes decorated in country, colonial, Federal, and such. But nowadays, stencils are also made for contemporary decor and eclectic looks.

❧Almost anyone can stencil. The secret is to work with a very dry brush. You get that by patting the wet brush on a paper towel or an absorbent paper plate.—*Zachariah Foss Guest House*

❧One of the ways we create an authentic look is through stenciling. Since the house is 200 years old, we didn't want the stencils to look as if they were put on yesterday. We applied them very unevenly and with a very light, delicate hand, even leaving out some parts. Sure enough, they look 200 years old.

Here's how: Use a standard, flat-tipped, round brush and acrylic paint. Tap out the brush, thereby removing excess paint and distributing the paint evenly on the bristles. Apply just a breath of color, missing some areas purposely—sometimes leaving out an edge, other times a tip of a leaf, and then the center part of the leaf in another section.

Sign your stenciling and date it with lettering in matching paint, either freehand or with a stencil.—*Brafferton Inn*

❧Stenciling our bathroom walls became our decorating solution when, year after year, many of our old walls rejected new wallpaper. The result of stenciling a wall is immediate, the effort minimal, and it is one sure way to create a soft country look inexpensively. In addition, the variation of wall stencil patterns today is endless.—*Barley Sheaf Farm*

❧Stenciling can also be done on the outside of some bathtubs. Our claw-foot tub was in bad shape, so we painted it, and then a friend stenciled over the paint. A nonglossy protective paint sealer was sprayed over the stencilings.—*Arcady Down East*

❧If you stencil around a room, extend the design to another part of the room—into the closet, onto a piece of furniture, a lamp shade, or even a wastebasket. You'll find that once you start stenciling, you'll want to keep on going.—*Nauset House*

❧Colorful stenciling on ordinary vinyl window shades is an inexpensive way to add a bit of color-coordinated zest to any room and make the shades more attractive.—*Quill and Quilt*

❧You can stencil on almost any fabric. Muslin is a popular choice, or use solid-colored chintz. You need to use specially made paint that is for washable items. It's easier to stencil on fabric, because you don't have to get into odd positions as you do when stenciling walls. The trick is to keep the fabric taut. Lay the fabric out on a long table and work with a different brush for each color. It goes faster that way.—*Locust Hill*

A beautifully coordinated room can be created with a few yards of muslin, some stencil paint and brushes, and a little effort. For one of our rooms, we made a stencil of the flower design in the wallpaper. We stenciled the design along the bottom edge of a muslin dust ruffle, along the edge of an opposite painted wall, on the ruffles of the curtains, and along the bottom of the window shade.

To stencil on the muslin, put a few layers of newspaper under the fabric and hold the fabric down with masking tape. Also hold the stencil in place on the fabric with masking tape. Then begin to stencil. The paint dries quickly, so you can move the stencil to the next area and just keep going.—*Glacier Bay Country Inn*

Stencil a lace-doily pattern around the ceiling light fixture. Guests enjoy seeing this as they retire at night. The delicate pattern

The sun rises in a friendly way shining on hard work, real progress, added peace, more joy in life, and your own comfortable home waiting around the corner.
—Old World Inn

adds softness and texture to a room. —*Heritage Park Inn*

Gail's Touch: It is so easy to use paper doilies to make a *trompe l' oeil* lace effect on a side table or candlestand. It looks as if there is a real table scarf or lace doily on the table.

First, prime your tabletop with white paint. Paint the rest of the table a solid rich color. (The dark colors show up the beauty of the lace better than pastels do). Then prepare a paper doily to become your stencil by placing the doily face down on top of a piece of butcher paper. Use stencil adhesive spray to spray the doily. Once the doily is dry and sticky, place it onto the tabletop with the sticky side down. Cover the doily with a piece of regular paper and press down firmly all around to secure the doily to the table.

Remove the paper and you're ready to stencil. Use a foam stencil brush and dip into the darker paint, drying off most of the paint with a paper towel. Pounce the color through the doily. Once you're done stenciling, carefully peel the doily from the table, revealing the white (prime painted) shape of the doily on the tabletop!

To be even more creative, you can have the side of the table stenciled as though the lace doily were hanging down from the table-top. Just get a large enough doily and turn the edges down when you secure it to the table prior to stenciling.

LOOK-OUT SPACES

❧Decorative fans—as large as the ones used as fireplace screens and done in such materials as fabric, brass, and heavy paper—make attractive decorations in front of a window. Placed on the ledge, they even provide added privacy.—*Quill and Quilt*

Gail's Touch: Dress up window shades with matching slipcovers or bedspread fabric, which you can have laminated to the shades.

Small grapevine wreaths make great tiebacks. So do dried flowers made into a ring.

❧Create an interesting window valance by using a twig-fence found in your local florist-supply shop, or make one of your own from grapevines.—*Heritage Park Inn*

For more information on inns listed in this book, see the directory beginning on page 203.

❧Consider stained-glass windows when redecorating a room. We installed them at the inn, and the soft, colorful light that comes through is soothing and romantic. —*The Shelburne Inn*

❧Curtainless windows can look barren, but all you need is a little natural enhance-ment. We added grapevine to a large picture window, surrounding the entire woodwork with the natural twig effect. It also enhanced the scene outdoors—most complementary. —*The Sugartree Inn*

❧Willow branches make great curtain rods for tabs or any stationary pocket cur-tains. We have them in several of our rooms.—*The Painted Porch*

❧A nice way to add a finished look to a window is to make a molding made from embossed wallpaper borders. These borders are left unfinished. You paint them a comple-mentary color and miter them appropriately to the inside window frame. We have even done rag and sponge brushing on the bor-ders.—*Nowlin Creek Inn*

❧We made some of my favorite window curtain treatments with lace ordered from

the bridal-veil section of sewing shops.
—*Williams House*

Rub candle wax on wooden curtain poles, and curtains will slide on easily.
—*Red Castle Inn*

A favorite window treatment uses old chintz draperies gathered on a wooden pole with a 3-inch header and poufed to one side. Use screw-in, bull's-eye drapery holders (round brackets) to push the fabric to the side. Let the curtains down for privacy. Another nice look is to use three bull's-eyes—one on each side and one in the middle of the window. Find the antique chintz at thrift shops or garage sales.—*Conyers House*

Wide, about 1 1/2- to 2-inch floral ribbon makes great casual curtain tiebacks. Look for the old-fashioned variety.
—*Summerport B&B*

Sheets make easy curtain treatments. Simply run a rod through the wide hem. Hang. Draw back with a lace tie, or gather and pouf the top.—*Palmer House*

Lace tablecloths can be made into curtains.—*Glenborough Inn*

You can cover a window with something as simple as a piece of fabric folded into a triangle and hung across the top of the window, point down. This covers half the window, and you don't even need rods. Velcro attached to the window and fabric will do.

At the inn our window treatments are also unusual. All the Priscilla-style curtains were made from curtain lining. This gives a soft look to all the rooms and is a very inexpensive way of creating a designer look.
—*Little River Inn*

Sheets can be used as lining for drapes.—*Chateau Victorian*

We use old monogrammed pillowcases as coverings for the tops of French doors and old damask tablecloths for the bottom halves. These let a wonderful old mellow light into the room. Cut and sew rod pockets to size.
—*Pride House*

BRIGHT IDEAS

Lighting is often overlooked when decorating. Yet it is most important from a functional and aesthetic view. In general, avoid overhead lighting. Use lots of small table lamps; over important pictures, use lights that can double as night-lights. Consider small lights in bookcases, cupboards, and shelves. And don't forget outdoor lighting. (Washes from below are best, not floods.) —*Bungay Jar*

Candlelight, exclusively in the living room, helps set the mood of our home, like a parlor in the 1800s.—*Bodine House*

Many a guest has gone home and immediately put this one to use: Night light in dim corners at Red Castle is provided by the lacy sparkle of miniature white Christmas lights inside a willow basket filled with airy, dried baby's breath and hydrangea blooms.

Lighting a favorite ficus or indoor palm tree from below creates a shadow pattern on the ceiling and is also effective as a night-light.—*Red Castle Inn*

Old flour-scoops reflect candlelight around the room. Hang them on the wall as sconces with the handle at the bottom. Mount a candle at the inside of the base.

How about a cheese-grater lantern? Wire a light bulb to any grater, antique or new. Hang it on a wall. Soft light peers through the tiny holes. (If the grater is new, rough it up and then tarnish it with varnish or stain.) You can

get the same effect on a table by placing the grater over a candle.—*Hopkins Inn*

You can color-coordinate a floor lamp with your decor. Try to find an old wrought-iron floor lamp; buy a glass globe and an attachment for it. Using ordinary latex paint to match paint and other trim in the room, brush two coats onto the inside of the globe.—*Hutchinson House*

A DECOROUS MIX

Don't forget to decorate behind the door. A bow wreath is hung on the back of each guest-room door. When the door is closed, it adds a special touch.—*Benner House*

You can add laths (flat narrow strips of wood) to the ceiling. Run them lengthwise and crosswise to make 1-foot squares. Gives an antique look.—*Park House*

An old pair of ice tongs makes a great paper-towel holder. Open the tongs and insert the roll, then hang the tongs or stand them on the handles.—*Out-the-Inn-Door*

Give a flat door interest by taking wood (even picture framing) and mitering it into squares for a paneled effect. We have done this on our parlor walls underneath the chair rail. It has an authentic look.—*Strawberry Inn*

Those once-useful, but big, flour sifters can make attractive dishtowel hangers. Nail the sifter to the wall. Hang a dishtowel through the handle. Put dish rags in the top of the sifter. And hang potholders from the knob that turns the sifter.—*Heritage Inn*

If you need bookcase space, try two ladders placed vertically opposite from one another with boards running across the rungs. If the ladder is wood, stain or paint it.—*Greenbriar Inn*

Leftover or new yarn, wound into a ball, makes a nice room accent when placed into a basket. Select complementary colors. Stick in a pair of large knitting needles. Don't be surprised if someday you have a guest who tries knitting.—*Gate House Inn*

We used an old floor joist to make the top of a kitchen counter. We cleaned and sanded it and put six coats of polyurethane on top.

The top of an early dough cabinet now hangs on a wall and holds our dishes. We found it at a farm sale.
—*Zachariah Foss Guest House*

In a room that needs more space and you have none, be creative and create that space. By using the area between the walls of the rooms—the width of the studs—you can sink a small bookcase and have the added bonus of an interesting architectural detail for the room. Here's how:

Simply cut out a rectangular space in the room's wall and frame it with wood on all four sides to create a box. Add shelving at desired heights and back the bookcase with wood or wallboard or with mirror. Frame the bookcase with wood molding of your choice, applying this outer frame flat to the surrounding wall space (as if you were placing a picture frame around the new opening). Stain or paint the bookcase to create the desired finish. Use the shelves to display objects or small antique books.
—*Rabbit Hill Inn*

Old ladders can have a variety of uses.

> *"Use what talents you possess; the woods would be very silent if no birds sang there except those that sang best." (Henry Van Dyke)*
> —Holden House

We have one leaning against a wall in our sun porch. The rungs are rounded, but we still display items such as our baskets and some dried flowers. And as long as your old ladder is freshly painted, you can even use it in the kitchen to dry homemade pasta and also to hold wet dishtowels for drying.
—*Main Street B&B*

❦Car-seat upholstery fabric is good for your heavily used furniture. I found a maroon fabric that gives the look of old-fashioned plush on our parlor couch. It doesn't fade or spot, wears like iron, and cost less than $5.00 per yard!—*High Cotton Inn*

Gail's Touch: If you don't have a foyer and your front door opens into the living room, create a place to receive guests. Add a coat rack just inside the door and a mirror for checking out the *chapeau* before exiting the house. An umbrella stand also helps create the illusion. One time we created a separate area, resembling an old colonial tavern. We placed wainscoting (narrow-grooved paneling) three-quarters of the way up the left entry wall and topped it with a wall-to-wall Shaker peg rail. Period hats hung from the rail, along with a wreath. We put a tavern table in the center of the wall, with a checker game in progress and a colonial pewter mug ready for a refill.

Gail's Touch: A decorator's touch can be accomplished by purchasing fairly wide molding (4–6 inches) and mounting it about one-third of the way down the wall from the ceiling. The wide top of the molding provides a small shelf all around the room and a border, should you decide to wallpaper.

❦Is a room so small that you want to make it appear larger? From the floor to ceiling, mount 1- to 2-inch strips of mirror in the corners, one on each side of the ninety-degree, concave angle. The eye defines size by the corners of the room. The mirror strips visually eliminate the corners altogether.
—*Queen Anne Inn*

❦Our spiral staircase is very high and has a lovely curved wall. It looked very bare, even with the Williamsburg Chinese-print wallpaper. So I hung an embroidered kimono on the wall.—*Four Chimneys*

> *You don't need to be the center of the universe; there are other stars out there who shine just as brightly.*
> —L'Auberge Provençale

Old hot-water or steam-heating radiators can be an eyesore. Here are ways to handle the problem: Build a ledgelike table around them. Put a thick slab of marble on top to make a usable surface. Or on shorter radiators, make window seats for cold days, cold people, or plants.—*Williams House*

Bathroom sinks that don't have a cabinet underneath can be dressed with fabric. Fasten the fabric skirt to the sink with a hot-glue gun. The fit is really tight and smooth.—*Kenniston Hill Inn*

Ordinary guest towels can be turned into beautiful ones with the addition of lace or a coordinating fabric sewn onto one edge.—*Victorian House*

ALOFT IN ROMANCE

It's easy to make a canopy for a bed. You'll need plant-hanger hooks, two 6-foot-long dowels (1-inch round) that you have stained or painted, and clear fishing line. Put four hooks in the ceiling above the four posts of the bed. Hang equal lengths of fishing line from the hooks, and attach each one to an end of the dowels. Drape sheets or other decorative fabric over the framework you've created.—*Glenborough Inn*

You can make a king-sized bed canopy by sewing together two lace tablecloths. —*Mercersburg Inn*

One of the most romantic canopy beds is to make tab curtains that fit the length of the bed. Keep them tied back with ribbon and tell your guests that they can drape the bed by unraveling the ribbon.—*Rabbit Hill Inn*

Old lace doilies, sewn together, make a great bed covering. Find them at thrift stores or flea markets, or check your own attic. —*Lanaux House*

Lace and eyelet trims can be sewn onto pillow cases and sheets to give them an instant designer look.—*Kingsley House*

If you find a headboard that you really like, but it is a double instead of a queen, just attach the headboard to the wall and then push the queen frame and mattress up to it. The effect will be dynamic.—*Holden House*

Instead of the usual headboards, our headboards at the inn have been made from many things: a pair of old porch posts, connected with a cornice; a section of old porch railing; a section of an old mantelpiece; an antique mirror; a quilt; old windows; a door, hung sideways; and an old pair of wooden window shutters.—*Clauser's B&B*

Make use of an old window frame by turning it into a headboard. We added a mirror to the back of the frame and hung it horizontally just over a bed. And we use a school desk as a bedside table.—*Pudding Creek Inn*

Here's an idea for decorating the space above a bed and creating drama if you don't have a headboard. Purchase a Battenburg lace tablecloth and cut it in half lengthwise. Hem the cut edges and sew the two short

---

PORTRAITS OF INN-SPIRATION

At the inn we love to be unobtrusive accomplices to romantic intrigue. We cannot believe how many men plan overnight "Just Because" getaways for their wives. They conceive the idea, make reservations, pack for the two of them, and enjoy dinner at the inn. Then, they pretend to show our lodging rooms to their wives and, lo and behold, there's the wife's bathrobe gently strewn across the bed.

As for the packing part, minor difficulties sometimes arise. One couple wanted to take a walk before dinner. The husband had carefully included dining attire, complete with high-heeled shoes, as well as a pair of casual jeans—but no other shoes except slippers. Luckily, I wear the same size shoe, so the woman very willingly borrowed my sneakers.

The Inn at Olde New Berlin

ends together. On the wall, 6 inches out and 17 inches above the headboard edges, hang two decorative swag curtain holders. Over the center of the headboard, about 23 inches up, drive a large, heavy nail into the wall. The long cloth, with the lace-trimmed edge facing down toward the bed and plain edge on the top, can then be swagged softly. A dried-rosebud covered, heart-shaped wreath can be hung over the exposed nail.—*Durham House*

Instead of the usual headboard, try using an antique Victorian (trifold) folding screen. Fabric to match the bedding can usually be inserted for a custom look.—*Rose Manor*

Here's a great way to hang a dust ruffle on an especially high bed. Use metal rods (1/4-inch diameter) cut to fit on three sides and foot of the bed. Buy the barrel curtain-rod holders for 1/4-inch rods, and mount them on the inside of the legs of the bed. The dust ruffle is gathered onto the rods like a curtain for the sides and foot of the bed. —*Captain's House*

Large lace tablecloths can work well as bed coverings.—*Ilverthorpe Cottage*

A warm, sparkling smile outshines any decor or cuisine!
—Lanaux House

When curtains and wallpaper are still good in a room, but the matching bedspread has worn out, cover the bedspread with a crocheted coverlet. The colors still show through this way, and you won't have to redo the entire room.—*Old Yacht Club Inn*

The headboards in one of our guest bedrooms are of pressed tin, which were the grate covers of ceramic gas heaters. When the heaters were in use during the winter in the twenties, the grate covers were removed. In summer they were put back in place, creating an ornate front. —*Inn of the Arts*

Gail's Touch: A friend of mine came up with the idea of using a colonial secretary desk to store her clothes. She selected one with glass doors on top so that her pretty sweaters would show through and add color. Other tops went in the drawers. She employed the tilt top and pigeon holes as a makeup storage area.

Iron Victorian tack-room brackets were placed over a bed for hanging a swag of fabric. The bracket was placed about 3 feet over the center of the bed. The fabric was draped over it and attached to the headboard with a bow, and then brought down the side of the bed.—*Silas Griffith Inn*

It is so easy to combine the warmth and comfort of a goose-down comforter with your room's decor. Merely buy a channel-stitched comforter of good quality. Have a cover made for it with complementary or matching curtain or other fabric in the room.—*The Wildflower Inn*

Chapter 9

BRINGING HOME THE SEASON

A GATHERING OF QUIET PLEASURES, THOUGHTFUL FEASTS, AND DAYS OF GRACE

*U*sually, most of us like to embrace the holidays with family and friends. But sometimes we are far from home. The innkeepers are aware of the traveler's need for the kind of welcoming atmosphere that eclipses the longing for home and family during the holidays. At some of the inns, everything done is targeted to the season—from breakfast to evening snacks and decorating.

Some inns, such as the Red Brook Inn in Old Mystic, Connecticut, bring guests to holidays past with their early American dinners. The innkeepers dress fashionably according to the era and serve meals reminiscent of the times.

We can imitate some of the inns' holiday celebrations by incorporating the innkeepers' festivities into our own family gatherings. This is bound to make the holidays a little different each year.

The innkeepers have also outlined some special events they have held at their inn. Let these ideas coax your own creativity. Consider that a theme will make planning your entire party or special dinner a lot easier. For example, have you ever become so confused by so many possible recipes that you do not know which dishes to make? A theme will narrow the choices and help you focus the meal plan.

KEEPING THE
HOLIDAY SPIRIT

Get plenty of rest during the holidays. Holidays are usually stressful. The whirlwind of parties, cooking, and shopping from before Thanksgiving through New Year's Day is enough to exhaust the strongest workhorse among us.

Don't try out intricate new menus or recipes. Save those for the March doldrums when a new idea in your kitchen will spread cheer throughout the house. During the holidays stick with food you can count on and you love. Remember that what may be an everyday snack or meal to you is special to your guests.—*The Half Penney Inn*

Better to do a little less than too much for holiday festivities. You enjoy the holidays more with less work and projects, so will everyone else around you.
—*The Mockingbird Inn*

We serve grape juice to our arriving holiday guests. It's a famous beverage here because the Welch's company is located in Westfield. Think about what's native to your area and plan your niceties around that.
—*William Seward Inn*

The holidays begin with a hike through the forest for the perfect tree. We usually choose a tree with two trunks, thereby naturally thinning the forest. During the outing we serve homemade fudge, cocoa, candy canes, and a lot of laughs.—*Mt. Juneau Inn*

Gail's Touch: I like to decorate for the holidays with seasonal cookbooks. The artistry of Susan Branch's Christmas cookbook, for example, is festive and country. Hers, and so many others, look pretty on a coffee table or on a cookbook holder next to the banquet table or simply on the kitchen counter. A cookbook can be a focal point when decorating for any season. I have a warm-weather book with a picture of a luscious watermelon on the front cover. The book takes center stage in summer. An added pleasure is that the book was given to me by my nephews as a thank-you for spending a week with me on their summer vacation. The grin delivered by the half slice of the watermelon on the front cover is them, smiling up at me.

On alternate years when our grown family is unable to join us, we gather together other less fortunate families, single parents, singles, or others who don't have families in our area. We serve a pancake breakfast with a simple menu of orange juice, coffee, tea, bacon, and pancakes. Remember, it is the attitude of gathering together, not the menu, that is important.

We do the same for people from our church. After an 8:00 P.M. candlelight service on Christmas Eve, we provide a place for refreshments and good conversation for those who have no family to be with.—*Garratt Mansion*

❧I use felt as a colored liner under lace tablecloths. It's inexpensive and so interchangeable for holiday entertaining. I keep a selection of colors, such as green for Saint Patrick's Day and pink for Valentine's.—*Robins Nest*

"Patience is the ability to idle your motor when you feel like stripping your gears." (author unkown)
—Whispering Waters

❧In the supermarkets at holiday time, you will find individually boxed liquor cakes (for one or two people per cake). Buy several packages of them and wrap each one differently. Place them under the tree. The boxes serve as additional decoration (especially when all the family presents have been opened on Christmas morning) when the tree base looks barren. The cakes are also presents for those unexpected friends and acquaintances who just happened to drop by—especially those who brought something for you and you weren't planning on a gift for them. The individual wraps make it seem as if the present was indeed special for someone.—*Ashling Cottage*

❧If you're having overnight guests for the holidays, remember to decorate their sleeping rooms festively. Let your cheer spread throughout.—*Edge of Thyme*

❧Many of our holidays are highlighted by a Victorian tradition. We place small flags on toothpicks on our muffins and fill tall vases with assorted sizes of flags whenever flowers are in short supply. The Victorian period was a very patriotic time, and the American flag was used extensively in decorating. If your home is Victorian, this practice would be particularly appropriate.—*Red Castle Inn*

❧Invite your holiday guests to decorate a Christmas tree for the birds. Save grapefruit halves and let them dry. String the dried fruit shells up with red yarn, putting holes through the bottom of the skins and knotting after each addition. Hang from a bough on an evergreen outside. Fill each shell with sunflower seeds.

Cut bagels in half and spread them with peanut butter. Sink sunflower seeds into the peanut butter. Run yarn through the hole and hang on the same tree.

String garlands of freshly popped corn and string with alternating raisins and cranberries.—*The Inn at Honey Run*

Your usual decorator pillows can be changed easily to coincide with a holiday. Take two napkins (or fabric you've hemmed in the size of a napkin) and place one on either side of the pillow. Take coordinating ribbon and gather the extra fabric at each of the corners. You have a new pillow in an instant. We do this at least during the Christmas season with our checked dinner napkins. The effect is versatility and a decorator's look for your holiday preparations.
—*Main Street B&B*

"I find that wherever I go, if I am willing to discard my concept of what I expect to find and I am willing to be open, adventurous, and genuine, people respond with much love. I do not go to any place to find what I have at home. I go to explore new realities —to understand. The planet is one very incredible family." (author unknown)
—Betsy's B&B

If you're invited to dinner and intend to bring a bottle of wine for the host, make the bottle a more attractive gift by adding a few fresh or silk flowers. Tie the flowers to the bottle with a piece of decorative twine or a ribbon.—*Kedron Valley Inn*

Gail's Touch: Small grapevine wreaths make splendid napkin holders. Dress them according to the season. A simple bow tied through the wreath will do nicely.

The holidays are times when home-baked goods are often given as gifts. Should you run out of gift tins, an inexpensive way to achieve the same results is to cover a coffee can in pretty holiday wrapping.
—*Triple T Ranch*

Gail's Touch: Gifts for all holidays and birthdays can be wrapped with colorful fabric that can be reused by the recipient. Leftover wallpaper can also make a memorable gift wrap.

Wrap a single-man's gift in the paper of your choice. Add a bow and attach a small black book (date book) to the bow. —*Glendale Farms*

VALENTINE'S DAY

Cupid reigns among our sugar cookies that are tied in plastic wrap with a red ribbon and placed on each guest pillow.

It's also nice to bring the holiday to your guests at the breakfast table. Our place settings are accented with large, homemade heart cookies bathed in pink frosting and topped with the word "Love" in white frosting.—*Covered Bridge Inn*

The names of our entrees change with the holiday. A sample for Valentine's Day: Cooing Duck, Heart Beet Soup, Passion Fruit Sorbet, Shrimps in Love, Nesting Greens, Sweet Ecstasy, Forever-after Coffee. Give your entrees seasonal names and announce them to your own dinner guests at home.—*Mercersburg Inn*

An easy touch for your guest's breakfast: We top eggs with red hearts that are made out of pimientos with a small cookie cutter.—*Edge of Thyme*

SAINT PATRICK'S DAY

On Saint Patrick's Day the local herb society meets at our inn. We serve green wine and green-herb hors d'oeuvres. We exchange herb recipes and green plants. —*Laurel Hill Plantation*

We serve green eggs and ham on Saint Patrick's Day. To a mixture of beaten eggs and half and half, add fresh parsley, scallions, steamed broccoli or asparagus, cubed cream cheese, and then julienne ham. Pour into skillet. Turn once. We garnish with avocado slices. So the eggs are not actually green, but the additional ingredients are, and they give the eggs a green theme.—*Ilverthorpe Cottage*

EASTER

Adults love to color Easter eggs. The leftover colors from our own Easter eggs are supplied to our guests after breakfast. They enjoy coloring their own and get to take the eggs home. If you have company coming the day before Easter, wait for them to work with you in coloring the eggs. It's one way of celebrating the holiday together.—*Wild Rose of York*

Dyed eggs with guests' names on them

are a nice place card for a table setting. An easy basket is a plastic strawberry basket. Weave a pretty ribbon around the top and fill it with grass and goodies.—*Garratt Mansion*

Mahogany eggs—dyed with onion skins and the outline of herbs—and marbleized eggs fill a twig basket at Easter and decorate the breakfast table. These eggs hail back to the early days of this country. Settlers used native plants—walnut hulls, pokeberries, goldenrod, cabbages, and onions—to create lovely colored eggs. A bit earlier in the season, the eggs are placed among freshly dug violets, sweet woodruff, and moss in a huge flat basket as the centerpiece for a buffet—the perfect harbinger of spring.

Here's how to make the eggs in your own kitchen:

You will need uncooked white eggs, a metal or enamel pan, nylon stockings, string, brown onion skins, turmeric, red cabbage leaves, vinegar, alum, young ivy leaves, and tiny sprigs of thyme, rosemary, and parsley or dried pressed flowers.

To decorate: Work with one color at a time. Start with the onion skins for mahogany eggs, as they are the easiest.

Dip 1/2 cup of brown onion skins into 2 cups of boiling water. Remove the skins and wrap around an egg. One layer will do. The wet skins will mold nicely to the egg.

Tie a string around the ankle of the stocking. Slip the wrapped egg into the stocking as far as the knot. Tie another knot at the opposite end of the egg.

Skip an inch and tie another knot, repeating with as many eggs as can fit in the pan.

Boil leftover skins for 10 minutes. Remove. Add eggs. Simmer for 10 minutes.

Carefully untie strings and unwrap eggs. They should be a lovely dark, yellow-brown, with a marbleized design. You can reuse these same skins for the next batch, although the color won't be as bright.

Let the eggs dry thoroughly. It was the custom in the Maryland colony to oil the eggs for a richer color. When they are completely dry, you can also use a little paste wax for a glowing shine. The eggs will dry up inside their shells and can be kept from year to year in a box.

> *Remember to take time to make the person you see in the mirror happy. Being happy with yourself helps you to see happiness in others.*
>
> —Captain Swift Inn

For your next batch, try something a little more challenging—a design on the egg:

Press a tiny herb sprig or a dried flower onto the egg before wrapping it with the onion skin. When it is unwrapped, it will have a tiny green print of the herb. Repeat as often as you like or until the color and skins wear out.

Directions for various colors:

Blue: Substitute red cabbage for the onion skins. Use 1 cup of chopped red cabbage leaves plus two or three of the softer leaves for wrapping. You need 2 cups of water and 1 tablespoon of vinegar. Boil all together for 10 minutes, removing the whole leaves as soon as they're soft. Wrap eggs with leaves as you did with the onion skins, or place the eggs, unwrapped, into the dye.

Yellow: Boil 1 teaspoon turmeric, 2 cups of water, 1 tablespoon of vinegar, and 2 pinches of alum together for 10 minutes. Apply herbs to eggs. Tie the eggs in the stockings and simmer in dye 10 minutes.

Green: Green eggs emerge from 1/2 cup young ivy leaves, 2 cups water, 1 tablespoon vinegar, and 2 pinches of alum. Follow the remaining procedure stated for the yellow eggs.—*Sage Cottage*

❧One year, an Easter table centerpiece consisted of Easter ornaments hung from a chandelier over the dining table at different heights and tied with pink ribbon. The table underneath had green grass and candles in the shape of eggs, plus wooden tulips and a lovely fresh flower arrangement.
—*Victorian B&B Inn*

❧For Easter, paper cupcake holders are filled with Easter grass and jelly beans and placed at each table setting.—*Hill Farm Inn*

MEMORIAL DAY

❧You can serve this on the Fourth of July as well as Memorial Day: It's a mock American flag made with food. Spread bread dough on a rectangular pan. Bake until done. On top, create the flag with blueberries in the corner for stars, strawberries for the red strips, and bananas for the white stripes. An alternative is to decorate a yellow cake baked in a shallow rectangular pan with the fruit. You can add a colorful selection of juices to serve with the cake in the red, white, and blue theme: tomato, grapefruit, and cran-blueberry.—*Ilverthorpe Cottage*

FOR MORE INFORMATION ON INNS LISTED IN THIS BOOK, SEE THE DIRECTORY BEGINNING ON PAGE 203.

INDEPENDENCE DAY

❧Breakfast on the Fourth of July is celebrated with French toast garnished with strawberries and blueberries and served to guests with a flaming sparkler.—*Kenniston Hill Inn*

HALLOWEEN

❧When pumpkins are growing on the vine, you can use a pin to scratch your name (we scratch the name of the inn) or a welcoming greeting on the surface. Your special welcome will grow larger as the pumpkin grows bigger.—*Hilltop Inn*

❧For a fall centerpiece hollow out small pumpkins and use them as vases filled with fresh flowers and autumn leaves. Group several filled pumpkins for a larger centerpiece, or place very small pumpkin vases at each place setting.—*Two Sisters Inn*

❧Deviled eggs are always popular, and we love to dress them for the particular occasion. At Halloween we make devilish eggs. Use your deviled-egg recipe and add slivers of green onions for the horns, ripe olives for the nose and eyes, parsley or poppy seeds for the beard or whiskers, and a pimiento for the tongue. (At Easter decorate the deviled eggs as a bunny with slices of cooked egg white for ears, small strawberries for pink eyes, and a black olive for the nose.)—*Robins Nest*

❧A wreath made of the mugwort herb guards the front door at Halloween to keep away the evil spirits. Here's how to make one. (Apply the same techniques to almost any wreath you make.)

Buy a wire ring at a crafts-supply store. They come in many sizes. For a large wreath gather lots of the plant or whatever material you are going to use as the basis of your wreath. (We use mugwort because of its herbal significance.) Divide the herb into branches, 3 or 4 inches long; then divide them into small bundles. Put one bunch on the outside of the frame in a spiral fashion, another in the middle, and one on the inside. Then, using a light wire, continue this spiral pattern around the ring, pulling the wire tightly after applying each bundle.

Wreaths 6 inches in diameter or smaller can be made by just wrapping a stem or two in a circle and securing the end with light

"Kindness is the oil that takes the friction out of life." (Author unknown)
— Whispering Waters

wire or heavy thread. Tiny dried flowers may be secured on any wreath with glue and very fine ribbon.—*Sage Cottage*

For a festive Halloween dinner, use grapevine-wreath or wooden napkin rings with white napkins that you set on top of an upside-down wine goblet. Adjust the napkins so that the head of the ghost is sitting upright.—*Victorian Oaks B&B*

A fun party idea is to take your guests to a local cemetery and do tombstone rubbings. Supplies are available at crafts stores or churches, usually for doing brass artistic rubbings. This unusual activity might inspire your guests to begin taking an interest in their own family genealogy.—*Eastlake Inn*

If you use fall leaves to decorate, dip them first in wax to give them strength and prevent crumbling.—*The Waverly Inn*

THANKSGIVING

For this holiday we pull cornstalks from the fields and create massive bundles attached to lightposts and columns on the porch. We tie the bunches with colorful orange and yellow ribbons. The look is country and festive.

You can buy cornstalks in the fall at many farmstands.—*Doubleday Inn*

CHRISTMAS
THE CHARMS OF CHRISTMAS

Gail's Touch: Treat yourself and your guests to an evening holiday concert. My favorites are a boys chorus and a handbell choir.

To add sparkle to any party from New Year's Eve on, decorate serving trays with shiny confetti and curls of ribbon.

We put up an abundance of lights—4,000 tiny whites—and seven Christmas trees to set the mood.

Guests names are written on gingerbread people and set out to honor them and, of course, to be eaten!—*Antique Rose Inn*

Mulled cider and hot toddies can be prepared ahead of time, and there is nothing like these libations during the holidays for warming the soul.—*L'Auberge Provençale*

Take advantage of Mother Nature when decorating for Christmas. Walk outside and pick ivy, grapevines, magnolia leaves, or any-

thing with red berries for the fireplace mantel, banister, or centerpiece.
—*The Mockingbird Inn*

❧Hang seasonal decorations with Velcro, instead of nails or wire, so that they may be easily changed.

Great idea: We hear that fruitcakes make great doorstops!—*Two Sisters Inn*

❧Get a couple of large planter pots and fill them with dirt to hold freshly cut small

pine trees. Decorate the trees with small white lights and red velvet bows and place them on your front steps. The trees will last for months.—*Shire Inn*

❧Horse-drawn sleigh rides are offered at the inn during the Christmas holiday season. Check out your own area. Many farms across the country still offer similar rides in old carriages or hay wagons.—*William Seward Inn*

❧Have a gift-wrapping party. Supply the

❧ PORTRAITS OF INN-SPIRATION ❧

A couple from California visited our bed and breakfast for their honeymoon. They told us an interesting story of how they first met:

Both were traveling on business and were seated next to each other on a transcontinental flight. There was quite a spark between them, but shyness had prevented the exchange of phone numbers. In due time the plane landed and passengers disembarked. As our female guest was exiting the terminal building, she spotted her seat mate leaving from a far door. She took a deep breath and shouted across the terminal, "My name is Susan and I work at the First Bank on East Center Street!"

They spent their honeymoon with us!

Deer Run Ranch

wrapping paper, ribbons, and bows. Provide small stencils for use on solid white paper. Have everyone bring their gifts and have a great time. Suddenly the wrapping process doesn't seem like a chore but a party! —*Blue Harbor House*

To make Christmas a bit more romantic, surround the tub with boughs of evergreen all around your whirlpool or soaking tub. Run a bubble bath for your significant other. When he or she gets into and out of the tub and enjoys the bath itself, they smell the scent of pine and cedar and the holidays all around them.—*Orchard Hill Country Inn*

An old sled, with an evergreen bough attached by a large bow, looks welcoming when placed next to the front door. —*Kingsley House*

Serve chocolate-chip-mint ice cream in individual-sized small clay flowerpots. Add a "dirt" layer of crushed chocolate cookies and a fake poinsettia plant. Your guests may be like ours and hesitate at first to eat what

When what I am doing stops being fun, I have learned to distance myself from it and take a new look. Then I must make objective decisions about what steps I can take to improve the situation.
—The King's Cottage

seems to be so real. But it's delicious and looks great on the table.—*Truffles B&B*

Gail's Touch: To make way for a more relaxing time with your guests during the holidays, here are some handy kitchen hints: Marinate in plastic bags instead of glass dishes to save cleaning time. Use nonstick cookware for easy cleaning. Dish up food in the kitchen; forget about serving dishes. Keep holiday cooking ingredients ready to go; roast nuts ahead of time; have candied fruits prepared in advance; keep citrus zests handy.

When decorating for the holidays, it's nice to give the decor a theme. Music is an especially important ingredient at Rabbit Hill during the holidays. We decorate our parlor with music as the theme. On the mantel are brass horn candle holders, wooden replicas of a harp and violin, and an antique music stand.

Our manger was handcrafted in Italy. On the sides of the manger, we have a jack-in-the-box featuring a pop-up Scrooge and scenes from Dickens's *A Christmas Carol.* We place music boxes in adjoining rooms. In the dining room we play tapes of music-box melodies. Guests, arriving to the sound of all these boxes playing, are enthralled. —*Rabbit Hill Inn*

Antique Santas are grouped together on the mantel in the main gathering room. Each Santa represents a different period and country.—*Captain Lord Mansion*

Strings of popcorn and cranberries are woven into our staircase railing.—*Inn on Golden Pond*

Our inn was part of a house tour one Christmas. To add to the holiday flavor, we dusted part of the table with flour and placed a rolling pin nearby, along with a few cooked gingerbread men on top of the flour. We wanted to give the illusion of just-baked cookies in the kitchen. This is a nice decorating idea for a holiday party in your own home.—*Main Street B&B*

When the holidays are over, don't throw away the popcorn-and-cranberry garland. Put it outside for the birds to eat. —*1830 Inn on the Green*

Kissing balls deck our home. To make your own seasonal Cupid of sorts, take a potato and stick boxwood stems into it from every direction. Attach a strong ribbon and hang it in a doorway.—*La Vista Plantation*

CHRISTMAS TREES

Every room of your home can have a Christmas tree. A friend taught us how to make small, fresh trees. Cut a block of florist oasis (a moist holder for flowers) to fit into a deep dish, standing upright. Wet the oasis. Stick fresh-cut evergreen branches into the florist oasis. You can decorate the trees with colored baby's breath, ribbons, toys, and even a string of tiny twinkling lights. —*Chestnut Hill on the Delaware*

Cover a Christmas tree with animal cookie cutters tied with red ribbons. —*Sage Cottage*

Old or new lace draped around the tree like a garland will give your tree an old-fashioned look.—*Alexander's Inn (New Jersey)*

When we decided to have a second tree—a large, 12-foot one—we didn't have the time to run out and buy new ornaments for it. Besides, decorating such a tree would cost a fortune in store-bought baubles. Instead, we took nuts and pinecones and sprayed them with gold paint, added ribbons, baby's breath, and tiny lights, and we had a tree that took our guests' breath away. Use imagination when decorating your own tree. Make it as personalized as you can.—*Main Street B&B*

TABLE ADORNMENTS

Buy the brightest apples you can. Core them and dip them into a crystal-clear floor wax. When they have dried, put a white candle in the cored area for truly authentic candle holders.—*Doubleday Inn*

A holiday centerpiece can be made from a small, white-birch log. Drill holes in it for candles, and decorate it with various yuletide greens and trimmings.—*Silver Maple Lodge*

Gail's Touch: You can also make natural candle holders from bagels. Just slip some tinfoil on the bottom of the candle and insert it in the bagel hole. Decorate the bagel with a hint of evergreen and a marble-sized Christmas ball.

Take an empty can (coffee can prefer-ably) and glue candy canes around the outside. The curved part should face out. Secure with a festive ribbon tied around the canes. Place holiday greenery or other flora inside. This also makes a nice container for cookies and candy.

Pineapples also make wonderful seasonal centerpieces. Wrap an evergreen bough around the bottom, and place colorful Christmas balls every 3 inches or so on top of the bough. Place a satin ribbon between each ball.

Scraps of felt and lace can be used to make holiday napkin holders. At Christmas, for example, they are red-felt mittens with a white-velvet ribbon cuff, topped by a green-felt holly leaf and a couple of red sequins for berries. When your napkin is rolled and slipped in, it looks like a sleeve going into the mitten. To make one, trace a mitten pattern onto felt. Sew together two pieces, leaving an opening where a hand would slip in, to be used for the napkin.—*Robins Nest*

SWEETS

Each year a different centerpiece of edible architecture greets guests and can be anything from a cracker cottage to a confectionery castle. You don't have to be a baker to start this tradition in your own home. If making a gingerbread house seems intimidating, relax and enjoy this similar but easier method of constructing a sweet building.

Anyone can mix up some royal icing (three egg whites to a pound of powdered sugar). This magic mortar dries to a sweet cement that will stick anything to anything. Your foundation can be square or round (for turrets) oatmeal boxes, cookie tins, or cardboard tubes. One year a row of jelly-bean town houses was constructed out of wine boxes from our vineyard. The royal icing covers your foundation. Add your own food accents.—*Hopkins Inn*

There is no reality except where you are.
—The River House

Winter holidays can be enhanced with frosted fruit as decorations. Here's a recipe for making your fruit glisten:

1 egg white
2 tablespoons water
1 cup sugar

In a small bowl beat the egg white and water lightly. Dip assorted fruits in the mixture. Drain the excess back in the bowl. Roll each piece in sugar until covered. Let them dry thoroughly on waxed paper.—*Arcady Down East*

NEW YEAR'S EVE

On New Year's Eve you can decorate a room inexpensively. We festoon our dining room with curly ribbon, and we fill the entire ceiling with helium balloons that have long strands of ribbon attached. Buy the ribbon in commercial-size rolls to save money.

Inside each wine glass we place a horn with long streamers. This makes for a colorful table before the clock strikes twelve.—*Ellis River House*

Gail's Touch: A cake complementary to the closing seconds of a New Year's Eve party is one decorated on top as though it were a clock. Use plastic numbers and hour hands, or make your own by piping black icing through a cake-decorating tip.

Entertainment for your New Year's Eve celebration can include something we do. Over our bar we fill a big net with black and white balloons. Then we pull the balloons down from the ceiling at midnight with a cheer.—*Black Lantern Inn*

FOR MORE INFORMATION ON INNS LISTED IN THIS BOOK, SEE THE DIRECTORY BEGINNING ON PAGE 203.

SPECIAL PARTIES

❧We use plain white china for all holiday and party occasions because it allows for the intermixing of seasons and colors. With a solid-color tablecloth, this allows for the seasonal accents to be the center of attention. Also, having one set of china allows me to concentrate on acquiring more table settings and saves storage space. Perfect for condo living!—*Mt. Juneau Inn*

Gail's Touch: No matter what the season, consider decorating with garlands that bespeak the time of year. In summer, for example, string together dried rosebuds and swag them across the top of a picture frame—the extra roses hanging from the side, and all tied at the top of the frame with a tassel or large bow.

For warm-weather time, how about a garland of hydrangea strung on the banister?

❧A few loaded instant-photo cameras can turn any party into a hilarious event. Here's one for Halloween, or omit the costumes and do it for any other occasion: Supply each guest with a camera (or ask them to bring one if they can). Depending on how many guests you have, divide them into small groups or couples. Send them out with the instant camera and a list of places where they must have their picture taken. All members of the group must be in the picture, so they will have to solicit strangers to take their snapshot.

A little advance preparation is necessary, since you need to scout out locations in your neighborhood that can be covered in the time allowed. You also need to add some bonus points to the scoring to break ties. For example, at one of our recent parties, we gave the groups ninety minutes to get their photos taken in a bowling alley, in a fire station, on a city bus, in a police car, in a grocery store checkout line, under a movie marquee, and in a cemetery. All the groups got all the photos in the time allowed. Bonus points for such items as the number of fire trucks in the fire-station picture, the number of additional people wearing bowling shirts in the bowling-alley shot, the number of heads of lettuce in the grocery-store picture, and so on, were the deciding factors for the winners.—*Quill and Quilt*

❧Check your local banquet and party-rental supply store for unusual and useful pieces to give your party an added flair. Lattice work and gazebos don't have to be just for wedding backgrounds, for example. Likewise, one or two unusual serving pieces you might find can add a lot to any party. —*Abriendo Inn*

Gail's Touch: Use bundles of wheat shafts tied together to decorate a buffet table for fall.

During an Iowa caucus we had thirteen candidates. For a political party we put up thirteen red, white, and blue balloons and cascaded them from a chandelier in various lengths. On the table we placed a donkey vase and an elephant vase, filled them with rice, and placed about three small flags in each, along with curled red, white, and blue ribbons. It made a lovely table setting.— *Victorian B&B*

The bottom line in entertaining is to keep it simple with style and prepare in advance. For a political fund-raising luncheon, we had the bakery slice 5-foot-long loaves of French bread lengthwise. On nice and new 1-by-12-inch boards, we made the bread into giant open-faced submarine sandwiches, which we decorated with ripe olives, cherry tomatoes, sardines, pickles, and other condiments. We used an electric knife to cut

the sandwiches into 4-inch sections and topped each one with a small American flag. They were a smash. We raised funds and later converted the boards into shelves. —*Robins Nest*

Have a summer-in-February party. Decorate with tropical posters and paper palm trees. Serve tropical fruits and other summer foods. Give everyone a lei, and turn up the heat so that they can wear shorts!— *Out-the-Inn-Door*

Gail's Touch: A useful centerpiece for a seasonal summer dinner is made by starting with a large bowl or basket filled with home-grown or fresh garden salad greens and vegetables. Use a small, colorful spade and rake as salad servers. Put a small, decorative watering can filled with an herb dressing nearby, and let your guests water their own garden-on-the-plate.

To decorate for a dinner with a Victorian theme, make some fancy napkin rings. Use wired ribbon to form the ring. Secure with a glue gun. Cut a small piece of lace from a damaged doily or another find. Starch the lace, and glue it to what will be the top side of the ribbon napkin ring. Then glue dried flower buds at the center of the lace. Add a short thin ribbon. (Note: These rings also make lovely curtain tiebacks.)

Make a complementary nosegay centerpiece. Select a paper or lace doily of desired diameter. Pierce the center and draw wired dried flower through it. Wind white florist tape around the wires, and curl the tape prettily at the ends. Next, pucker the doily from its center by gathering it underneath, and glue in place with a glue gun to shape it around the flowers. Glue dried leaves around the flowers to make a pretty arrangement. Add a crystal bead to resemble a dewdrop and thin ribbon streamers. Place at the center of the table or on the side, or make nosegays to decorate each place setting.—*Rabbit Hill Inn*

Gail's Touch: Have a Western Party. Set the table with bandannas as your napkins. You can use place mats or make a tablecloth out of burlap. Napkin rings can be round, slotted, wooden clothespins upon which you write your guest's name. Another napkin ring idea that also doubles as a place card is using a small cowboy hat from a doll. Write the guest's name on a piece of paper attached to

> *If I have made you smile, you have made my day worthwhile*
> —The Mellon Patch Inn

the hat with a straight pin. The elastic hatband wraps nicely around the napkin. For a centerpiece use something western, such as a small rocking horse or an agate coffeepot filled with fresh baby's breath. You can also place two candlesticks with a string between them. Using tiny clothespins and doll clothes, hang a pair of overalls and a checkered shirt on the line to dry! Pewter plates are a nice complement, if you have them.

Tell guests it's a jeans party, so they will wear denim. Serve a barbecue dish as the main entree, perhaps with wagon-wheel pasta and pesto sauce as one of the side dishes. Green and yellow squash slices, sauteed in butter and sprinkled lightly with salt and pepper, also go well. A loaf or two of braided bread to resemble the rope of rough riders will look attractive on the table and complement the theme.

Gail's Touch: I sometimes use restaurant menus to coincide with my dinner-table theme. For example, I once had a bon-voyage dinner party for my in-laws bound for vacation in France. The centerpiece was a menu from a French restaurant. I inserted a list of the evening's dishes, giving them

Parisian titles. The menu sparked jovial conversation. My father-in-law started it off with, "Does this restaurant take a credit card?"

I have a collection of menus to complement many themes for the table, having collected them when I used to review restaurants for a newspaper column. Now I have to depend on the generosity of the restaurant to give me one or else pay a few dollars for one.

(Incidentally, some menus look great in a custom-made picture frame, hanging in the kitchen.) One of my favorites is from The Settlers Inn in Hawley, Pennsylvania, with its fresh-from-the-garden watercolors.

❧"Of the gladdest moments in human life, methinks is the departure upon a distant journey to unknown lands. Shaking off with one mighty effort the fetters of habit, the leaden weights of routine, the cloak of many cares, and the slavery of home. Man feels once more happy. The blood flows with the fast circulation of childhood. Afresh dawns the morn of life." (Sir Richard Francis Burton)
—*Blue Lake Ranch*

❧We, who work and share ourselves here at The Inn at Olde New Berlin and Gabriel's Restaurant, aspire to be inspirational to each and every one of our guests. Our desire is that memories will be created, a relationship will be enhanced. We desire that our hospitality— the treating of others lovingly, gently, and respectfully—will extend within and beyond our doors into everyday life. We know that when we give, we are also inspired and open to receiving the spirit of life from others.
—*The Inn at Olde New Berlin*

❧ DIRECTORY OF INNS ❧

Call the inns directly or consult inn guidebooks for current
information when making travel arrangements.

Abriendo Inn
300 West Abriendo Avenue
Pueblo, CO 81004
(719) 544–2703

Academy Street Bed and Breakfast
528 Academy Street
Hawley, PA 18428
(717) 226–3430

Adams Edgeworth Inn
Monteagle Assembly
Monteagle, TN 37356
(615) 924–4000

Adams Hillborne
801 Vine Street
Chattanooga, TN 37403
(423) 265–5000

Alaska Ocean View B&B
1101 Edgecumbe Drive
Sitka, AK 99835
(907) 747–8310

Alexander's Inn
529 East Palace Avenue
Santa Fe, NM 87501
(505) 986–1431

Alexander's Inn
653 Washington Street
Cape May, NJ 08204
(609) 884–2555

Annie Horan's
415 West Main Street
Grass Valley, CA 95945
(916) 272–2418

Antique Rose Inn
91 Gresham Street
Ashland, OR 97520
(541) 482–6285

The Arcadian Inn
328 East First Street
Edmond–Oklahoma City, OK 73034
(405) 348–6347

Arcady Down East
South Street
Blue Hill, ME 04614
(207) 374–5576

Ash Mill Farm
Route 202, P.O. Box 202
Holicong, PA 18928
(215) 794–5373

Ashling Cottage
106 Sussex Avenue
Spring Lake, NJ 07762
(908) 449–3553

Audrie's Cranbury Corner
RR 8, Box 2400
Rapid City, SD 57702
(605) 342–7788

B.D. Williams House
1505 Fourth Avenue North
Seattle, WA 98109-2902
(206) 285–0810

Balcony Downs
P.O. Box 563
Glasgow, VA 24555
(703) 258–2100

Barley Sheaf Farm
Route 202, Box 10
Holicong, PA 18928
(215) 794–5104

Barry's Gull Cottage
116 Chesapeake Street
Dewey Beach, DE 19971
(302) 227–7000

Bay Moon B&B
128 Kings Highway
Lewes, DE 19958
(302) 644–1802

The Beal House
247 West Main Street
Littleton, NH 03561
(603) 444–2661

Beazley House
1910 First Street
Napa, CA 94559
(707) 257–1649

The Bechtel Mansion Inn
400 West King Street
East Berlin, PA 17316
(717) 259–7760

Benner House
645 Main Street
Weston, MO 64098
(816) 386–2616

Betsy's Bed and Breakfast
1428 Park Avenue
Baltimore, MD 21217
(301) 383–1274

The Birchwood Inn
Route 45
Temple, NH 03084
(603) 878–3285

Black Dog Inn
650 South St. Vrain Avenue
P.O. Box 4659
Estes Park, CO 80517
(303) 586–0374

The Black Lantern Inn
Route 118
Montgomery Village, VT 05470
(802) 326–4507

Blossom Tyme
P.O. Box 54
Gambier, OH 43022
(614) 427–3300

Blue Harbor House
67 Elm Street
Camden, ME 04843
(207) 236–3196

Blue Lake Ranch
16000 Highway 140
Hesperus, CO 81326
(970) 385–4537

Bluebelle House
263 South State Highway 173
Lake Arrowhead, CA 92352
(714) 336–3292

Blueberry Hill
Goshen, VT 05733
(802) 247–6735

Bluff Creek Inn
1161 Bluff Creek Drive
Chaska, MN 55318
(612) 445–2735

The Bodine House
307 South Main Street
Muncy, PA 17756
(717) 546–8949

Borgman's Bed & Breakfast
Arrow Rock, MO 65320
(816) 837–3350

The Boxwood Inn
P.O. Box 203
Akron, PA 17501
(800) 238–3466

Boydville The Inn at Martinsburg
601 South Queen Street
Martinsburg, WV 25401
(304) 263–1448

The Brafferton Inn
44–46 York Street
Gettysburg, PA 17325
(717) 337–3423

The Bramble Inn
Route 6A
Brewster, MA 02631
(508) 896–7644

The Brass Bed
719 Columbia Avenue
Cape May, NJ 08204
(609) 884–8075

The Briar Rose B&B
2151 Arapahoe Avenue
Boulder, CO 80302
(303) 442–3007

Britt House
406 Maple Street
San Diego, CA 92103
(619) 234–2926

Bungay Jar
Route 116 (P.O. Box 15, Franconia)
Easton, NH 03580
(603) 823–7775

Butterfield B&B
2284 Sunset Drive
P.O. Box 1115
Julian, CA 92036
(619) 765–2179

The Butternut Inn
Route 16 and Genesee Road
Chaffee, NY 14030
(716) 496–8987

Campbell Ranch Inn
1475 Canyon Road
Geyersville, CA 95441
(707) 857–3476

Candlelite Inn
5 Greenhouse Lane
Bradford, NH 03221
(603) 938–5571

Canyon Villa
125 Canyon Circle Drive
Sedona, AZ 86351
(520) 284–1226

Captain Dexter House
100 Main Street, P.O. Box 2457
Vineyard Haven, MA 02568
(508) 693–6564

Captain Ezra Nye House
152 Main Street
Sandwich, MA 02563
(800) 388–2278

The Captain Lord Mansion
P.O. Box 800
Kennebunkport, ME 04046
(207) 967–3141

Captain Nickerson Inn
333 Main Street
South Dennis, MA 02660
(508) 398–5966

The Captain Stannard House
138 South Main Street
Westbrook, CT 06498
(203) 399–7565

Captain Swift Inn
72 Elm Street
Camden, ME 04843
(207) 236–8113

The Captain's House
371 Old Harbor Road
Chatham, MA 02633
(508) 945–0127

Carter House
1033 Third Street
Eureka, CA 95501
(707) 445–1390

Casa de las Chimeneas
405 Cordoba Road
P.O. Box 5303
Taos, NM 87571
(505) 758–4777

Cedarcroft Farm
431 SE "Y" Highway
Warrensburg, MO 64093
(816) 747–5728

Cedarym: A Colonial Bed and Breakfast
1011 240th Avenue Northeast
Redmond, WA 98053
(206) 868–4159

Center Street Inn
169 East Center
Logan, UT 84321
(801) 752–3443

Château du Sureau
48688 Victoria Lane
Oakhurst, CA 93644
(209) 683–6800

Chateau Victorian
118 First Street
Santa Cruz, CA 95060
(408) 458–9458

The Chatelaine B&B
P.O. Box 326
Pine Grove Mills, PA 16868
(814) 238–2028

The Checkerberry Inn
62644 C.R. 37
Goshen, IN 46526
(219) 642–4445

Chestnut Hill on the Delaware
63 Church Street
Milford, NJ 08848
(201) 995–9761

The Chetwynd House
Chestnut Street, Box 130
Kennebunkport, ME 04046
(207) 967–2235

Chicago Pike Inn
215 East Chicago Street
Coldwater, MI 49036
(517) 279–8744

Churchtown Inn
Route 23
Churchtown, PA 17555
(215) 445–7794

Clauser's Bed and Breakfast
201 East Kicklighter Road
Lake Helen, FL 32744
(904) 228–0310

Clayton Country Inn
Route 1, Box 8, Highway 271
Clayton, OK 74536
(918) 569–4165

Clements Inn
1712 Center Avenue (M–25)
Bay City, MI 48708
(517) 894–4600

Cliff House
122 Fairmount Drive
Madison, IN 47250
(812) 265–5272

Clifton Country Inn
Route 13, Box 26
Charlottesville, VA 22901
(804) 971–1800

Conover's Bay Head Inn
646 Main Avenue
Bay Head, NJ 08742
(908) 892–4664

The Conyers House
Slate Mills Road, Route 707
Sperryville, VA 22740
(703) 987–8025

The Corner Cupboard Inn
50 Park Avenue
Rehoboth Beach, DE 19971
(302) 227–8553

Countryside Bed & Breakfast
P.O. Box 57
Summit Point, WV 25446
(304) 725–2614

Covered Bridge Inn
990 Rettew Mill Road
Ephrata, PA 17522
(717) 733–1592

Crystal Rose Inn
789 Valley Road
Arroyo Grande, CA 93420
(805) 481–1854

Cypress Inn
407 Mirada Road
Miramar, CA 94019
(415) 726–6002

Dairy Hollow House
515 Spring Street
Eureka Springs, AR 72632
(501) 253–7444

Davy Jackson Inn
85 Perry Avenue
P.O. Box 20147
Jackson, WY 83001
(307) 739–2294

The Decoy
958 Eisenberger Road
Strasburg, PA 17579
(717) 687–8585

Deer Run Ranch
5440 Eastlake Boulevard
Carson City, NV 89704
(702) 882–3643

Doanleigh Wallagh Inn
217 East Thirty-seventh Street
Kansas City, MO 64111
(816) 753–2667

The Doctor's Inn
RR#1, Box 375
Saranac Lake, NY 12983
(518) 891–3464

The Doubleday Inn
104 Doubleday Avenue
Gettysburg, PA 17325
(717) 334–9119

Duggan Place
151 Nile Street
Stratford, Ontario
Canada N5A 4E1
(519) 273–7502

Durham House
921 Heights Boulevard
Houston, TX 77008
(713) 868–4654

Eastlake Inn
1442 Kellam Avenue
Los Angeles, CA 90026
(213) 250–1620

The Edge of Thyme
6 Main Street
Candor, NY 13743
(607) 659–5155

Edgewood Manor
Route 2, Box 329
P.O. Box 509
Bunker Hill, WV 25413
(304) 229–9359

The 1819 Red Brick Inn
2081 Route 230
Dundee, NY 14837
(607) 243–8844

Ellis River House
Route 16, Box 656
Jackson, NH 03846
(603) 383–9339

The Elms Bed and Breakfast
84 Elm Street
Camden, ME 04843
(207) 236–6250

Emersons' Guest House
82 Main Street
Vergennes, VT 05491
(802) 877–3293

The English Manor
540 El Paso Street
Jacksonville, TX 75766
(800) 866–0946

Eton House
1485 Eton
Fayetteville, AR 72703
(501) 521–6344

Fairfield Farm Inn
10 Main Street (Highway 1)
Box 1287
Middleton, Nova Scotia
Canada BOS IPO
(902) 825–6989

The Fairhaven Inn
RR 2, Box 85, North Bath Road
Bath, ME 04530
(207) 443–4391

Federal House
P.O. Box 4914
Ithaca, NY 14852
(607) 533–7362

Folkestone Bed and Breakfast
Martinsburg Road
Berkeley Springs, WV 25411
(304) 258–3743

Foothill House
3037 Foothill Boulevard
Calistoga, CA 94515
(707) 942–6933

The Forsyth Park Inn
102 West Hall Street
Savannah, GA 31401
(912) 233–6800

The Four Chimneys B&B
38 Orange Street
Nantucket, MA 02554
(508) 228–1912

Freedom House Bed 'n Breakfast
1 Maple Street
Freedom, NH 03836
(603) 539–4815

Garnet Hill Lodge
North River, NY 12856
(518) 251–2821

Garratt Mansion
900 Union Street
Alameda, CA 94501
(510) 521–4779

Gate House Inn
1330 Jackson Gate Road
Jackson, CA 95642
(209) 223–3500

The Gingerbread House
141 Division Street
West Harwich, MA 02671
(508) 432–1901

The Gingerbread Mansion
400 Berding Street
Ferndale, CA 95536
(707) 786–4000

Glacier Bay Country Inn
Box 5
Gustavus, AK 99826
(907) 697–2288

Glen-Ella Springs Inn
Bear Gap Road
Clarkesville, GA 30523
(706) 754–7295

Glendale Farms
224 Bostwick Road
Ithaca, NY 14850
(607) 272–8756

The Glenborough Inn
1327 Bath Street
Santa Barbara, CA 93101
(805) 966–0589

The Governor's Inn
86 Main Street
Ludlow, VT 05149
(802) 228–8830

Governors' Inn
611 West Twenty-second Street
Austin, TX 78705
(512) 477–0711

The Green Tree Inn
15 Mill Street, P.O. Box 96
Elsah, IL 62028
(618) 374–2821

The Grey Whale Inn
615 North Main Street
Fort Bragg, CA 95437
(707) 964–0640

The Groveland Hotel
P.O. Box 481
Groveland, CA 95321
(209) 962–4000

Grace Hall Bed and Breakfast Inn
506 Lauderdale Street
Selma, AL 36701
(334) 875–5744

Graham's Bed and Breakfast Inn
150 Canyon Circle Drive
Sedona, AZ 86336
(520) 284–1425

Grant Corner Inn
122 Grant Avenue
Santa Fe, NM 87501
(505) 983–6678

Greenbriar Inn
315 Wallace
Coeur d'Alene, ID 83814
(208) 667–9660

Greenhurst Inn
Bethel, VT 05032
(802) 234–9474

Haikuleana
69 Haiku Road
Haiku, HA 96708
(808) 575–2890

The Half Penney Inn
Box 84, Handy Road
West Hartford, VT 05084
(802) 295–6082

Hamilton House
500 West Main Street
Decatur, IL 62522
(217) 429–1669

Hannah Marie Country Inn
RR 1, Highway 71 South
Spencer, IA 51301
(712) 262–1286

Hannah's House
Route 3, Middle Creek Road
Pigeon Forge, TN 37863
(615) 428–2192

Healdsburg Inn on the Plaza
116 Matheson Street
Healdsburg, CA 95448
(707) 433–6991

Heartstone Inn
35 Kingshighway
Eureka Springs, AR 72632
(501) 253–8916

Heritage Inn
510 Lena Street
Salmon, ID 83467
(208) 756–3174

Heritage Park Inn
2470 Heritage Park Row
San Diego, CA 92110
(619) 299–6832

High Cotton
214 South Live Oak
Bellville, TX 77418
(409) 865–9796

Highland Lake Inn
Highland Lake Drive
Flat Rock, NC 28731
(704) 693–6812

Hill Farm Inn
RR 2, Box 2015
Arlington, VT 05250
(802) 375–2269

The Hilltop Inn
Main Street, Route 117
Sugar Hill, NH 03585
(603) 823–5695

Holden House
1102 West Pikes Peak Avenue
Colorado Springs, CO 80904
(719) 471–3980

The Hopkins Inn
Hopkins Road
New Preston, CT 06777
(203) 868–7295

The Horatio Johnson House
36 Church Street
Belfast, ME 04915
(207) 338–5153

The Hutchinson House
305 NW Second Street
Faribault, MN 55021
(507) 332–7519

The Hutchinson Mansion
220 West Tenth Street
Michigan City, IN 46360
(219) 879–1700

Ilverthorpe Cottage
41 Robinson Street
Narragansett, RI 02882
(401) 789–2392

Inn of the Arts
618 South Alameda
Las Cruces, NM 88005
(505) 526–3327

The Inn at Buckeystown
Buckeystown, MD 21717
(301) 874–5755

Inn at Cedar Falls
21190 State Route 374
Logan, OH 43138
(614) 385–7489

The Inn on the Common
Craftsbury Common, VT 05827
(802) 586–9619

Inn on Cove Hill
37 Mount Pleasant Street
Rockport, MA 01966
(508) 546–2701

The Inn at Depot Hill
250 Monterey Avenue
Capitola-by-the-Sea, CA 95010
(408) 462–3376

The Inn at 410
410 North Leroux Street
Flagstaff, AZ 86001
(520) 774–0088

The Inn on Golden Pond
Route 3, P.O. Box 126
Holderness, NH 03245
(603) 968–7269

The Inn at Gristmill Square
P.O. Box 359
Warm Springs, VA 24484
(703) 839–2231

The Inn at Honey Run
6920 County Road 203
Millersburg, OH 44654
(216) 674–0011

The Inn at Manchester
Box 41
Historic Route 7A
Manchester Village, VT 05254
(802) 362–1793

The Inn at Maplewood Farm
447 Center Road
P.O. Box 1478
Hillsborough, NH 03244
(603) 464–4242

The Inn at Merridun
100 Merridun Place
Union, SC 29379
(803) 427–7052

The Inn at Mitchell House
Box 329, RD 2 (Tolchester Estates)
Chestertown, MD 21620
(301) 778–6500

The Inn at Olde New Berlin
321 Market Street
New Berlin, PA 17855-0390
(717) 966–0321

The Inn at Ormsby Hill
Historic Route 7A
Manchester Center, VT 05255
(802) 362–1163

Inn at Playa Del Rey
435 Culver Boulevard
Playa Del Rey, CA 90293
(310) 574–1920

The Inn at Starlight Lake
Starlight, PA 18461
(717) 798–2519

The Inn at the Shore
301 Fourth Avenue
Belmar, NJ 07719
(908) 681–3762

The Inn at Weathersfield
Route 106, Box 165
Weathersfield, VT 05151
(802) 263–9217

Inn at Willowbend
3939 Comotara
Wichita, KS 67226
(316) 636–4032

Isaiah Hall Bed and Breakfast Inn
152 Whig Street
Dennis, MA 02638
(508) 385–9928

The Jabberwock
598 Laine Street
Monterey, CA 93940
(408) 372–4777

Jakobstettel Guest House
16 Isabella Street
St. Jacobs, Ontario N0B 2N0
Canada
(519) 664–2208

The Jefferson Inn
Route 2
Jefferson, NH 03583
(603) 586–7998

The John Brady Inn
18-20 N. Main Street
Muncy, PA 17756
(717) 546–3480

The John Palmer House
4314 North Mississippi Avenue
Portland, OR 97217
(503) 284–5893

Kedron Valley Inn
Route 106
South Woodstock, VT 05071
(802) 457–1473

Kenniston Hill Inn
Route 27, P.O. Box 125
Boothbay, ME 04537
(207) 633–2159

King's Cottage
1049 East King Street
Lancaster, PA 17602
(717) 397–1017

The Kingsley House
626 West Main Street
Fennville, MI 49408
(616) 561–6425

Kirschke Hour B&B
1124 West Third Street
Grand Island, NE 68801
(308) 381–6851

Knoll Farm Country Inn
Bragg Hill Road
Waitsfield, VT 05673
(802) 496–3939

L'Auberge Provençale
P.O. Box 119
White Post, VA 22663
(540) 837–1375

La Maida House
11159 La Maida Street
North Hollywood, CA 91601
(818) 769–3857

La Maison
404 Jersey Avenue
Spring Lake, NJ 07762
(908) 449–0969

La Vista Plantation
4420 Guinea Station Road
Fredericksburg, VA 22401
(703) 898–8444

The Lamplight Inn
2129 Lake Avenue (Route 9N)
Lake Luzerne, NY 12846
(518) 696–5294

Lanaux House
Esplanade Avenue at Chartres
P.O. Box 52257
New Orleans, LA 70152
(504) 488–4640

Langdon House
135 Craven Street
Beaufort, NC 28516
(919) 728–5499

Laurel Hill Plantation
P.O. Box 182
McClellanville, SC 29458
(803) 887–3708

Little River Inn
Box 116
Aldie, VA 22001
(703) 327–6742

Locust Hill B&B
1659 East U.S. 22–3
Morrow, OH 45152
(513) 899–2749

The Lord Proprietors' Inn
300 North Broad Street
Edenton, NC 27932
(919) 482–3641

The Lovelander Inn
217 West Fourth Street
Loveland, CO 80537
(303) 669–0798

Lynchburg Mansion
405 Madison Street
Lynchburg, VA 24504
(804) 528–5400

Madame Dyer's B&B
1720 Postoffice Street
Galveston, TX 77550
(409) 765–5692

The Maidstone Arms
207 Main Street
East Hampton, NY 11937
(516) 324–5006

Main Street Bed and Breakfast
739 West Main Street
Madison, IN 47250
(812) 265–3539

The Maine Stay
34 Maine Street
P.O. Box 500A
Kennebunkport, ME 04046
(207) 967–2117

The Mainstay Inn
635 Columbia Avenue
Cape May, NJ 08204
(609) 884–8690

Manor House
P.O. Box 447
69 Maple Avenue
Norfolk, CT 06058
(203) 542–5690

The Manor House
57 Maine Avenue
West Yarmouth, Cape Cod, MA 02673
(508) 771–3433

The Manor at Taylor's Store
Route 1, Box 533
Smith Mountain Lake, VA 24184
(703) 721–3951

The Maples Inn
16 Roberts Avenue
Bar Harbor, ME 04609
(207) 288–3443

Marlborough Inn
320 Woods Hole Road
Woods Hole, MA 02543
(508) 548–6218

The Mason Cottage
625 Columbia Avenue
Cape May, NJ 08204
(609) 884–3358

Mayhurst Bed and Breakfast
P.O. Box 707
Orange, VA 22960
(703) 672–5597

McKay House
306 East Delta Street
Jefferson, TX 75657
(903) 665–7322

The Meadowlark Manor
241 West Ninth Avenue
Red Cloud, NE 68970
(402) 746–3550

The Mellon Patch Inn
3601 North A1A
North Hutchinson Island, FL 34949
(407) 461–5231

The Mercersburg Inn
405 South Main Street
Mercersburg, PA 17236
(717) 328–5231

The Middlebury Inn
14 Courthouse Square
Middlebury, VT 05753
(802) 388–4961

Mill Brook Bed & Breakfast
Route 44, P.O. Box 410
Brownsville, VT 05037
(802) 484–7283

Mill Creek Homestead
2578 Old Philadelphia Pike
Bird-in-Hand, PA 17505
(717) 291–6419

Mill Farm Inn
P.O. Box 1251
Tryon, NC 28782
(704) 859–6992

The Mockingbird Inn
305 North Gloster
Tupelo, MS 38801
(601) 841–0286

The Montford Inn
322 West Tonhawa
Norman, OK 73069
(405) 321–2200

Morning Star Inn
480 Flat Mountain Estates Road
Highlands, NC 28741
(704) 526–1009

Mt. Juneau Inn
1801 Old Glacier Highway
Juneau, AK 99801
(907) 463–5855

The Nauset House
Beach Road, P.O. Box 774
East Orleans, MA 02643
(508) 255–2195

Neil Creek House
341 Mowetza Drive
Ashland, OR 97520
(503) 482–6443

North Garden Inn
1014 North Garden Street
Bellingham, WA 98225
(206) 671–7828

The Notchland Inn
Hart's Location, NH 03812
(603) 374–6131

Nowlin Creek Inn
660 East Broadway
Jackson Hole, WY 83001
(307) 733–0882

O'Duach'ain Country Inn
675 Ferndale Drive
Bigfork, MT 59911
(406) 837–6851

Oceancrest House
15510 Pedrioli Drive
Harbor, OR 97415
(503) 469–9200

October Country Inn
P.O. Box 66
Bridgewater Corners, VT 05035
(802) 672–3412

Olallieberry Inn
2476 Main Street
Cambria, CA 93428
(805) 927–3222

Old Broad Bay Inn
Main Street
Waldoboro, ME 04572
(207) 832–6668

Old Church House Inn
P.O. Box 295
Mossville, IL 61552
(309) 579–2300

Old Drover's Inn
Old Route 22
Dover Plains, NY 12522
(914) 832–9311

Old Pioneer Garden Country Inn
No. 79
Unionville, NV 89418
(702) 538–7585

The Old World Inn
1301 Jefferson Street
Napa, CA 94559
(707) 257–0112

The Old Yacht Club Inn
431 Corona Del Mar Drive
Santa Barbara, CA 93103
(805) 962–1277

Orchard Hill Country Inn
P.O. Box 425
Julian, CA 92036
(619) 765–1700

Out-the-Inn-Door
P.O. Box 633
Freeport, ME 04032
(207) 865–3688

The Over Look Inn
Route 6, P.O. Box 771
Eastham, MA 02642
(508) 255–1886

The Painted Porch
P.O. Box 3965
Jackson, WY 83001
(307) 733–1981

Palmer House
81 Palmer Avenue
Falmouth, MA 02540
(508) 548–1230

The Palmer Inn
25 Church Street
Noank, CT 06340
(203) 572–9000

The Park House
888 Holland Street
Saugatuck, MI 49453
(616) 857–4535

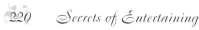

Partridge Brook Inn
Hatt Road, P.O. Box 151
Westmoreland, NH 03467
(603) 399–4994

Pheasant Field B&B
150 Hickorytown Road
Carlisle, PA 17013
(717) 258–0717

Pilgrim's Inn
Deer Isle, ME 04627
(207) 348–6615

Pine Knob Inn
Route 447
Canadensis, PA 18325
(717) 595–2532

Pineapple Hill
1324 River Road
New Hope, PA 18938
(215) 862–9608

Pratt Guest House
105 North Iuka Street
Pratt, KS 67124
(316) 672–1200

Pride House
409 East Broadway
Jefferson, TX 75657
(214) 665–2675

Prince of Wales
133 Thirteenth Avenue East
Seattle, WA 98102
(206) 325–9692

Pudding Creek Inn
700 North Main Street
Fort Bragg, CA 95437
(707) 964–9529

Queen Anne Inn
2147 Tremont Place
Denver, CO 80205
(303) 296–6666

Quill and Quilt
615 West Hoffman Street
Cannon Falls, MN 55009
(507) 263–5507

Rabbit Hill Inn
Lower Waterford, VT 05848
(802) 748–5168

Randall's Ordinary
Route 2, P.O. Box 243
North Stonington, CT 06359
(203) 599–4540

Randolph House
Fryemont Road
Bryson City, NC 28713
(704) 488–3472

Ravenwood Castle
Route 1
New Plymouth, OH 45654
(614) 596–2606

Red Brook Inn
P.O. Box 237
Old Mystic, CT 06372
(203) 572–0349

Red Castle Inn
109 Prospect Street
Nevada City, CA 95959
(916) 265–5135

The Red House
Lincolnville Beach, ME 04849
(207) 236–4621

Red Willow Farm
224 East Street Road
Kennett Square, PA 19348
(215) 444–0518

The Reluctant Panther
West Road, Box 678
Manchester, VT 05254
(802) 362–2568

The River House
Route 1
Boyce, VA 22620
(703) 837–1476

Riversbend Bed and Breakfast
42505 Highway 160
P.O. Box 861
Mancos, CO 81328
(970) 533–7353

Riverwind
209 Main Street
Deep River, CT 06417
(203) 526–2014

The Roaring Lion
75 Main Street, P.O. Box 756
Waldoboro, ME 04572
(207) 832–4038

The Robins Nest
Highway 49, P.O. Box 1408
San Andreas, CA 95249
(209) 754–1076

Rose Inn
813 Auburn Road, Route 34
Ithaca, NY 14851
(607) 533–7905

Rose Manor B&B
124 South Linden Street
Manheim, PA 17545
(717) 664–4932

Roses and the River
7074 CR 506
Brazoria, TX 77422
(409) 798–1070

Rowell's Inn
RR 1, Box 267-D
Simonsville, VT 05143
(802) 875–3658

Run of the River
P.O. Box 285
Leavenworth, WA 98826
(509) 548–7171

Sage Cottage
112 East Main Street
Trumansburg, NY 14886
(607) 387–6449

San Ysidro Ranch
900 San Ysidro Lane
Santa Barbara, CA 93108
(805) 969–5046

Sassafras Inn
785 Highway 51
Hernando, MS 38632
(601) 429–5864

School House Bed and Breakfast
Third and Clark Streets
P.O. Box 88
Rocheport, MO 65279
(314) 698–2022

Schoolhouse Inn
106 East Beck
Melvern, KS 66510
(913) 549–3473

Schumacher's New Prague Hotel
212 West Main Street
New Prague, MN 56071
(612) 758–2133

The Seal Beach Inn
212 Fifth Street
Seal Beach, CA 90740
(310) 493–2416

Settlers Inn
Four Main Avenue
Hawley, PA 18428
(717) 226–2993

The Seymour House
1248 Blue Star Highway
South Haven, MI 49090
(616) 227–3918

The Shaw House
8 Cyprus Court
Georgetown, SC 29440
(803) 546–9663

The Shelburne Inn
P.O. Box 250
Seaview, WA 98644
(360) 642–2442

Shellmont Bed and Breakfast
821 Piedmont Avenue N.E.
Atlanta, GA 30308
(404) 872–9290

Shire Inn
P.O. Box 37
Chelsea, VT 05038
(802) 685–3031

Silas Griffith House
RR 1, Box 66F
Danby, VT 05739
(802) 293–5567

Silver Maple Lodge
South Main Street
Fairlee, VT 05045
(802) 333–4326

The Simmons Homestead Inn
288 Scudder Avenue
Hyannisport, MA 02647
(508) 778–4999

Simmons' Way Village Inn
Main Street
Millerton, NY 12546
(518) 789–6235

Six Water Street Bed and Breakfast
6 Water Street, Box 1295
Sandwich, MA 02563
(508) 888–6808

Sleepy Hollow Farm
Route 3, Box 43
Gordonsville, VA 22942
(703) 832–5555

Sooke Harbour House
1528 Whiffen Spit Road, RR 4
Sooke, British Columbia VOS 1NO
Canada
(604) 642–3421

The Southern Hotel
146 South Third Street
Ste. Genevieve, MO 63670
(314) 883–3493

Spring Bank Inn
7945 Worman's Mill Road
Frederick, MD 21701
(301) 694–0440

Squire Tarbox Inn
RR 2, Box 620
Wiscasset, ME 04578
(207) 882–7693

Stonehedge Inn
160 Pawtucket Boulevard
Tyngsboro, MA 01879
(508) 649–4400

Strawberry Inn
17 Main Street, P.O. Box 237
New Market, MD 21774
(301) 865–3318

The Sugartree Inn
Sugarbush Access Road
Warren, VT 05674
(802) 583–3211

The Summer Cottage
613 Columbia Avenue
Cape May, NJ 08204
(609) 884–4948

Summerland Inn
2161 Ortega Hill Road, P.O. Box 1209
Summerland, CA 93067
(805) 969–5225

Summerport Bed and Breakfast
17 South Avenue
Schroon Lake, NY 12870
(518) 532–9339

Sunning Hill
Arch Street
Pittsford, VT 05763
(802) 483–9402

Sweet Adeline's
949 F Street
Salida, CO 81201
(719) 539–4100

Sweet Onion Inn
P.O. Box 66
Hancock, VT 05748
(802) 767–3734

Sweetwater Farm
Sweetwater Road, Box 86
Glen Mills, PA 19342
(215) 459–4711

Teton Tree House
Box 550
Jackson, WY 83014

Thomas Huckins House
2701 Main Street, Route 6A
Barnstable, MA 02630
(508) 362–6379

Thompson Park House
118 Front Street
Owego, NY 13827
(607) 687–4323

Trail's End Country Inn
Smith Road
Wilmington, VT 05363
(802) 464–2727

Trezona House
315 East Washington Street
Ely, MN 55731
(218) 365–4809

Trillium House
P.O. Box 280
Nellysford, VA 22958
(804) 325–9126

The Triple T Ranch
Route 1, Box 93
Stanley, ND 58784
(701) 628–2418

Trojan Horse Inn
19455 Sonoma Highway
Sonoma, CA 95476
(707) 996–2430

Troutbeck Inn
P.O. Box 26
Amenia, NY 12501
(914) 373–9681

Truffles B&B
43591 Bow Canyon Road
P.O. Box 130649
Big Bear Lake, CA 92315
(909) 585–2772

Turtleback Farm Inn
Crow Valley Road, Route 1
Orcas Island, WA 98245
(206) 376–4914

Twin Gates B&B
308 Morris Avenue
Lutherville, MD 21093
(410) 252–3131

Two Brooks
Route 42
Shandaken, NY 12480
(914) 688–7101

Two Sisters Inn
Ten Otoe Place
Manitou Springs, CO 80829
(719) 685–9684

Tyler Hill Bed and Breakfast
Route 371, P.O. Box 62
Tyler Hill, PA 18469
(717) 224–6418

Ujjala's Bed and Breakfast
2 Forest Glen
New Paltz, NY 12561
(914) 255–6360

Under Mountain Inn
Route 41
Salisbiry, CT 06068
(203) 435–0242

Victorian House
11 Cadiz Street
St. Augustine, FL 32084
(904) 824–5214

Victorian Oaks B&B
435 Locust
Minonk, IL 61760
(309) 432–2771

Victorian Rose Garden B&B
314 Washington Street
Algonquin, IL 60102
(847) 854–9667

Wanek's Lodge
560 Ponderosa Drive
Estes Park, CO 80517
(303) 586–5851

The Waverly Inn
783 North Main Street
Hendersonville, NC
(704) 693–9193

The Wedgwood Inn
111 West Bridge Street
New Hope, PA 18938
(215) 862–2570

Wellington Bed and Breakfast
800 West Fourth Street
Waterloo, IA 50702
(319) 234–2993

Whispering Waters B&B
Outlet Bay Road
HCR5 Box 125B
Priest Lake, ID 83856
(208) 443–3229

White Goose Inn
Route 10, P.O. Box 17
Orford, NH 03777
(603) 353–4812

White Lace Inn
16 North Fifth Avenue
Sturgeon Bay, WI 54235
(414) 742–1105

The Wild Rose of York
78 Long Sands Road
York, ME 03909
(207) 363–2532

The Wildflower Inn
Teton Village Road
Jackson, WY 83001
(307) 733–4710

The Wildwood Inn
121 Church Street
Ware, MA 01082
(413) 967–7798

William Seward Inn
RR#2, South Portage Road
Westfield, NY 14787
(716) 326–4151

Williams House
420 Quapaw
Hot Springs National Park, AR 71901
(501) 624–4275

Willow Brook Inn
44255 Warren Road
Canton, MI 48187
(313) 454–0019

Windermere Manor
P.O. Box 2177
Lake Arrowhead, CA 92352
(909) 336–3292

Windfields Farm
RR 1, Box 170
Cummington, MA 01026
(413) 684–3786

Window On The Winds B&B
10151 Highway 191
P.O. Box 135
Pinedale, WY 82941
(307) 367–2600

The Winter House
3522 Arsenal Street
St. Louis, MO 63118
(314) 664–4399

WinterGreen Country Inn
16330 Thelan Road
Mountain, WI 54149
(715) 276–6885

Winters Creek Inn
1201 U.S. 395 North
Carson City, NV 89701
(702) 849–1020

Wisconsin House
2105 East Main
Hazel Green, WI 53811
(608) 854–2233

Zachariah Foss Guest House
4 Lafayette Street
Washington, MO 63090
(314) 239–6499

INDEX

C